S0-BUF-865

BILINGUAL EDUCATION

Professor Joshua A. Fishman
Distinguished University Research Professor
Emeritus
Yeshiva University, New York

BILINGUAL EDUCATION

FOCUSSCHRIFT IN HONOR OF JOSHUA A. FISHMAN ON THE OCCASION OF HIS 65TH BIRTHDAY

Volume I

Edited by

OFELIA GARCÍA
City College of New York

LC
3715
.B56
1991
West

JOHN BENJAMINS PUBLISHING COMPANY
AMSTERDAM/PHILADELPHIA

1991

Library of Congress Cataloging-in-Publication Data

Bilingual education / edited by Ofelia García.
    p.   cm. -- (Focusschrift in honor of Joshua A. Fishman on the occasion of his 65th birthday ; v. 1)
Includes bibliographical references and index.
1. Education, Bilingual. I. García, Ofelia. II. Fishman, Joshua A. III. Series.
LC3715.B56   1991
371.97 -- dc20   91-16166
ISBN 90 272 2080 8 (Eur.) / 1-55619-116-2 (US) (alk. paper)   CIP

© Copyright 1991 - John Benjamins B.V.
No part of this book may be reproduced in any form, by print, photoprint, microfilm, or any other means, without written permission from the publisher.

Preface

In the academic world we often pause to honor and celebrate a colleague's birthday or passage into retirement with a *Festschrift*. On rare occasions we attempt to focus such volumes on the topic which the celebrant pioneered and devoted his life and work to. Just such an occasion, Joshua A. Fishman's sixty fifth birthday, has caused us to produce not only a *Festschrift*, but also this three volume *Focusschrift*. It was indeed necessary to divide the effort, first because Professor Fishman has touched and influenced so many people around the world, that only through multiple volumes could we even begin to include all those who wanted to participate. Secondly, however, and far more importantly, it was necessary because Joshua Fishman has in fact pioneered, worked in and on, and he has contributed an enormous body of literature to each of the areas in this trilogy, so that it seemed only appropriate to call for focused studies on each of the topics he devoted his academic and personal life to. This three volume set thus focuses on *Bilingual Education* edited by Ofelia García, *Language and Ethnicity* edited by James R. Dow, and *Language Planning* edited by David Marshall. Each volume contains recent studies by well-known scholars from around the world, and each one attempts to document at this point in time (1990) where we are in the study of these topics.

With these volumes we want to indicate to the contemporary world of linguistics, sociolinguistics, and sociology just how great an impact Joshua Fishman has had on all of us. For future generations we want to leave a record of our respect for this man, by furthering areas of academic research which he helped found, promote, and shape. Here then are three collections on topics which Fishman researched and wrote about throughout his entire academic career. All of us, editors and authors alike, hope that our work will contribute still more to our understanding of these complex but very gratifying subjects, and that they will thus be challenging and stimulating to the readers.

Ames, IA
New York, NY
Grand Forks, ND
July 1991

PARA RICARDO,
MI OTRA VOZ

Table of Contents

Intertextuality is a patchwork, a fusion, a mosaic of allusions.

Humpty Dumpty, in
Alice in Wonderland

Bilingual education itself is not a discipline, it is an interdisciplinary activity.

Joshua A. Fishman, 1976a: 124

A Gathering of Voices, a 'Legion of Scholarly Decency', and Bilingual Education: Fishman's Biographemes as Introduction

Ofelia García

The City College of New York

1. Intra/Intertextuality and Fishman's Contribution to Bilingual Education

Joshua Fishman's voice in support of bilingualism, bilingual education, and cultural pluralism has been heard loud and clear in all academic arenas. His article, "A gathering of vultures, the 'Legion of Decency' and bilingual education in the USA" (1978a) denounced enemies of bilingualism. Our own gathering of voices echoes a response to those vultures, and forms "a legion of scholarly decency" in defense of bilingualism and bilingual education. As students, friends, and colleagues of Joshua Fishman, this volume pays tribute to his contribution by acting as the intertext of his bilingual education discourse.

In her *Séméotikè: Recherches pour une sémanalyse*, Julia Kristeva has said: "Every text is built as a mosaic of quotes, every text is absorption and transformation of another text" (1969: 146). Fishman's sociology of language, and his shaping of the discipline's contribution to bilingual education, is built on other texts, sometimes those of others, and sometimes his own. In Fishman's case, intertextuality many times absorbs *his own* intratextuality, for often his later texts are transformations of earlier ones (compare, for example, his views on the ethnic mother tongue school in Fishman [1988b: 363-373] with those in Fishman [1949]). Fishman himself has said: "I've never closed a book, even though I've said I wanted to ... My old work is usually stimulating, open-ended and growing" (García 1990).

Fishman's own life has acted as an important text in the formation of his scholarly text. One can hardly understand Fishman's work without also knowing Fishman the man – the son, the student, and the father; the husband, the teacher, the grandfather, and the colleague; the Yiddish activist, the Orthodox Jew, the helping neighbor in the Bronx, and the supporter of Latino Doctoral students at Yeshiva University. "Biographèmes", defined by Roland Barthes (1953) as elements from the life of writers that are paradigmatically related to their text, are then crucial to our understanding of Joshua Fishman's work.

Inspired on Fishman's intra/intertext, and on the plural quality of his work, this volume is built as an interdisciplinary mosaic approximating an open, rather than closed, text on bilingual education. Roland Barthes has said that "To interpret a text is not to give it meaning, but it is, on the contrary, to appreciate the plurality of which it is made" (1970: 11). And so, Fishman's open text is here not explained, but "pluralized" through the contributor's different voices, different nationalities and ethnicities, their different languages, different disciplines, and their different societal realities.

Fishman's emphasis on the study of language in society parallels closely that of the father of modern linguistics and semiology, Ferdinand de Saussure. In the first decade of the 20th century, Saussure (1916: 16) identified semiology (or semiotics) as the science "which would study the life of *signs* within society" (my emphasis). Only a semiotic study of Fishman's text will now reveal his interest in the use of *language* within society, and especially in bilingual education.

2. Joshua A. Fishman's Intra/Intertext on Bilingual Education

When Joshua Fishman was asked to write his own biography, he entitled it, "My Life from My Work; My Work from My Life" (forthcoming a). Four elements of Fishman's life are important to understand his ideology on bilingual education, a philosophy dominated by the four principles that he outlined in *Bilingual Education: An International Sociological Perspective* (1976a):

a. Bilingual education as a vehicle to support the "*little languages*" of "little people".
   ("Bilingual education is good for the minority group", p. 11.)

b. Bilingual education to help stabilize the *functional complementarity* of the languages and cultures in society.
   ("Bilingual education is good for language learning and language teaching", p. 32.)

c. Bilingual education as an expression of a societal arrangement for the support of true *cultural pluralism* and the development of plural intellectual and educational experiences.
   ("Bilingual education is (also) good for the majority group", p. 3.)

d. Bilingual education as the means to promote *biliteracy* as a plural expression.
   ("Bilingual education is good for education", p. 23.)

The first two elements in Fishman's life and work (a & b above) relate to his "narrow" loyalty as a Jewish man: his *Yiddish* activism and his Jewish *neo-orthodoxy*. But the last two elements (c & d above) relate to his "broad" loyalty as a man with an intellectual contribution to humanity: his *cultural pluralism* not only in relationship to society in general, but also to the academic/ intellectual community of which he is part, as well as his plurality as an avid and *biliterate writer*. Fishman's life reflects his belief that "[n]arrower and broader loyalties must coexist if mankind is to survive in time" (Fishman, 1974). When explaining his support of compartmentalized behavior between minorities and majorities in order to maintain their ethnolinguistic continuity, Fishman said: "The choice is not one between diametric opposites, but between two unaccepted (though opposite) extreme monolithic solutions, on the one hand, and an *ecclectic selection and combination of features*, on the other" (Fishman 1980b: 171, emphasis mine). Fishman's life and work attempts to combine the Ying and Yang of life, and it tries to reach that Supreme Surrealist Point where all antinomies will cease to be contradictory.

We will first turn to Fishman's "narrow loyalty", an ecclectic and most often unaccepted view of what it means to be a Jew, which encompasses being both a Yiddish activist (in the tradition of secularists) and a neo-Orthodox Jew.

2.1 *The Yiddish Activist*

Fishman's commitment to the language of the Askhenazy diaspora starts in
the "beehive of Yiddish" (Fishman 1981c) which was his parents' home in
Philadelphia. His father, a dental mechanic from Bessarabia who had been a
member of the Bund in Czarist Russia, and who continued his commitment to
Socialism in the US, and his mother, who came to the US from the Ukraine,
were fervent Yiddish loyalists. At home they demanded that both Shikl (Fishman's Yiddish nickname) and his sister, Rukhl, speak, read, and write Yiddish. They also organized Yiddish conferences, poetry recitals, theater performances, and other activities. (Much of their Yiddish advocacy efforts are
documented in the Fishman Family Archives, The Aaron and Sonia Horwitz
Fishman Collection.)

In his biographical account, Joshua Fishman has said: "I continue to try to
extrapolate validly and provocatively from the supra-rational concerns, sensi-
tivities, responsibilities, insights, fervent wishes and moral principles that I
most frequently derive from 'listening to Yiddish with the third ear'" (forthcoming a: 15). It is obvious that Fishman's experience with Yiddish schools
has shaped his ideology about bilingual education. His enrichment model of
bilingual education, his support of certain types of bilingual schools, as well
as his communicative and functional approach to second language acquisition, are derivatives of his early experience at the Workmen's Circle Schools
in Philadelphia. These supplementary Yiddish schools had a linguistic and
secular function. Their emphasis was on the development of the students'
Yiddish, as well as on their understanding of Yiddish literature and history.
At the same time, and in keeping with the narrow and broad loyalties theme,
these schools had a Socialist orientation and focused on current events, especially those related to the exploitation of workers. Fishman remembers learning about the Spanish Civil War, about the major role that minority groups
such as the Basques and the Catalans had in the resistance. He also remembers marching on picket lines in support of local Unions. At the same time,
however, he remembers the very advanced literary program in the school and
his broad exposure to literary genres and to modern Yiddish literature. These
schools provided a highly intellectual forum in which to discuss social problems, as well as ideas. And he claimed that it was done "at a much higher
intellectual level than in public school" (García 1990).

His experience in these schools nourished his vision of enrichment bilingual education, for he learned early that "it was possible to do well, to do *out-*

standingly well in two schools" (García 1990). And he also discovered that things that were learned in one school were easily transfered to the other.

The distinction made by Fishman and Lovas (1972) between Type III schools (Partial Bilingualism) and Type IV schools (Full Bilingualism), and their insightful discussion of these two types of schools, are also a direct result of Fishman's own schooling experience. In schools with a partial bilingual program, "literacy in the mother tongue is restricted to certain subject matter" (1972: 87). And although schools with full bilingualism programs are seen as ideal in the linguistic and psychological literature, Fishman and Lovas warn:

> [A] fully balanced bilingual speech community seems to be a theoretical impossibility because balanced competence implies languages that are functionally equivalent and no society can be motivated to maintain two languages if they are really functionally redundant. Thus, this type of program does not seem to have a clearly articulated goal with respect to *societal* reality.

This criticism of an ideal full-bilingual programs was a lesson learned by Fishman not in the literature, but in his early experience with schooling. The Workmen's Circle Schools focused on using Yiddish to teach Yiddish literature, history and the Socialist content of Jewish secularism. The schools did not attempt to teach all subjects in Yiddish, and yet, Fishman himself became successfully bilingual and biliterate. And thus, when it came time to think about typologies of bilingual schooling (especially applicable to the United States), Joshua Fishman did not fall into the trap of supporting an "ideal" kind of full-enrichment program. Rather, he was content with supporting an enrichment program that established particular societal roles for the minority and majority languages.

The way in which Yiddish was taught in the Workmen's Circle Schools has also supported Fishman's vision that bilingual education is "good for language learning and language teaching" (1976a: 32). In *Bilingual Education: An International Sociological Perspective* (1976a) Fishman said: "There is simply no way in which language teaching which focuses on language as a *target of instruction* can fully capture the total impact upon the learner which is available to language teaching which also capitalizes upon language as the *process of instruction*" (1976a: 36, emphasis in the original). This claim, which has been supported in research carried out in Canadian French immersion programs (Cummins and Swain 1986, Lambert and Tucker 1972), was based on Fishman's own personal experience. In the Workmen's Circle Schools there was no emphasis on teaching the structure of Yiddish; children (who were mostly English speaking) were "immersed" in Yiddish and they simply "spoke it, heard it, read it and wrote it" (García 1990).

And such was the hold of Yiddish on Joshua Fishman that it became his first public language. At the age of eight he wrote his first Yiddish poetry (a genre in which his late sister, Rukhl, would later excel), and his first publication was a short story written in Yiddish in 1938 at the age of 12. And at the age of 14, Fishman became the founding editor of a Yiddish youth journal (*Ilpik*, later *Yugntruf*).

Fishman's commitment to Yiddish did not end when he graduated from the Workmen's Circle Schools. Under the sponsorship of Max Weinreich, Fishman continued taking Yiddish courses at the Yivo Institute for Jewish Research while studying for a B.S. and M.S. at the University of Pennsylvania (1944 to 1948) and while doing his doctoral work at Columbia University (1948 to 1953). During those years, he supported himself by teaching in both elementary and secondary Jewish secular schools in New York. And it is most significant that his first publication in English and his first book-length study was devoted to a Yiddish school.

"Bilingualism in a Yiddish School: Some Correlates and non-Correlates" (1949) was written for the Yivo and received the Yivo Social Science Research Award in 1950. Although it remains unpublished, it already raises the important questions about bilingualism and bilingual education that later came to dominate Fishman's work. Speaking of the waste of non-English language resources in the United States, and anticipating his 1956 call in *Language Loyalty in the US* and his 1988 position in *The Rise and Fall of the Ethnic Revival*, Fishman wrote: "America will perhaps some day realize how wasteful, in terms of human emotions, efforts and abilities, and how undemocratic, in terms of basic self-respect, freedom and equality, such a policy has been" (1949: 1).

The research methodology used by Fishman to study the Yiddish-English bilingualism of children in that particular Sholem Aleichem Folshul in 1949 also contains the key elements in Fishman's future research into the Sociology of Language. The "Bilinguality Relationship Scale" used in the 1949 study contains questions that foreshadow Fishman's now famous "Who speaks what language to whom and when": "Do your grandparents speak

Yiddish to you ... usually, sometimes, rarely or never?" "Do you speak Yiddish to your grandparents ... usually, sometimes, rarely or never?" (1949: 7). And the independent variables identified in the study: play preferences, school adjustment, family adjustment, number of friends, self-identity with nationality, and attitude toward Yiddish, are all variables that come up in numerous future studies of language and ethnicity.

It is also no accident that Fishman met his wife, Gella Schweid Fishman, at a date to discuss the possible renewal of *Yugntruf*. Gella, who married Fishman in 1951, was a Yiddish teacher at a Sholem Aleichem school and has remained the champion of Yiddish throughout their lives. And much of Fishman's vision of bilingualism and bilingual education has been shaped not only through his own schooling experience (as a student and teacher), but through Gella's, who had studied in the Jewish Teachers Seminary in Montreal. Gella's dream when they got married was to open a Yiddish school in which she would be the Head Teacher and Shikl would be the Principal (García 1990). And although that dream never materialized, the Fishman home has been school to many young Yiddish activists, and in particular, to their three sons and three grandsons. Just recently, I witnessed the development of "Kemp Fishman", a total Yiddish immersion week-long summer "camp" at the grandparents' for two of their grandsons. And the development of children's books and materials in Yiddish for the grandchildren is a continuation of their experiences as Consultants for a Title VII Bilingual Education Curriculum Center at the New York City Board of Education in the early 1970s. In 1965 Joshua and Gella Fishman established The Aaron and Sonia Fishman Foundation for Yiddish Culture Papers. This Foundation, in memory of Joshua's parents, supports projects that further the use of Yiddish by young people.

Fishman's experiences with Yiddish schooling, Yiddish language development and the relationship of Yiddish to Jewish ethnicity has informed much of Fishman's work on bilingual education, bilingualism, and the sociology of language. But yet, Yiddish itself was not an object of study until 1973, when Fishman assisted Shlomo Noble in the translation of Max Weinreich's *Geshikhte fun der yidisher shprakh* (*History of the Yiddish Language*, Chicago: University of Chicago Press, 1980). Since then, four book-long publications have related the Sociology of Language concerns that Fishman discovered through Yiddish to Yiddish itself, yielding again a dynamic continuous intertext in which *Never Say Die! A Thousand Years of Yiddish in Jewish*

Life and Letters (1981d), *Readings in the Sociology of Jewish Languages* (1985b), *Ideology, Society and Language: The Odyssey of Nathan Birnbaum* (1987a) and the forthcoming, *Yiddish: Turning to Life: Sociolinguistic Studies and Interpretations*, reflect and interact with more general and earlier works, such as *Readings in the Sociology of Language* (1968), *Advances in the Sociology of Language I & II* (1971a and 1972a), and *The Sociology of Language: an Interdisciplinary Social Science Approach to Language in Society* (1972d).

Again, Fishman's life and work provides an open and continuous intertext, in which, as in the famous Chinese boxes, one contains the other. His intellectual contribution is the work of a weaver, "a patchwork" or "a fusion" as Humpty Dumpty would have said, for Fishman himself has said: "I have never found that an initial idea was full of holes, just incomplete" (García 1990). As an experienced weaver, able to combine two worlds, two languages, two schools, he looks for the threads that unite, rather than the holes that separate; but he also looks for the different colors and textures of the threads, so that the rich cultural tapestry which he weaves is a "multisplendored" one ("The entire beast is a multisplendored thing", Fishman has said, 1976a). And thus, he can also say: "The unity of mankind is a unity of fate and not a unity of face; it is a unity of ultimate interdependence, not of ultimate identity" (Fishman 1978d: viii).

2.2 *The Neo-Orthodox Jew*

In keeping with the philosophy of not closing the book, not finding the holes but the distinct threads, Joshua and Gella Fishman moved from the secularism of Yiddish to a modern, orthodox Jewish traditionalism which does not reject Yiddish. With characteristic nonconformity, Fishman attributes their initial interest in Jewish Orthodoxy to their participation in a Sholem Aleichem summer camp ran by a Jewish secular traditionalist by the name of Lehrer. It was there that Joshua and Gella first saw the need for a life style that went beyond just a different language in order to guarantee ethnolinguistic continuity (García 1990). The change in life-style was gradual and did not fully take place until the early 1970s when the family lived in Israel (1970-1973) while Fishman participated in the Ford Foundation study of Language Planning processes in East Pakistan, India, Indonesia, and Israel.

But the Fishman's kosher kitchen and their strict compartmentalization of secular and religious behavior may be the practical realization of one of

Joshua Fishman's most important theoretical contributions. One can hardly read his definition of diglossia without thinking of the Fishman's kitchen: "[I]f the roles were *not* kept separate (compartmentalized) by the power of their association with quite separate though complementary values, domains of activity and everyday situations, one language or variety would displace the other as role and value distinctions became blurred or merged" (1972b: 140). This is not to say that the kosher kitchen came before diglossia, because even chronologically that would be incorrect. But in Fishman's search for ethnolinguistic intergenerational continuity, he had to adopt a life-style that was clearly separate from his secular one. And orthodoxy and diglossia are thus deeply interrelated, just as his Yiddish activism and diglossia are also intertwined.

2.3 *The Cultural and Intellectual Pluralist*

Joshua A. Fishman's interest in cultural pluralism started early, when at eight years of age he began stamp-collecting, and thus learned the names (even in non-Latin letters) of the countries and their location in the map (Fishman, forthcoming a). And it was also stamp collecting that first encouraged his copious multinational correspondence, for he regularly wrote to US ambassadors all over the world requesting stamps. And to this date, Fishman does not hesitate to write to the most remote corners of the world, to the most renown international scholars, to ask for information about a particular problem, to request a contribution for a particular journal or book, to give advice and help, so that many of his own books and scholarly contributions are built on others' quotes, others' stories. For example, his forthcoming *Reversing Language Shift* required a copious and intricate correspondence with international scholars who provided the context from which the case studies were written. Fishman's intertext is not solely built on published "closed" works, but on an open dialogue with others who informally contribute to his work, comment upon it and share in the multiple revisions.

Fishman's multinational interest has allowed his broad definition of bilingual education within an international context. One of his major works on bilingual education is precisely the study of its international sociological perspective (1976a). Besides using the international context in order to enlighten the US bilingual education reality, Fishman has contributed much to its shaping. When Crosain Seamus from Ireland was asked for a personal testimony bearing tribute to Joshua Fishman on his 60th birthday, he wrote: "Few Irishmen and no foreigner have contributed so significantly to the shaping and clarification of language policy in Ireland over the past few decades". In fact, Fishman has been deeply involved in the shaping of bilingual education policies in many countries of the world, especially in Ireland and most recently, in the Basque country.

In a recent interview with this author (García 1990), Fishman said: "I've cultivated the world by reading and correspondence. I've read a lot, written a lot, spoken a lot ... I'm a student of countries.... Very early on I established a file on every country and every language, and very soon I came to realize that there was non-symmetry between languages and countries". It is this early realization of the existence of language minorities in an international context, reflected in his personal situation as a Yiddish speaker in an English speaking society, that shapes Fishman's advocacy of language minorities.

It is important to underline that Fishman's fascination with cultural pluralism was not limited to an interest in an exotic international context or a multinational elite. We must remember that his early intellectual readings on the subject were those of two Jews whose theoretical stance on cultural pluralism was always applied to their immediate reality in the United States: Louis Adamic and Horace Kallen. And Fishman's early interest in cultural pluralism was also a direct result of the Socialist ideology of the Workmen's Circle Schools in Philadelphia and of the secularist Yiddish tradition. In school he engaged early in discussions of social problems, exploitation of workers, oppression of minority groups. And he recalls with affection the "Holiday of Nations" that was celebrated in the Yivo Summer Camp, with each bunk taking on the identity of a different people of the world and singing their songs in Yiddish (García 1990). This celebration of cultures, focusing not only on their surface features but also on their deep socio-historical issues, shapes Fishman's attack of what he calls the "trivializations of biculturism that are currently common in US bilingual education programs" (Fishman 1977b: 43). This trivialization consists of portraying the marked culture only through "show and tell" items ("thingification") or costumed pageantry and "song-and-dance". These early attacks of the cultural component of bilingual education programs, or of what has become known as "multicultural education", anticipates recent criticism of this movement in the light of the anti-racist literature (see, for example, Cummins 1988, Mullard 1985, 1988). Criticizing current schools efforts in promoting biculturism and multiculturism, Fishman continues: "The basic ingredient lacking in all of the above approaches ... is the finespun web of ethnic self-beliefs, behaviors and *Weltanschauungent* that are reflected primarily in intragroup life" (1977b: 43). It is the belief that "[i]n the United States tradition, *unum* and *pluribus* go hand in hand" (1989b: 652) that makes Fishman a constant critic of Title VII bilingual education and its "transitional and transethnifying" components, and a committed supporter of the ethnic mother tongue schools.

Just as he has studied the enrichment context of international elite bilingual schools, the cultural pluralistic context of ethnic mother tongue schools in the United States has been the object of much of Fishman's scholarly attention. As early as 1964, Fishman co-authored an article with Vladimir Nahirny entitled "The ethnic group school and mother tongue maintenance in the United States", later reprinted in *Language Loyalty in the United States.* And almost twenty years later, he returned to the study of these schools (see, for example, 1980a,b and 1985a). In effect, these studies are expansions of his 1949 study of a Yiddish school.

Fishman's vision of cultural pluralism has never reduced the importance he attaches to the ethnolinguistic minority's command of the majority language. He has devoted much time to studying the spread of English (see, for example, Fishman, Cooper and Conrad 1977), at the same time that he contributes to the stabilization of English in a diglossic or triglossic pattern with other societal languages.

The international/intercultural/intereducational/interlinguistic/intertextual character of Fishman's intellectual contribution, can only be understood in the "open" and "plural" context in which he views traditional academic disciplines. Fishman (1976a) has said that bilingual education is an interdisciplinary activity. And in fact, this is just how he defines all academic and intellectual endeavors. Cultural pluralism, this time relating to the academic/intellectual society of which he is part, informs and transforms his work.

Joshua Fishman's own academic training was interdisciplinary in nature. His early training in Yiddish linguistics at the Yivo, his B.S. and M.S. in Education, his Ph.D. in Education and Social Psychology, his post-graduate work at the Social Science Research Council, prepared him early on for his interdisciplinary venture.

From the beginning of his academic career, Fishman maintained a "plural" and interdisciplinary character. During his years as Assistant Director and then Director of Research at the College Entrance Examination Board

(1955-1958), Fishman held his first teaching job in the Department of Psychology at the City College of New York. Even then, he used Bram's *Language and Society* (1955) for the course he taught on Social Psychology. When in 1958 he became Associate Professor of Psychology and Human Relations at the University of Pennsylvania and Director of Research at Albert Greenfield Center for Human Relations, he started offering a year-long course called "Human Relations and Language". This course consisted of one semester of "Psychology of Language" and one semester of what he then called "Sociology of Language".

It wasn't until 1964, after four years at Yeshiva University, when he came into contact with "official sociolinguistics" during the seminal Summer Linguistic Institute at Indiana University. Funded by the Social Science Research Council's Committee on Sociolinguistics, and chaired by Charles Ferguson, this Institute brought together the other major actors in what would be the sociolinguistic enterprise: Gumperz, Labov, Bright, Ervin, Rubin, Grimshaw, among others.

Joshua Fishman's contribution to the sociolinguistic venture has been a major one. Although he has expressed disappointment with the narrow linguistics-only approach of today's sociolinguistics, he has chosen to impact upon it by reminding linguists of the importance of "the shell", rather than by alienating "Sociology of Language". Reacting to criticism by a linguist that his work is "tantamount to cracking an egg, pouring out its contents and concentrating on its outer shell", Fishman has said:

> I have never argued with this implication of peripherality ...; I have merely insisted that the shell too is part of the egg and that without it the so-called "contents" would soon be little more than an intellectually trivial, formless and lifeless mess. (Fishman, fortchoming a: 15)

And thus, rather than developing an organized and closed Sociology of Language enterprise, Fishman's interest in macro-sociological, historical and quantitative aspects of language continue to impact on sociolinguistics. His editorship of *The International Journal of the Sociology of Language* since 1974 and of the Mouton de Gruyter series on "Contributions to the Sociology of Language" are proof of his broad and encompassing definition of sociolinguistics and sociology of language.

Joshua Fishman has continuously tried to shape the interdisciplinary nature of the academic preparation required for students of Sociology of Language. After his Deanship at Yeshiva University (the Graduate School of Education from 1960 to 1963 and Ferkauf Graduate School of Humanities and Social Sciences from 1964 to 1966), Fishman proposed the merging of Education, Liberal Arts and Behavioral and Social Sciences saying that: "[Teacher education] is first and foremost an intellectual endeavor striving to increase knowledge about man and the process whereby he learns, grows, changes, and influences others" (Congressional Record A, 3594, July 11, 1966). His Doctoral Program in Language and Behavior (1966-1972) became the first interdisciplinary program at Ferkauf, later succeeded by the recent Ph.D. Program in Bilingual Educational/Developmental Psychology (1981-1989).

But in keeping with the narrow and broad loyalty theme in Fishman's life, his link to a Jewish institution, Yeshiva University, and to a Department of Psychology within the University, has made it difficult to develop a following of students of Sociology of Language educated to Fishman's liking. At Yeshiva University, Fishman has had to teach courses outside of the sociolinguistic enterprise to psychologists with little interest in Sociology of Language or ethnolinguistic minorities. Yet, his teaching of courses such as Medical Anthropology and Test Construction have allowed him to conserve his interdisciplinary and pluralistic focus. In recent years, the presence of the Latino Doctoral students in the Bilingual Educational/Developmental Psychology Program at Yeshiva University has been living proof of his commitment to cultural pluralism.

Academically and intellectually, Fishman's life reflects his personal *ecclectic* choice as a Yiddish activist and a neo-Orthodox Jew. At Yeshiva University, colleagues in the School of Psychology found it difficult to understand his work and interest as a Psychologist/Sociologist/Linguist/Yiddish scholar. They also found it difficult to understand his commitment to ethnolinguistic minorities all over the world (and to Latinos, in particular, within the institution), at the same time that he was committed to Jewish ethnolinguistic continuity. He, however, never asked for understanding or inclusion, he merely continued to insist that history, society, culture and language be seen as an intricate part of studies of human psychology.

2.4 *The Plural Writer*

Joshua Fishman has been an avid writer and bold editor all of his life. When at fourteen he needed a forum for the publication of his Yiddish writing, he did not hesitate to start a journal for children. When years later he wanted to develop a field of study which he had shaped, he did not hesitate to contact Mouton to start both a journal for the Sociology of Language, as well as a book series. One can hardly ignore the primary force of the Word in a religious sense when studying Joshua Fishman's work.

In the Hebraic and Christian tradition, "The Word was God" (John 1:1-3). In India, "the Word is the Imperishable, the firstborn of the eternal Law, the mother of the Veddas, the navel of the divine world" (Taittiriya Brahm, 2,8,4). In the same sense, Fishman, the writer, has created the reality of Sociology of Language, while at the same time conserving its plural and generative aspects. He has said:

> I feel strongly that there is more 'out there' (even more to the sociology of language) than science can grasp, and I have a personal need for poets, artists, mystics and philosophers too for a deeper understanding of all that puzzles me. (Fishman, forthcoming a)

Fishman's words reflect this puzzlement by the dense and poetic style which characterizes his work. Even the results of his most quantitative studies are not expressed in absolute terms, for as he said very early: "Research operations ... are never-ending, for their value resides in their provocativeness and in their fruitfulness with respect to future research" (Fishman 1959: 62). And Fishman's words constantly provoke others. He writes quickly and avidly (in long-hand before the computer age, and with two fingers at the keyboard since then), and the process often reminds us of the "automatic texts" of the Surrealist writers, who like him, were searching for the Supreme Point where all contradictions cease to exist.

Fishman's text is plural because it is a constant intra-text, and the 544-item bibliography which Gella Fishman has compiled (G. Fishman, forthcoming) bears witness to the many reprints of Joshua Fishman's work. His text is plural because it reflects others' intertext, not just that of Ancient texts such as the Bible, but even those of his contemporary colleagues whom he engages in continuous correspondence. But the plural and generative character of his writing is a direct result of his biliteracy: the concrete understanding that the Word is multiple even as a *signifiant* and certainly as a *signifié*.

During the last decade, Gella Fishman has devoted much time to the creation of the inter-generational Fishman Family Archives. Presently located in the Archives Room of the Fishman home in the Bronx, the many file cabinets in the Joshua A. Fishman Collection bear witness to the proliferation of Fishman's written word.

3. Our Intertext on Bilingual Education

The voices in this volume interact with those of our colleague, friend and teacher, Joshua A. Fishman, in extending the plural text which informs work on bilingual education.

This is an interdisciplinary text, and thus, there are contributions of anthropologists (Trueba), linguists (Abdulaziz, Baetens Beardsmore, Bratt Paulston, Clyne, Sridhar), psychologists (Cummins, Hakuta), sociologists (Verdoodt), Yiddishists (Roskies), bilingual education policy makers (Benton, Sibayan, Zondag), bilingual education pedagogues (Casanova, Torres), as well as interdisciplinary bilingualism/bilingual education specialists (Skutnabb-Kangas, Hornberger, Mackey). It is often difficult to place the contributions and the authors within a discipline, since following Fishman, all voices are interdisciplinary, reflecting the nature of the bilingual education activity.

This text is also international in scope, containing contributions about bilingual education in Africa (Abdulaziz), Australia (Clyne), Canada (Mackey and Roskies), Friesland (Zondag), India (Sridhar), Luxembourg (Baetens Beardsmore and Lebrun), New Zealand (Benton), Philippines (Sibayan), Sweden (Skutnabb-Kangas), as well as the United States (Casanova, Cummins, Hakuta, Hornberger, Paulston, Torres). Some of the articles address policy and curricular issues with regards to the minority language, whereas others focus on the majority language. Some consider the enrichment aspect of bilingual education for some students (Clyne, Sibayan), for some ethnic communities (Mackey) and for some multilingual societies (Baetens Beardsmore); others focus on the language maintenance aspects of bilingual education for the ethnolinguistic minority (Casanova, Roskies) and on its language revitalization features (Benton, Zondag); still others look at ways in which bilingual education could stabilize the functions of the societal languages (Abdulaziz, Sridhar). All the articles, however, support bilingualism in society, and consider how bilingual education could promote that goal.

The book is divided into five sections, each reflecting a different aspect of the Sociology of Bilingual Education, and each echoing and pluralizing the words of Joshua A. Fishman that title each of the sections:

Section I   :   "Ethnicity recognized and liberated"
                   Languages in Education: Theoretical Considerations

Section II   :   "We all need rhinoceros and orangutans"
                   Languages in Education: Planning

Section III :   "Multilingualism for minnows and whales"
                   *Languages in Education: Policies and Implementation in an
                   International Context*

Section IV   :   "Yes, Virginia, we too have language problems"
                   Languages in Education: US Policies and Politics

Section V   :   "The beast as a multisplendored thing"
                   Languages in Education: Practices

And following the plural construction of Fishman's discourse, the epigraphs
which I have placed before each of the articles echo the words which title
each of the sections. The Fishman discourse is then expanded by the contributors; thus creating the plural intra/intertext which this volume attempts.

    In the first section, articles by Skutnabb-Kangas and Trueba provide the
theoretical underpinnings for the recognition of ethnicity and the inclusion of
cultures, as well as languages, in education. The articles in the second section
address *language planning issues* in education. Verdoodt describes a study
that should precede use of regional languages in education. Two case studies
of language in education planning then follow, one in three East African
countries (Abdulaziz) and the other one in India (Sridhar).

    The third and fourth sections contain articles that address bilingual educa-
tion *policies*. The *international* context is described in section three with contributions about the past and present school policies on the use of Luxemburger (Letzeburgesch), German and French in Luxembourg (Baetens Beardsmore and Lebrun), Frisian in Friesland (Zondag), Maori in New Zealand
(Benton), and Yiddish in Montreal (Roskies). The *US* bilingual education policies that have turned outright political are discussed in section four. The first
two articles in this section (Casanova and Cummins) must be read as reflec-
tions of each other. The discussion of the politics of bilingual education
research by Casanova and Cummins contextualize for the reader the first person account of the researcher which follows (Hakuta). The last article in this
section discusses and clarifies the numerous typologies of bilingual education
and portrays one successful enrichment program (Hornberger).

Practices of bilingual education are discussed in the last section. The first two articles of this section, present two successful experimental programs to promote bilingualism, one in Acadia, Canada (Mackey), and the other in Australia (Clyne). The article which follows (Torres) discusses active pedagogy within the bilingual education classroom. Finally, the last two articles focus on children's acquisition of English. One is a first person account by a major Philippine language planner of his own education through English (Sibayan). The other is a brave attempt by a Swedish American to discuss language practices within the bilingual classroom and their relationship to children's acquisition of English (Paulston).

A word must be said about my own voice as it has been influenced by reading Fishman's work. I was a Fellow in the NEH Seminar that Fishman conducted at Yeshiva University in 1981. Since then I have been involved in the Ph.D. Program in Bilingual Educational/Developmental Psychology at Yeshiva University, teaching occasional courses on Bilingual Education and Bilingualism, helping students complete Pre-Doctoral Projects and Doctoral Dissertations, but most of all, continuing to learn from Joshua Fishman. In the last decade, he has provided me with more guidance and support than I had a right to expect, meeting with me frequently, discussing my work, sharing his, sending me articles, giving me books.

Since 1980 I have taught in the School of Education at City College in New York. It might be a coincidence that Fishman's first full-time academic job was, like mine, at City College, and that the Chair of my Department, Miriam Dorn, had been the Fishman's eldest son's Kindergarten teacher and shares with Gella a Yiddish Canadian experience. But beyond these coincidences, the multiple magic boxes of Fishman's life and work continue to give meaning to mine. As the wife of a linguist, Ricardo Otheguy, and mother of three bilingual children, Eric, Raquel, and Emma, as a Latina born in Cuba who grew up in a Hispanic neighboorhood in New York City, I have often gathered strength as a wife, mother, ethnic advocate, and committed bilingual educator from the Fishman's family context, and especially from Gella. The best lesson learned has been the human one.

SECTION I:

"ETHNICITY RECOGNIZED AND LIBERATED"

Languages in Education: Theoretical Considerations

Ethnicity grows stronger when denied, oppressed, or repressed, and becomes more reasonable and more tractable when recognized and liberated.

Joshua A. Fishman, 1976a: 118

Swedish Strategies to Prevent Integration and National Ethnic Minorities

Tove Skutnabb-Kangas

University of Roskilde

1. Introduction

A national ethnic minority has many more internationally coded rights than an immigrant group. When a minority, created through migration, wants to change its status from a migrant group to a national ethnic minority group, with corresponding legal rights, the validity of this new status must be negotiated with the state. There are then possibilities of agreement and/or disagreement as discussed below.

If both the state and a migrant group itself see the group as temporary migrants, there is no conflict. This was the situation of Italian migrants into Sweden in the fifties – even if most of them in fact have stayed. If both see the group as a national ethnic minority, there is no conflict either. In Sweden this is the situation for the indigenous (Sami) minority. If the group sees itself as temporary, whereas the state sees the members as immigrants, there may be conflict – this is the situation with some refugee groups in Sweden today. And if a group wants to have a national ethnic minority status whereas the state sees it as an immigrant group, there is also conflict. The options left open by the state to this type of a migrant minority group are thus either to assimilate or to remain immigrants forever. This is the situation of Sweden Finns today (see Skutnabb-Kangas 1987, forthcoming a, b, c; Widgren 1986).

Finns in Sweden, the largest labour migrant group in Scandinavia, may be of international interest for several reasons. On the one hand, they resemble many other labour migrants. The majority of them are among those many millions who came to industrialised European countries during the last two or three decades in search of work and who stayed in the new country. They moved from the old colony to the country which earlier colonised them (Finland was colonised by Sweden approximately from 1150 to 1809 and was a Russian Grand Duchy between 1809-1917). Some Finns in Sweden are descendants of indigenous Finns who were left on the Swedish side of the border in 1809, i.e. a situation reminiscent of that of Mexican-Americans with both native and migrant groups. On the other hand, Finns differ from many traditional labour migrants on some dimensions in ways which may become more frequent also globally in the future. They moved from one highly developed industrialised country, now one of the richest in the world, to another industrialised country. There are few cultural differences between them and "the hosts" (partly because of the long colonisation) and there is no difference in skin color. Even if the Finnish minority is largely working class, everybody has at the least a basic education and there are no more illiterates among the Finns than among the Swedes. Thus it is difficult to legitimate the poor school achievement of Finnish children in Swedish schools or the factual unequal division of power and resources between the Swedes and the Finns with "racial", cultural or social difference explanations such as are often used in relation to migrant groups globally (see Churchill 1986). The only major difference is one of *language* (Finnish is Finno-Ugric, Swedish is Germanic, Indo-European). Language-related explanations for the generally poor school achievement of Finnish children in Sweden have therefore been used (and elaborated – see e.g. Pertti Toukomaa's and my reports for UNESCO) earlier than in most comparable countries.

Language seems to be one of the important core values (Smolicz 1979) in Finnish culture, and a *sine qua non* for Finnish ethnic identity. This is easy to understand because the Finnish speakers in Finland had to struggle for centuries to maintain their language in the colonial era under Swedish rule when it had few rights, and to some extent during the last decades of the 108 years of Russian rule. The Swedish language in Sweden has, on the other hand, not been threatened by other languages, regardless of the influences of, respectively, Latin, German and French, as (additional) languages for certain ruling sectors in earlier centuries. There seems to be little awareness among the Swedes of the importance of one's mother tongue, almost regardless of what indicators are used (see examples in Westin 1988, Skutnabb-Kangas and Phillipson 1987). The Finnish language has taken on a heavy symbolic and signalling load in Sweden, because it is the main noticeable differentiator between the Finns and the Swedes and because of the relative Finnish awareness and Swedish lack of awareness of the importance of the mother tongue.

Sweden is known for one of the world's most progressive general immigrant policies. The official rhetoric about equality, partnership and freedom of choice (main principles in Swedish immigrant policy, SOU 1976), and minorities as an enrichment, active bilingualism as an educational goal, and intercultural education as a way towards harmony and international understanding (SOU 1983) is impeccable. On the other hand, Swedish attitudes towards the Finnish language in the processes of both interpreting and implementing these centrally defined goals are often extremely negative. This can be seen in the slow development, extreme insecurity and instability, and the harsh opposition in relation to the use of Finnish as the medium in day-care centres, schools, further education and adult education, in the lack of any mother tongue questions in the census despite demands of it, in the lack of requirements of competence in Finnish in jobs, etc. The Finns in Sweden (e.g. The National Union of Finnish Associations) want to have mother tongue medium education for their children, because they know it leads to good results.[1] The Swedes have tried and still try to prevent it. The struggle for the right to mother tongue medium education seems to have functioned as the main mobilising factor in the development of the Finns in Sweden from an immigrant group to a group which demands acceptance as a national ethnic minority group (Peura, forthcoming).

Negative attitudes toward Finnish have been explicitly expressed in a recent decision (January 22, 1990) by the City Council in Haparanda (where sixty-five percent of the population has Finnish as their mother tongue, mostly descendants of the old border minority). The Council has fobidden the staff in all day-care centres to speak anything else but Swedish when communicating with each other both in their planning work and in the children's presence; the same prohibition is planned to be extended to the schools too. A complaint about this is being investigated by both the Ombud of Justice and the Ombud against Discrimination. Normally, negative attitudes toward Finnish are expressed in much more sophisticated ways (see Municio 1983, 1987, and forthcoming, for thorough analyses of some concrete cases). There is an obvious lack of correspondence between realities in Sweden for minorities and the picture which this "conscience of the world" likes to project for itself. At the same time that Sweden both actively and passively tries to prevent regular mother tongue medium education, much of the official rhetoric supports bilingualism and biculturalism for minorities.

Both Finland and Sweden are consensus-seeking societies in their general political decision-making. But consensus is reached in very different ways. In Finland it is often reached through aggresive debates, strikes, etc., whereas in Sweden it is often accomplished diplomatically, softly, negotiating behind closed doors, or by treating the other party as a non-party (Municio, forthcoming), ignoring the conflict and pretending that consensus has been reached. Conflict avoidance is one of the most typical Swedish cultural traits (Daun 1984, 1989, Daun and Ehn 1988, Daun, Mattlar and Alanen 1989, Ehn and Arnstberg 1980). This makes Sweden an excellent conflict mediator internationally. It also makes it difficult then to analyse conflicts between the Swedish rhetoric and immigrant realities.

In this paper I analyse the kinds of conceptualisations of integration and ethnicity that are most profitable when trying to understand the extremely covert conflicts in Sweden in relation to the future of (Finnish) immigrants. The theoretical framework presented here has been applied to empirical material from a project among Finnish youngsters in mother tongue medium classes and their working class parents in Sweden (see Skutnabb-Kangas 1987 and forthcoming a, b, c, for a fuller treatment).

2.   Integration and Ethnicity: Characteristics or Relations?

2.1 *How Is "Difference" Constructed?*

Principles of democracy and equality presuppose that power and resources are distributed equally between people. In order to legitimate an unequal distribution, the ones who get more have to show that the ones who get less are somehow "different" in a way which appears to demonstrate that they do not *deserve* a fair share. If we are interested in a more equal distribution of power and resources, it is important to understand how "differences" are constructed. "Being ethnic" and "not being integrated" are in some views **characteristics** which "legitimate" that individuals/groups with these "different" characteristics should have less power and resources, until they have stopped "being different", i.e. lost their ethnic traits and become integrated. If you are "different", you have to be different **from** something which is seen as constituting a (desirable) norm. It is only comparison which brings out a difference. The theoretical stance taken here is that differences can be more profitably understood if they are conceptually treated as *socially constructed mutual* **relations** *between the definer and the defined, not as characteristics of the defined.* I will show some of the consequences of defining integration and ethnicity either as *characteristics* or *relations*.

2.2.1   *Covertly Assimilationist Rhetoric, Overtly Assimilationist Implicit Assumptions*

Both integration and ethnicity have in much of the earlier research literature been treated as (static, final) *characteristics of a minority group or individual.* The reasoning goes approximately like this: A minority group or individual goes through different phases in the process of becoming integrated. In the final phase it/she *is* integrated into the new society. Likewise, the minority group/individual *possesses* a certain ethnicity (or ethnic identity).

In this reasoning, it is mostly only the newcomer or the minority person/group who is seen as possessing ethnicity, and having to change and to embrace the goals, ideals and identity of the new country and become integrated into a "mainstream society". Methodologically, it has been only the newcomer's "degree of integration" and "ethnic identity" which is discussed and assessed, not the degree of integration or the ethnic identity of the majority. If the newcomer has to fit into a virtually unchanged society, this society can continue to regard itself as the mainstream. "Being in the mainstream" is thus also treated as a characteristic, a characteristic of the majority, which they somehow possess in a natural way.

This static and ethnocentric view, where the whole burden of integration is on the incomer alone, and where the dominant group's values are presented as somehow "shared" and "universal" values (see Zubrzycki's criticism, 1988) in which the minority groups have to participate (rather than particularistic and changing, like all values are), still prevails in many countries. When the majority population is presented in this way as an integrated mainstream, homogeneously sharing universal cultural values, this characteristic legitimates its access to power and resources (which are, of course shared unevenly on a class and gender basis *within* the majority population, but this is often not mentioned in the integration discourse).

If "being integrated" is seen as a characteristic which the majority population possesses "naturally", and if this "integrated" majority is seen as non-ethnic (= only minorities are ethnics), that means that "being integrated" entails "disappearance of ethnic characteristics". This view of integration and ethnicity in fact leads to "integration" becoming synonymous with "assimilation". But this is often not apparent, because the brutally assimilationist rhetoric of earlier times is absent. Those who hold these views are not even always themselves aware of the assimilationist implications of their concepts. The *rhetoric* used is thus *covertly assimilationist*, but the *implicit assumptions* are *overtly assimilationist* in relation to *integration* and *ethnicity* (overt because they are clear to the observer; they follow logically from the way the concepts integration and ethnicity are constructed).

If integration is seen in this way as something that only the minority group has to do and can choose to do or not to do, the minority can also be held responsible for the results, which are seen as reflecting its members' *wish* to integrate. The retaining of their ethnic identity and their lack of integration (which are in this view seen as their own fault) can then be used as a legitimation for the unequal division of power and resources which prevails in majority/minority relations. This is done in Sweden (and several other countries). The final report of the Swedish State Committee Against Racism and Xenophobia says: "There is reason to believe that some groups of immigrants will little by little integrate into the Swedish society. But a probable development is also that other groups will maintain and specifically emphasize their ethnic distinctiveness" (SOU 1989: 13, 115, my translation). According to the Swedes, then, a group is not integrated if it maintains its ethnic distinctiveness, they have to lose it and become Swedes in order to be integrated, i.e. they have to assimilate and become non-ethnic.[2]

Integration and ethnic identity are judged following *exo-definitions*, definitions by others. It is the representatives of those "already integrated" and those who "possess no ethnicity" who are the arbiters of to what extent an immigrant (group) has integrated or still behaves as ethnic. In these phases, minority members are also mostly seen by researchers/politicians within a deficiency-based framework, as problems (of their own making), until they have integrated/assimilated (see Skutnabb-Kangas 1988). They are seen as possessing integration-preventing characteristics which cause their problems and which they consequently have to get rid of (see Jayasuriya 1986, Skutnabb-Kangas and Cummins 1988). They are defined *with the majority population as a norm* and *negatively*, according to what they are not, do not have, or do not represent (= majority-language-speaking middle class "modern" majority members). For instances, LEP or NEP children in the United States (Limited or No English Proficiency) or NESB students in Australia (Non-

English-Speaking-Background) or *fremmedsprogede* in Denmakr (foreign speaking) represent these definitions. The problems which minorities face are *not* analysed in terms of the racism, ethnocentrism and discriminatory practices of the majority society (i.e. in terms of *relations* between the minorities and the majority), but are seen as resulting from handicaps and deficiencies (*characteristics*) in the minorities themselves.

2.2.2 Overtly Liberal/Intercultural Rhetoric, Covertly Assimilationist Implicit Assumptions

Another way of seeing integration and ethnicity often follows the more crudely assimilationist views described above. Here the *rhetoric* is *overtly liberal/ intercultural* whereas the *implicit assumptions* are *covertly assimilationist* with regards to *integration/ethnicity*. Now it is overtly acknowledged that the migrant may have something to contribute, but it is the host society which decides what of it is accepted as enriching, and thus allowed to exist as part of the "mainstream" (often ethnic food, dances, clothes, etc). The rest, meaning many of the more vital non-material group-reproduction-oriented parts of minority cultures, are seen as belonging to the domain of the private sphere.

However, the same attributes are *not* seen as part of any private ethnicity when it comes to the majority population. *Their* "private ethnicity" is of course being supported by public institutions like schools. Majority language schools for majority children "naturally" maintain *their* language, which should logically also be seen as a private aspect of *their* ethnicity. This lack of consistency is a logical consequence of seeing ethnicity as something that majorities are devoid of.

In this phase integration is defined in a way which allows the minority to categorise itself to a larger extent, to use *endo-definitions*. The minority is allowed to retain what it wants of its own cultural heritage, in addition to being allowed to learn and use cultural and structural features of the host society on an equal basis, i.e. it is allowed to become structurally incorporated and bicultural. But in this more progressive atmosphere, in an intercultural phase, the host society may still not see the need to change. It just lets a bilingual, bicultural migrant (group) incorporate structurally into an unchanged "mainstream" culture and structure.

All these ways to construct the concepts of integration and ethnicity can be used to legitimate less access to power and resources for minority groups, which are seen as being unintegrated because they "cling" to their original

ethnic identity. At the same time, integration is defined for minorities in a discriminatory way because it forces them to assimilate, whereas no change is
required in the majority population or society. These deficit theories also do
not challenge the static, ethnocentric view of majorities as devoid of ethnicity.
In thus making invisible those "characteristics", on the basis of which the
majority group gets access to more power and resources, and reconstructing
minorities' *resources* (their "differences" and their ethnicity) as *handicaps*,
these definitions implicitly legitimate and reproduce this unequal access.
They function in a racist/ethnicist/linguicist way.

2.2.3 *Democratic/Intercultural Rhetoric, Intercultural Harmony-Oriented Implicit Assumptions*

In contrast to these definitions, Drobizheva and Gouboglo (1986) define integration as the "formation of a series of common features in an ethnically heterogenous group". This definition of integration where the *rhetoric* is *demo-
cratic/intercultural* and the *implicit assumption* is one of *intercultural harmony* with regards to *integration/ethnicity, uses ambo-definitions.* It sees integration as a process, (not a product) with several participants, all equal,
regardless of size, and it sees all groups as ethnic. As an example of the use of
the definition we can consider the present changes in Europe. If an *integrated
Europe* is to be "an ethnically heterogenous group", one implication of the
definition is that majority ethnicities have to be acknowledged and made
visible. Secondly, *all* groups have to change, not only old or new minorities,
or Eastern Europeans now entering what many Western Europeans have
defined as "Europe". There cannot be any kind of "mainstream European-
ness", that we "in the fringe areas" are invited to join.

But the features which the Drobizheva and Gouboglo definition talks
about can still be seen as *characteristics* in a group, even if all participants are
allowed to participate in defining the legitimate characteristics. And there is
nothing in the definition to suggest that the formation of the common features
might be something conflictual, something where the power relations
between the different groups involved might influence the outcome. It presupposes *harmonious relations* where everybody is prepared to give and take on
an equal basis. Conflicts are not discussed or conceptualised within the definition and thus harmony becomes deceptive.

2.2.4 *Various Rhetoric, Intercultural Conflict-Oriented Implicit Assumptions*

Barth's way of seeing *boundaries* between ethnicities as the focal point of ethnicity is a conceptualisation approximating a *relational* outlook. The essence of ethnicity is for Barth (1969) the very existence of the boundaries, not their content. But in the end, the binary oppositions used to constitute a boundary function as characteristics, even if they are constantly changing not static characteristics. Since the *content* of the boundaries is not important, the conflict in negotiating whose content definitions should be valid does not become salient for Barth – both groups define the boundaries for themselves and their conceptions of the boundaries do not necessarily need to coincide. It is not a contest about whose boundaries and world views are valid.

Deirdre Jordan (1984, 1988), building further on Barth, Berger and Luchmann, and others has studied the construction of ethnic identity by Aborigines in Australia. The negative white-constructed identities (exo-definitions) which Aborigines have been offered in most of their earlier contacts with the colonisers, (and which some accepted as their endo-definitions, leading to a behaviour which confirmed the negative identity) has to some extent been rejected by both groups. But the definition which Aborigines negotiate are socially constructed in a power relationship where they are the weaker party. Jordan's analysis of the Aboriginal theorising sees ethnic identity as a relation, where the outcome depends on the power relations between the negotiating groups. Her conceptualisation of ethnicity comes very close to the one advocated here.

Fishman has seen ethnicity in terms of both characteristics and relations. Fishman's (putative) biological origins-related "paternity" concept which "the notion of ethnicity requires (as) a central concept or chord around which all others can be clustered" (1989b: 24) can be seen as a characteristic, and so can "patrimony", the "behavioral or implementational or enactment system" of ethnicity (1989b: 27-28). His ethnicity "is viewed as having both inner and outer characteristics and consequences, causes and effects" (1989b: 6). In the same way as Barth, Fishman sees boundaries (contrast) and fully articulated opposition across boundaries as something that ethnic identity logically requires, but "there can be no boundaries unless there is a heartland", i.e. characteristics to relate to. Fishman also discusses ethnicity in relational terms in most of his articles, and recognises fully the power relations involved. This recognition of the complexity of ethnic relations seems to lead to an intellectually laudable but at the same time (politically and otherwise) frustrating stance that it is still too early to come up with a comprehensive theory of ethnicity (or integration), or even a definition. This seems to lead to a certain avoidance of fully exploiting power relations as causal factors in empirical analyses.

All these conceptualisations of integration/ethnicity come with implicit assumptions of *intercultural conflict* sometimes abstract (between definitions) and sometimes concrete (power conflict between groups), despite using different types of *rhetoric*. Whereas some conceptualisations stop with description, explanation and understanding, some go further to advocacy. All use *ambo-definitions*.

2.3 *Some Methodological Considerations*

In the *assimilationist phase* when the *migrant* has to do the integrating into an unchanged "host" society, researchers only study the migrant (group), and compare it with the host population. Deviations from the norm are seen as deficiencies to be compensated, and often subtractive changes (changes where the migrant adopts the hosts' behaviour at the expense of her own, not in addition to it) are applauded (see e.g. Jeppesen 1989 who has done this).

In the *liberal/intercultural phase, both minority and majority individuals/ groups* are seen as the ones to be studied. While the migrant (group) is still compared with the majority and deviations judged negatively, the majority are often compared with themselves earlier, and small deviations from earlier behaviour-attitudes are often seen as positive as long as they are additive, not subtractive.

In the *democratic/intercultural harmony phase*, when integration is seen as socially constructed, in the same way as gender, class and ethnicity, it is somehow assumed that the negotiation of legitimate features to be included just happens more or less "naturally", as a result of a state which promotes "international understanding" between the different nationalities/ethnicites. *All groups are studied, but in a way which emphasizes their equality and resources.* They are in principle judged according to the same criteria, but the majority's unwillingness to change is often "glossed over" or "understood" as rational. Power conflicts are not supposed to exist and are therefore not studied. As we can see from the recent occurences in the Soviet Union, this implicit assumption of harmony has been to some extent false; the conflicts had merely not been acknowledged enough.

This is what is explicitly done in the *intercultural conflict phase*. Since the integration relation is here seen as socially created and constructed through interaction between the parties to be integrated, the *conditions for this interaction should be equally important as objects of study* as the actors in this intercultural conflict view. If there is unequal access to power and resources in the negotiation process, there is a risk that some features are being forcibly imposed as "universal" and "common" to all, and these are invariably features of the powerful groups. Integration has not commonly been studied in this way in empirical studies.

The treatment of ethnicity has had a similar development. When ethnicity is seen as a characteristic of a group or a person, certain criteria are needed in order to differentiate ethnic groups from other types of groups. Allardt and Starck (1981: 43) identify the following criteria for an **ethnic group**:

1. Self-categorization (self-identification).
2. Common descent ("real" or "imagined").
3. Specific cultural traits, for instance, language.
4. Social organisation for interaction both within the group and with people outside the group.

According to Allardt, there are no criteria for membership in an ethnic group that would hold for *all* the members, but at least *part* of the members must fulfill *all* the criteria before one can speak of an ethnic group, and *every* member must fulfill at least *one* of them. Often most members fulfill all the criteria, but there is also a number of "ethnic lukewarms" and "ethnic self-haters" who do not self-categorise as members despite fulfilling all the other criteria except self-categorisation and despite being categorised as members by others.

One problem with such situations of cognitive dissonance is that forced external categorisations, *exo-categorisations* which do not agree with people's own categorisations, are, according to many researchers, "experienced as an insult to basic human rights" (e.g. Liebkind 1984: 19). According to a human-rights-oriented argumentation, it should be the right of every individual and group to have *endo-categorisations*, their own definitions of ethnic group membership or degree of integration accepted and respected by others.

On the other hand, according to Allardt, self-categorisations and other-categorisations have different logical structures. Other-categorisations imply reference to other superficial criteria (like cultural traits, language or organisation) which are part of his definition anyway, whereas self-categorisation presupposes a wish to identify or categorise as a member of the group (but see Fishman 1989b: 52, footnote 3 about the difference between ethnic self-recognition, awareness and consciousness). Therefore, Allardt sees it as unnecessary to have exo-categorisations as a part of the definition, but on different grounds from the human-rights-oriented argument of Liebkind and others. Fishman (1989b: 6), on the other hand, sees both endo- and exo-categorisations as part of ethnicity: "Above all, ethnicity is phenomenological, i.e. it is self-perceived or attributed", and ethnicity is "an aspect of a collective self-recognition as well as an aspect of its recognition in the eyes of outsiders" (1989b: 24). The criteria for belonging to an ethnic group as outlined by Allardt are all seen as *characteristics* in individuals making up that group or in the group itself.

By contrast, if ethnicity is treated as a *socially constructed relation*, the necessity of considering both endo- and exo-categorisations can be motivated differently. Relations cannot be decided by one party in the relation alone, relations are to be negotiated. Ethnicity is not a characteristic that a member of an ethnic group "possesses", it is something that the individual or group must negotiate about with significant others. If ethnicity is seen in this way, as something to be negotiated, something that *needs validation from both parties in order to exist*, all the parties involved in the negotiation process must be taken into account when defining somebody's ethnicity. If this is so, then the power relationships between the parties in the definition process become a primary object of study, just as when studying integration.

One consequence of this approach, in contrast to the human-rights-oriented demand for self-categorisation (which represents an intercultural harmony-oriented approach), is that other-categorisations have to be seen as a part of somebody's ethnic identity and ethnicity (as Fishman 1989b: 24 does). Self-categorisation is not enough. We can draw a parallel to a state. A state is also a relation, not a characteristic of the supposed state. It is not enough for the PLO to proclaim a state (which is an act of self-categorisation). The state does not "exist" before (at least some) other states have accepted its existence, meaning exo-categorisations are needed as validation, and thus *ambo-categorisation* becomes necessary.

The development of the definitions in constructing ethnicity can be seen from a dialectic point of view. The *thesis* is the phase (still the most common one) when the majority defines (and names) the ethnic identity and the ethnicity of the minorities, meaning only other-categorisations (and the names for an ethnic group given by others, exo-ethnonyms) are valid. This would correspond to all the assimilationist phases in studying integration. The progressive *anti-thesis*, represented by Allardt, Liebkind, Drobizheva and Gouboglo (but all with different arguments) is that the minority itself defines or has the right to define (and name) itself, i.e. only endo-categorisations and endo-ethnonyms (the names used by ethnic groups themselves about themselves) are valid. During both the thesis and the anti-thesis phase, cognitive dissonance, conflict between exo-ethnonyms and endo-ethnonyms, is possible and often probable, but since only either one or the other categorisation is seen as valid, the conflict does not become apparent. All treat ethnicity as a characteristic of the group to be characterised and named, and all concentrate, accordingly, on a study of the group or groups involved.

The *synthesis* which I try to develop here, sees the ethnonym, the name by which the group is characterised, as a signifier of the power relation between the groups. Cognitive consonance can only be reached (and exo- and endo-ethnonyms can only coincide) in a situation of balanced power between the parties. In this phase it is again, as in the study of integration, the negotiation process between the parties, the conditions for negotiation, and thus the power relations between them which should become the main object of study. Ethnicity has not commonly been studied in this way.

2.4 *Conclusion: The Power of the Definer Can Prevent Integration and the Development of National Ethnic Minorities*

I see both a high degree of bilingual and bicultural competence and a wish to self-categorise as a national ethnic minority group (as opposed to an immigrant group or just an ethnic group) as a prerequisite for an immigrated minority group to do its part of the integration. But the majority also has to do its part.

If a minority group persists in an interpretation of integration as a *mutual* process, and demands that the majority also change, an unwilling majority (as in Sweden) can either dictate terms or cease negotiating. It can revert back to (or never stop) seeing integration as a characteristic, and claim that the majority is integrated anyway, because it represents the mainstream. Thus a powerful majority may subvert the integration process, and simultaneously arrogate to itself the power to define the minority as non-integrated and itself as integrated. Research about integration should, in the view taken in this article, mainly study the *structural and ideological conditions for the negotiation, in-cluding the power relationships between the actors.* By researching the migrants/minorities and "their" characteristics, the conditions for real integra-tion, most importantly *the power of the majority to prevent integration,* are neglected. Thus the concept of integration is constructed in a way which per-mits it to be used in legitimating new forms of racism.

The human right to self-definition makes sense only when the parties are equal. If minorities are defined on the basis of power, not numbers, minorities are per definition not equal parties in the negotiation process about "their" ethnicities or "their" degree of integration.

The powerful party is able to prevent a migrant minority group from con-structing itself as a national ethnic minority by refusing to do "its" (i.e. the majority's) part in the validation process. In relation to itself, the majority can refuse to change. In relation to the minority, the majority can, in the first place, prevent the minority from acquiring the bilingual, bicultural compe-tence needed as a prerequisite for integration. This is what Sweden does when organising minority education so that it leads to linguistic and cultural assimi-lation (which is what Swedish medium classes do, see e.g. Boyd 1985). Sec-ondly, if a migrant minority group struggles to get this competence, feels ready to integrate and wants to change its ethnic identification from Xish (e.g. Finnish) to an ambo-categorisation, often a hyphenated term (e.g. Sweden-Finn), the majority can refuse to accept the new categorisation as a *positive* categorisation and can redefine it in negative, deficiency-based terms. This is also what Sweden does. Identifying as anything that contains "Finnish" is not interpreted by Swedes as a positive endo-ethnonym, denoting a valued ethnic minority identity, but as a *linguonym* (Skutnabb-Kangas 1987, forthcoming a, b, c). As a linguonym, "Finnish" should, of course, denote a (positive) capac-ity to speak Finnish. But according to monolingual norms, a capacity to speak a *marked language* (and all non-majority languages are marked in a monolin-gually-oriented society) is also, or even mainly, taken as indicative of the possibility that one is **not** able to speak the unmarked majority language. The linguonym is *not* interpreted in a positive way, in line with enrichment theories, as denoting a *positive competence in an additional language.* It is interpreted negatively, according to a deficiency-theoretical interpretation, where "Finnish" stands for "lack of competence in Swedish". This is how the defiency hypothesis (see Skutnabb-Kangas and Leporanta-Morley 1988) is operationalised with regards to language. Being able to speak language X is not taken to indicate a **capacity**, a competence, but rather a suspicion of **lack of capacity** to speak language Y. As long as the Swedes do not accept "Finnish" as a *positive* official (as opposed to private: "home language") ethnonym which does *not* mean being less loyal to Sweden, and as long as "Swedish" is an exclusive and unmarked ethnonym, Sweden cannot have national ethnic minority groups, regardless of how ready for this and for integration these groups are. Swedish racism towards the inhabitants of Finland, its colony for 650 years, had to use *language* as the main basis for dividing groups to be given unequal access to power and resources because there were few biological differences like skin colour. And that is why Swedish racism and ethnicism from so early on has crystallised in **linguicism** ("ideologies, structures and practices which are used to legitimate, effectuate and reproduce an unequal division of power and (both material and non-material) resources between groups which are defined on the basis of language". Skutnabb-Kangas 1988). One strategy in linguicism is to restrict an ethnonym so that it becomes a linguonym only, and then to redefine the linguonym in a deficiency-theoretical framework (for more detailed accounts of how linguicism works see Phillipson 1990, Phillipson and Skutnabb-Kangas 1986, Skutnabb-Kangas 1988, 1990).

In educational planning linguicism is operationalised as a combination of L2-related handicaps and L1-deprivation (see Churchill 1986, Skutnabb-Kangas 1988). Being "Finnish" thus becomes an illness. It signals "lack of Swedish (competence) = in need of compensatory support". Earlier the cure was "more Swedish". And now the treatment is about to change again: "freedom of choice must not be interpreted as freedom from the daily educational cumulative dosis of school Swedish". Answers by representative samples of Swedes to questions about immigrants show marked changes during the 1980s towards more assimilationist demands, especially in relation to language (see Westin 1988 and Skutnabb-Kangas forthcoming a, b).

If Swedish society wanted to support the development of national ethnic minority groups, it would help to organise conditions conducive to the further development of *specific* cultural traits (e.g. bilingualism and biculturalism). The knowledge of the minority culture, especially the linguistic competence, seems to have a fair chance of developing fully only in mother-tongue-medium education which continues throughout the comprehensive school. This would also be a well suited social organisation to support. Mother-tongue-medium education also leads to ambo-categorisations and can also develop high competence in Swedish. This type of education is what Sweden opposes.

The Finnish minority, represented by the parents and children in my study, has the prerequisites for forming a national ethnic minority. Now it is up to Sweden to do its part. If Sweden does not even acknowledge that there is conflict, we are far from a solution. It is important in such a situation to make the study of the conditions for *negotiation* central in research, and to show how different ways of conceptualising can either hide the conflict or illuminate it.

The role of researchers in supporting one or the other party in a conflict of this kind is important. By choosing how to define and study "integration" or "ethnicity", by treating them as characteristics or relations, researchers can present evidence to legitimate or delegitimate the results of the unequal relations between immigrant minorities and the majority. As researchers we can either function as parts of the repressive state apparatus or participate in delegitimating racist ideologies and structures.

Notes

1. Less than 20 percent of the Finnish children in Sweden are in Finnish medium education, despite a general wish of this type of education. The large majority of Finnish medium classes are in the lower grades, and very few municipalities have been allowed to have instruction through the medium of Finnish in grades 7-9. The results from these few experiments (see e.g. Hagman and Lahdenperä 1988) break the pattern of extremely low achievement which the Finns until now have shown. In my longitudinal study of 20 youngsters in Finnish medium classes in two metropolitan Stockholm municipalities, the youngsters (born in Sweden, of working class parents, in grades 8-9 during the project, i.e. 14-16 years of age and trained as co-researchers during the project) did almost as well as a Finnish control group in Finland in a Finnish language test and slightly (but not significantly) better than a Swedish control gorup (53 youngsters, mostly middle class in parallel classes in the same schools) in a Swedish language test. Their school achievement was slightly better than that of the Swedish controls, and they continued their education to a somewhat higher extent than the Swedes (for details see Skutnabb-Kangas 1987).

2. My interpretation of Sweden here is at a general level based on reading, observation and active professional and non-professional participation in minority policy and practice during at least the last 25 years. At a more specific level it is based on research done by a multidisciplinary team during 1984-1989 in the project "The Education of the Finnish Minority in Sweden" which I directed (see Peura and Skutnabb-Kangas, forthcoming).

A minority student who is confident of and recognized in his more intimate primary-group membership relates more positively both to school and to society (both of which are majority-dominated) and, as a result, profits more from schooling.

Joshua A. Fishman, 1976a: 30

The Role of Culture in Bilingual Instruction: Linking Linguistic and Cognitive Development to Cultural Knowledge

Henry T. Trueba

University of California

1. Introduction

Classroom instruction both in the mother tongue and in the language of the larger society has been a central concern in Joshua Fishman's work (Fishman 1976a, 1977a, 1978c, 1979, etc.). The fundamental rights of ethnic groups to maintain their language and culture and the resulting enrichment of a country in which linguistic resources are truly appreciated have been championed by Joshua Fishman with distinction in the last three decades. One of his most significant contributions to linguistics and education was the publication of *Language Loyalty* (1956). Now considered a classic volume, *Language Loyalty* is of unique importance in the context of continuing attacks against the language and culture of ethnic groups in the United States.

2. Rights of Linguistic Minorities

Ethnic and other minority communities in the U.S. and in other countries are excluded from educational benefits on the grounds that their lack of proficiency in standard English prevents them from participating in regular classroom instructional activities (Cummins 1984, 1986, 1989). Fishman has warned us (1979) that looking at bilingual education as a panacea for curing the underachievement of linguistic minorities is a serious mistake and a political setup for the perpetuation of their academic failure. Language rights of ethnolinguistic minorities are not detachable from their basic human rights, their right to their culture and their civil rights. Minorities should be able to retain their cultural values and religious beliefs without jeopardizing any benefits associated with full participation in the social, economic and political institutions of United States' democracy.

As an internationally recognized scholar who has inspired language policies based on solid research and respect for human rights, Fishman insists that learning English is not the same as being educated, and that the learning of academic subject matter can at times be pursued equally or even more effectively through the home language of students rather than through a second language. Joshua Fishman, who stresses the significant role that the mother language plays in the acquisition of knowledge and the desirability for all students to develop proficiency not only in their mother tongue but in other languages as well, has invited reflection in sociolinguists, sociologists, anthropologists and psychologists.

Social scientists have since the early 1960s made significant contributions to the study of language, and its essential relationship to learning, as well as its joint role with culture in the cognitive development of children, especially in the context of instruction in the public schools. Sociolinguists have been highly instrumental in the study of the role of language in communicative settings (Cazden 1985; Cheng 1987; Cohen 1975; Cook-Gumperz 1986; Gumperz 1982, 1986; Gumperz & Hymes 1964, 1972).

Educational anthropologists have worked on issues of differential achievement in minorities and on the importance of the context of knowledge acquisition, as well as on the role of culture and language in instructional effectiveness (Au 1981; Au & Jordan 1981; Boggs 1985; Delgado-Gaitan 1986, 1987a, 1987b,1988a, 1988b, 1990; Delgado-Gaitan & Trueba 1991; Erickson 1984, 1986, 1987; Heath 1983b; McDermott 1987a, 1987b; Ogbu 1974, 1978, 1983, 1987a, 1987b, 1989; G. Spindler 1955, 1963, 1977, 1987a, 1987b, 1987c; Spindler & Spindler 1987a, 1987b, 1987c, forthcoming; Suárez-Orozco 1989; Trueba 1983, 1987a, 1987b, 1987c, 1988a, 1988b, 1989; Trueba & Delgado-Gaitan 1988; Trueba, Spindler & Spindler 1989; Trueba, Jacobs & Kirton 1990). Psychologists have done research on the joint role of language and culture for cognitive development (Cole 1985; Cole & Scribner 1974; Diaz, Moll & Mehan 1986; Goldman & Trueba 1987; Moll & Diaz 1987). Social scientists have increasingly come to recognize the essential relationship between the home language and the home culture, and between learning processes and the linguistic and sociocultural context of learning. Researchers understand the enormous pressure placed on ethnolinguistic communities to acquire the language of the dominant society and to conform with its norms and etiquette. The consequences of this pressure have been eloquently depicted in the work by De Vos and associates (1973, 1980, 1983, 1988; De Vos and Wagatsuma 1966; Wagatsuma and De Vos 1984), Cummins (1986, 1989), Hornberger (1988a), Suárez-Orozco (1987, 1989), Trueba, Jacobs & Kirton (1990), and others.

3. Demographic Trends of Linguistic Minorities in the United States

If we examine the demographic distribution of language minority groups given in the 1980 Census data, as well as advance analysis of recent demographic data (U.S. Bureau of the Census 1984; and U.S. Department of Commerce 1987), we find that linguistic minority enrollment in our public schools will increase dramatically in the last decade of this century and in the following years. Therefore, the issues of cultural understanding and compassion become issues of survival and protection of the North American dream, because the future of our technological development, economic power and military power will be to a large extent in the hands of children whose mother tongue is other than English.

There are approximately 35 million persons in the United States who speak a language other than English at home, of whom about 20 million are not fluent in English. Almost 11 million of them are school age children. Almost fifty percent of this linguistic minority population (about 16 million) are Spanish-speaking. Together, French, German and Italian speaking linguistic minorities make 8.4 million (or twenty-four percent). The Spanish-speaking population is concentrated in the Southwestern states of California (7 million), Texas (3.8 million), Arizona (727,000), New Mexico (618,000), and Colorado (475,000) (U.S. Bureau of the Census 1984; U.S. Department of Commerce 1987).

School is a microcosm of the larger society, and as such reflects the same biases and prejudicial attitudes which become a barrier to democratic ideals of equity and educational opportunity for all. A few pseudo-scientists (see, for example, Dunn 1987 and Jensen 1981) have argued that genetic differences (from a perspective of biological determinism) explain the low achievement of Blacks and Hispanics. For the most part, these individuals are not taken seriously. Nevertheless, the devastating implications of their prejudicial position for instructional policy and practice has been felt in some circles. Their misunderstanding of what tests mean and in what ways they measure cultural differences rather than intelligence seems to bias their findings.

From a cultural perspective (Cummins 1986; Spindler 1977; Spindler & Spindler 1983, 1987a; Trueba 1989) intelligence is the ability to pursue individual and group cultural goals through activities perceived as enhancing the home culture values. Intelligence is definitely not the ability to score high in tests constructed by individuals from a foreign culture, based on narrowly defined literacy and problem-solving settings. Cultural anthropologists (De Vos 1983; De Vos & Wagatsuma 1966; Ogbu 1974, 1978, 1987a, 1987b; Wagatsuma & De Vos 1984; and others) have documented the differential performance of the same ethnic group immigrating to diverse countries, and who are collectively low achieving in one country, but high achieving in another. The Koreans, for example, are considered outcast in Japan, yet they get recognition as outstanding students in the continental U.S., Hawaii and Europe.

In the United States English is seen as an indispensable instrument in order to adapt to North American life style and achieve in public schools. But the loss of the home language and culture is seen by some people as a necessary condition for the acquisition of English. While most ethnic community members see the importance of learning English and indeed seek opportunities to do so even at a high personal cost, extreme isolation and continued rejection experienced by minorities persuade them of the impossibility of ever belonging in the United States. Some members of ethnic minority groups rightfully perceive the loss of the home language and culture as a factor undermining their personal identity, and therefore resist pressures to conform with mainstream societal norms.

4. Language Minority Children in Europe and the United States

Immigrant and refugee families in both Europe and the United States venture into a new cultural world in their effort for socio-economic improvement. The case of immigrants in Belgium is here particularly relevant:

There is only one way to achieve this improvement, and this route inevitably runs through extended schooling or an intensive training period in an industry. Even if Belgian schools were to incorporate special immigrant language and cultural courses into their curricula, the logic of competitive technological Western society and its attendant service sectors would impose a certain degree of uniformity on the life pattern of immigrant pupils, and this could not be reconciled with large portions of the culture from their countries. Such pupils would only be able to maintain some traits of the symbolic-expressive sector of their culture. However, this does not prevent people who assimilate large portions of the surrounding culture from firmly maintaining their own *ethnic identity*. (Roosens 1989: 90-91) (Italics in original.)

The case of the Netherlands is also most revealing of the dilemmas faced by European countries today. In 1987 there were 570,000 immigrants (Turks, Moroccans, Surinamese, Antilleans and Moluccans – most of them living in rural areas) composing five percent of the entire population (Eldering 1989: 111). Early official policies on immigrants were based on the assumption that immigrants would be returning home within two years. Since 1980, however, the Dutch government has established three policy goals: "improving the social position of residing immigrants (as well as restricting further immigration), preventing and combating prejudice and discrimination, [and] furthering the emancipation of the immigrant groups by respecting their cultural, religious and linguistic backgrounds" (Eldering 1989: 115-116). School is expected to prepare immigrants for returning to their home countries, and therefore supports the use of the home language, but the policy also attempts to integrate the immigrants into the Dutch school system.

In Germany the number of migrant pupils went from 35,100 in 1965 to 150,000 in 1970 to 386,000 in 1975, to finally 637,180 (or seven percent) in 1980 and a peak of 720,700 (or nine percent) in 1982. There is now a serious problem with unemployed and unschooled migrant youngsters (not in training programs or paid work). Ethnic young persons between 15 and 18 years of age in the above category arose from twenty-six percent of the total population in those age brackets to thirty-four percent in 1984. But the highest proportion of these persons were Turkish. More recent policies stress the need of helping migrant children and youngsters to adjust to German society by preparing them to enter German schools (Boos-Nunning & Hohmann 1989: 39-59).

In the United States, immigrant and refugee populations are willing to do anything to share in the North American dream, and they often believe that giving up their language and culture is necessary in order to adopt American values and become more acceptable to all members of our society. The loss of the home language and culture in children of immigrants and refugees – very costly in terms of loss of personal identity and of emotional bonds with senior members of family and community – is often compounded by the unexpected rejection these children experience from mainstream community persons. Here is the crux of the conflict faced by linguistic minorities, that having given up their language and culture in order to belong in United States' society, they find out that minority persons are unaccepted by both their own ethnic community and by members of the society at large. Not being able to belong anywhere, they become isolated, disenfranchised and transitional between their parents' culture and that of their new country. This phenomenon is frequent in many modern industrial nations. Roosens, who has studied European ethnic migrations states:

> It is commonplace to say that the second generation sits between two cultures. In fact, this expression conceals as much as it reveals. There is evidence that the immigrant family never perfectly maintains the culture it acquired in the home country. Instead, an immigrant version of the home culture is created, in which the social context that gives many elements of a culture meaning and significance has been lost. (Roosens 1989: 88)

The cultural conflict faced by many immigrant children in the United States is very similar to that suffered by other immigrant children in Europe and Asia (Eldering & Kloprogge 1989; Trueba 1987b; Trueba & Delgado-Gaitan 1988; see especially, Roosens 1989: 85-106). The outcome of such conflict can be the gradual disempowerment (or "castification" as some call it) of ethnic groups alluded to by Delgado-Gaitan (forthcoming), Delgado-Gaitan & Trueba (1991), De Vos (1967, 1973, 1983, 1988), Freire (1970), Ogbu (1974, 1978, 1983), Roosens (1989), Spindler (1987c), Suárez-Orozco (1987, 1989), and notably Cummins (1986, 1989).

At the root of the disempowerment of ethnic minorities in the United States is a profound insensitivity of members of educational institutions (reflecting the insensitivity of society at large). This insensitivity can take the form of indifference, lack of advocacy, ethnocentrism, or plain racism and it is reflected in the way the needs of linguistically and culturally different children are handled. Rather than questioning the system, educationists assume that there is something wrong with children.

5. English and the Academic Achievement of Minorities in the United States

Cummins summarizes the institutional position of North Americans regarding the academic failure of linguistically and culturally different children as follows:

> Lack of English proficiency is the major reason for language minority students' academic failure. Bilingual education is intended to ensure that students do not fall behind in subject matter content while they are learning English, as they would likely do in an all-English program, since limited English proficiency will no longer impede their academic progress. (Cummins 1989: 21)

The above position has, in Cummins' opinion, serious problems because it ignores the sociohistorical and cultural factors determining children's failure. Cummins voices the public opinion which attributes low school achievement in ethnolinguistic minority children to their inability to communicate in English. This inability is presumed to imply some deficit on the part of those students. The reality is that these children are often normal and even high achievers in their own language when attending school in their home countries. To expect that a child can take full responsibility for the consequences of an abrupt change in language and culture is unfair to the child. To demand that a child start achieving at grade level immediately after arriving to a new country with a new language and culture is equally unfair and unrealistic. Furthermore, the underachievement of linguistic minority students in the host country is often related to the inability of the school personnel to understand the overwhelming effort required from the minority child to adapt to a new set of values and a new symbolic system of communication. The child's failure is in reality the school's failure to recognize the impossible demands placed on a language minority child in the new country. Besides the fundamental myopia implied in this position, it reflects serious misconceptions regarding the nature of language proficiency and of the relationship between language, culture and learning. Language minority children not only have to acquire phonetic skills in making new sounds and develop conversational skills in the new language, they also must redefine cognitively the world around, and re-interpret all the new relationships to space, individuals, objects and to themselves. Assuming that a child is "learning handicapped" because she/he speaks a non-standard variety of English or a non-standard of her/his mother tongue is a serious mistake commonly made by individuals who have rather simplistic notions of the learning and teaching processes.

Language is a system for social communication, as such it is anchored in culture; but language, as an instrument to capture and organize new knowledge, is further related to cognitive structuring and development. In order for language to be used effectively in learning settings, it presupposes a series of joint efforts in the exchange and interpretation of messages. Messages are tailored to specific contexts by gauging the knowledge shared by interaction participants. Thus, the development of learning skills and the transmission of academic content is dependent upon language control (not necessarily on the control of the language of instruction – often the second language for ethnic children). Language control is here understood as the ability to use a given linguistic system with mastery of its grammar, lexicon, semantics and discourse, especially in usages that establish conceptual relationships and properties of language domains, taxonomies or forms. The organization of information in appropriate linguistic categories requires a profound knowledge of a linguistic system. The interpretation and generation of these categories is vitally related to the culture associated with a given language. Language control is related to high levels of literacy because it is required to handle abstract knowledge in highly decontextualized interactional settings (including interaction with text). Highly literate children in their home language often process (interpret and organize) information passed to them in a second language better than less literate children who share with the teacher the language of instruction (see for example, Saville-Troike and Kleifgen 1989).

There are other problems, however, for culturally different children. Because ethnic children have coded their experiences in their mother tongue and have thus acquired cultural knowledge not shared with the teacher and peers – knowledge necessary to process information given to them in their countries of origin or their home environments, an abrupt change of language and culture imposes on children the impossible task of recoding old experiences and/ or coding new experiences in an unknown linguistic system. To make matters more difficult, these children often lack the social or cultural structures associated with the new language.

Cultural structures are understood here to be the contextual frames in which we place meaning, or culturally defined cognitive domains and categories. Frames are needed, for example, in the interpretation of face-to-face discourse, in the identification of semantic ranges and relationships, or in the reading of text. These required frames are missing, for example, when a child is asked to point to the color relationship between two flowers unknown to the child, or flowers whose colors are not semantically distinguished in the home language, or when a child is asked to assess the differential degree of urgency in the commands given by a teacher who in apparently the same context sometimes says: "Juan, you must..." and others "Juan, would you please..." Take, for example, a series of classroom micro-political events. The interpretation of a History lesson on the reunification of the two Germanies that alludes to political movements from the radical right requires an understanding of broader European and United States historical and sociopolitical contexts. The understanding of this lesson by Jewish and Afro-American students will be different. And the teacher's understanding will likewise be different. Furthermore, because of different interpretations and experiences, the participation structures of the students will most likely be different.

A student whose language and culture matches that of the teacher has a definite advantage in obtaining a positive evaluation from the teacher simply because the communication is linguistically clear and culturally congruent.

The United States continues to attract many immigrant and refugees who endure hardships and drastic changes in pursuit of their dream to be rich, free and happy. They clearly buy into North American ideals of mass education, political participation and economic opportunity equally accessible to all. Indeed, they believe with the rest of North Americans that the very foundations of democratic institutions are linked to peaceful and productive working relationships with a culturally diverse immigrant population eager to succeed. Indeed cultural and linguistic diversity are the cornerstone of United States democracy and the source of its continued strength over the last two hundred years (Spindler 1977; Spindler & Spindler 1983, 1987a, 1987b).

The successful adjustment of immigrant and refugee families depends a great deal on their ability to integrate United States' values with their ethnic values and thus resolve the conflicts associated with drastic cultural change. New beliefs, codes of behavior, communication patterns and stress faced on account of their differences are often compounded with prejudice. It is precisely in this social, political and cultural context that the work by Fishman has been so inspiring and instrumental for educators attempting to resolve the educational problems of minority students. The fundamental concern for respect to language and culture rights of ethnic populations, transparent in the work by Fishman, has deeply impacted my work (Trueba 1983, 1987a, 1987b, 1988a, 1988b, 1989) and that of many other researchers. Teachers are not only the key persons responsible for delivering packages of academic knowledge (in the form of lessons) to students regardless of their linguistic or cultural background, but also are the role models and cultural brokers for ethnic children. They are responsible for helping all children internalize cultural knowledge and values congruent with the U.S. democratic structures and instrumental for participating in social institutions in the United States. One of these values is precisely our appreciation for cultural and linguistic resources.

Because refugee and immigrant children cannot succeed in our society without a high level of literacy in English, the acquisition of the English language is crucial for them. However, overall adjustment and participation in social institutions (including school) depends on the ability of these children to integrate their cultural values with those acquired in the new country. The loss of the mother tongue is often the first step in the process of total rejection of one's own linguistic and cultural heritage. Richard Rodriguez, with his own testimonies in *Hunger of Memory* (1982) and other writings (1985, as cited by Cummins, 1989: 103-108) has typified the price of language and culture loss. Arguing against bilingual education he feels that bilingualism is only "a way of exacting from gringos a grudging admission of contrition – for the 19th century theft of the Southwest, the relegation of Spanish to a foreign tongue, the injustice of history..." (1985: 63) and that the reaffirmation of an ethnic identity is only a way of delaying assimilation to the United States. Then he describes what he went through:

> The child's difficulty will turn out to be psychological more than linguistic because what he gives up are symbols of home. I was that child! *I faced the stranger's English with pain and guilt and fear.* Baptized to English in school, at first *I felt myself drowning – the ugly sounds forced down my throat* – until slowly, slowly ... suddenly the conviction took: English was my language to use. (Rodriguez, 1985: 63) (Emphasis mine.)

6. Home Language Loss and Disempowerment of Minorities

The work by De Vos (1980, 1988) and Suárez-Orozco (1987, 1989) regarding systematic degradation of minority groups suggests similar consequences of self-rejection, disempowerment and cultural conflicts in minorities across cultures. The fundamental dilemma faced by minorities is to make a decision regarding means to empowerment that are not destructive of their ethnic identity and their ties with the community. Minorities are often asked to become mainstream members, to exhibit behavioral patterns and conformity with societal norms, yet, these minorities often are not accorded the status and recognition as bona fide members of the society.

Persistent low academic achievement in public schools and the resulting disempowerment of ethnic minorities is a central concern of educational anthropologists and other social scientists (G. Spindler 1974; Spindler & Spindler 1983, 1987a, 1987b). Researchers have documented the tragedy exemplified by Rodriguez and repeated in many children of immigrants, and they have discussed the false assumptions about the role of the home language and culture shared by ethnic families under the pressure of the dominant society (Delgado-Gaitan 1990; Delgado-Gaitan & Trueba forthcoming; Goldman & Trueba 1987; Ogbu 1974, 1978; Suárez-Orozco 1987, 1989; Trueba 1987a, 1987b, 1988a, 1988b, 1989; Trueba & Delgado-Gaitan 1988; and many others).

Many immigrant and refugee children have a life of poverty and rural isolation in crowded dwellings where they lack privacy, toilet and shower facilities, comfort, and basic medical attention. In some cases migrant life for children means abuse, malnutrition, poor health, ignorance and neglect. Uprooting a child from his/her land can lead to a life of stigma and low status. In turn, this status is acted upon in school during the process of second language acquisition.

The result of the "drowning" experience described by Rodriguez is precisely self-rejection as a member of an ethnic group. In more technical terms, these children's experience as they are formally stigmatized as "learning handicapped", as they attempt to "passing for" and survive are discussed eloquently by Rueda and other scholars (Rueda 1983, 1987; Rueda & Mehan 1986).

The close relationship between language, culture and cognition, and the significance of socially- and culturally-based theories of cognitive development are proposed by the sociohistorical school of psychology (Diaz, Moll and Mehan 1986; Scribner & Cole 1981; Vygotsky 1962, 1978; Wertsch 1985). The central question is: How do we create a culturally-appropriate learning environment (congruent with the values of home culture) in order to maximize cognitive development in ethnic children? In order to answer this question we must recognize the role of the mother tongue and the home culture in the acquisition of literacy in a second language. More specifically, we should ask:

1. What is the most effective use of language in the classroom if the primary goal of instruction is to foster learning in children?
2. What is the effect of using the home language in the overall cultural adjustment of ethnic children to school?

The education of linguistic minorities is primarily intended to help students acquire high levels of literacy so they can process information and develop their cognitive skills. Cognitive skills (the ability to handle learning tasks and to process knowledge effectively) can be best acquired through the language best known and then easily transferred to a second or third language. The use of the home language facilitates children's ability to develop critical thinking skills for the same reason listed earlier, that knowledge is best processed through a well-known language. What is less often mentioned in the literature is that cognitive structuring (the mental classification of experiences and knowledge acquired) is patterned not only by linguistic knowledge, but also by cultural knowledge and the social and cultural context in which knowledge is obtained. We know that many schools do not always have the resources or commitment to instruct children in their own language. The use of adult and peer tutors can be affordable and may significantly help ethnic children in the early stages of adjustment to the new school. Ethnic children must have a way of acquiring the new cultural knowledge presumed by the instructors and writers of textbook materials, and teachers must have a way of learning about ethnic children's culture in order not only to respect their home life style and values, but also to help other educational personnel (textbook writers especially) to make school-work more meaningful, to prevent negative ethnic or racial stereotypes, and raise awareness of ethnic children's learning potential.

Effective instruction for ethnolinguistic minority children in cultural transition should be conducted in their mother tongue, and within a flexible organizational structure in which teachers have a great deal of control of instructional strategies and activities. Children should also be able to take advantage of school instructional resources – tutors, translators, parental groups, audiovisual, computer and other technological packages – which increase comprehensibility. In other words, learning for these children must be guaranteed to become successful and satisfying to them. Schooling, in brief, must empower ethnic children to succeed, rather than setting them up for failure and thus disempowering them for life.

Fishman's inspirational work in linguistics, psychology and education has some long-term, forceful and profound implications for educational reform. A better understanding of the role of language in education, and of languages as national resources, requires drastic changes in the training of teachers, in the organization of Schools of Education and in the reorganization of Elementary and Secondary schools. The United States is, and will continue to be, a country of immigrants who will pursue the North American dream and in this pursuit recreate the making of United States' democracy.

SECTION II:

"WE ALL NEED RHINOCEROS AND ORANGUTANS"

Languages in Education: Planning

Who needs a rhinoceros or an orangutan?
We all do, for they enrich our lives.

Joshua A. Fishman, 1976a: 7

Writing and Schooling in the Regional Languages of the Member States of the Council of Europe

Albert Verdoodt

Université Catholique de Louvain

1. Introduction

The use of regional and minority languages in the education of linguistic minorities requires textbooks and print in those languages. And therefore, a study of the *written regional and minority languages of Europe* sheds some light on the the possibility of using these languages in education along with a majority language.

The International Centre for Research on Bilingualism (ICRB) at Laval University, Québec, along with the Standing Conference of Cultural and Regional Authorities (SCLRA) of the Council of Europe have supported the preparation of information files on the *written regional and minority languages of Europe.* Both ICRB and SCLRA have shared a political preoccupation to promote, or even provoke, a true decentralization of cultural policy in countries that are members of the Council of Europe.

It was Heinz Kloss who initially undertook the initiative to set up a data bank on the written languages of the world. And in 1969, Kloss and Verdoodt planned to carry out a systematic inventory of those languages worldwide. Our first research project consisted of studying the use of languages and their social relations for learning in the world's 172 bilingual universities (Verdoodt 1969).

The present article reports on the results of a research project focusing on *written regional and minority languages of Europe* (Verdoodt 1989). A clarification about our object of study is now in order. The sociolinguistic survey included only *written languages*. This restriction, however, was related only to financial limitations and in in no way undermines the importance of oral language.

In our study, *regional and minority languages* have the following characteristics:

1. They are used only in a particular geographical area of a State.
2. They are numerically weak or juridically limited in their usage.

The regional and minority languages studied have written forms, although they are not entitled to the same rights as the major official language(s). For these reasons, then, we include in our study Rhaeto-Romance and Swiss German in Switzerland, but not German, French or Italian which are officially recognized. We use States as units of analysis, and languages are considered to be regional or minority in relation to each of the States that is a member of the Council of Europe.

2. Some Useful Theoretical Positions

There has been little study of the use of written regional and minority languages in society. And so, there are few general or specific theories which serve as the framework to our study.

Sociology and political science have only very slightly delved into the study of the general use of languages, and almost not at all into the issue of regional and minority languages. When specialists from these fields show an interest in languages, they do so under the cover of culture, but seldom do they offer a coherent set of the most typical indicators of culture and the role of language in that set.

Our study is based on the principle that culture constitutes an all-encompassing phenomenon in which language plays an important role. However, the extent of this role may vary, depending on the group (Smolicz 1983). Furthermore, two distinct languages do not necessarily correspond to two cultures. It is possible to have a single underlying culture for several languages in one given area. The case of the Grand Duchy of Luxemburg, where French, German and Luxemburgian are all used, is a good illustration of this point (see Baetens Beardsmore, this volume).

It is also possible for two languages to correspond to two cultures. This is undoubtedly the case in Finland for Sami in relation to Swedish, but it is not the case for Finnish in relation to Swedish. It is even possible for one language, English or French for example, to be part of many cultures. And many immigrant groups create quite different cultures in their new settings even if they still remain largely faithful to their language.

The relationship between language and culture has been studied by theoreticians such as Bourdieu, Petrella and Rokkan. But we prefer the concepts introduced by Fishman and Kloss in this field of study.

The role of culture, and especially art, plays a central role in the work of *Bourdieu* (1979). Bourdieu emphasizes that symbolic interests may determine the use of a particular language by a certain group (Bourdieu 1975 and 1977). He admits, however, that it is difficult to apply these theoretical concepts to a concrete situation, and that such a task should be the object of sociolinguistics. Bordieu compensates for his lack of empirical research by introducing concepts which take into account the complexity of reality. His notion of "habitus" was one such concept:

> Habitus, as the term denotes, is that which one has acquired, but which is steadfastly internalized ... as permanent behaviour.... But why not use the term "habit"? Because habit is spontaneously considered to be repetitive, ..., rather reproductive than generative. So, I wished to insist on the idea of habitus as a powerful generator. (Bourdieu 1980: 134)

Within this notion of "habitus", which can be attributed to all stable social behaviour, lies the outline of another useful concept which we will discuss below, that of diglossia.

Petrella (1971 and 1978) studied what he considered to be deviant territories of the European Economic Community. His observations and classifications are based mainly on regions governed by nationalist movements. Although the use of two languages does not necessarily lead to a difference of opinion or identity (Lamy 1975), descriptions of these regions are useful in clarifying conflicts.

Rokkan's work (1968, 1971 and 1975) studies how language is used in national construction. He only considers language as an entity, separate from religion, education and judicial traditions, if it has political impact. In evaluating linguistic communities, Rokkan (1971: 35) judges the general level attained by standardized written publications, and literary production in particular, as being most important.

Many of the sociologists who have studied linguistic minorities have underlined the competition, struggle and conflict that surrounds them. *Fish-*

man, however, has focused on the stable and peaceful coexistence of more than one language in a given community. Fishman (1970) has stated that a bilingual situation can only be long-lasting if it is upheld by a certain amount of *diglossia*, which ensures its continuance. And Fishman's theoretical concepts have been tested against empirical reality (Fishman et al. 1971b).

Although the theoretical concept of *diglossia* has been developed by Fishman (1971a, 1981d), it was Ferguson (1959) who initially popularized the term. Ferguson described the situation of Arabic, Greek, Swiss-German and Haitian Creole as using language A in religion, education and other official aspects of life, and the use of language A' or B in daily activities, either at home, among family and friends or in the work place. In Ferguson's use of the term *diglossia*, the two languages or varieties always stem from the same linguistic origin, as is the case of German and Swiss German in Switzerland.

Fishman attributes the expansion of the notion of diglossia to Gumperz (1961, 1962, 1964), who described multilingual societies, such as India, that recognize languages of different language families, for purposes of communication within one group. While understanding that each language corresponds to a particular *domain* or sphere of life, Fishman defined *diglossia* as the stable existence of two or more complementary, not conflicting, languages within one group.

Our research study was limited to one domain: that of *written production*. And this domain was further divided into levels. Written production was used because it leads to distinct and verifiable *products*, even though the linguistic distance may be small. *Kloss* (1978) calls this linguistic distance *Abstand*. For example, there is a very weak *Abstand* between Corsican and Italian, or between Galician and Portuguese. But, although the linguistic distance is small, two forms of what were historically considered one language can and do appear because of the acquisition of very distinct functions and written products. This is what Kloss calls *Ausbausprache* and it is this concept that served as the framework for our study.

The concept of *Ausbau* or language development, as formulated by Kloss (1976 and 1983), constitutes the backbone of our questionnaire. According to Kloss (1976: 308) the written form of a language generally begins with poetry, short stories, and then fiction. Another stage unfolds once a language is used for *dialectic* or *non-narrative* prose (*Sachprosa*). This stage contains three distinct levels of language, represented by numbers 1, 2 and 3 in the diagram:

3. *Popular* dialectic prose, that is, simple writings in the form of pedagogical, political or religious materials.

2. *Refined* dialectic prose which englobes more sophisticated writings, such
as essential findings pertaining to the language group in question or to
pure sciences and the humanities.

1. *Learned* dialectic prose which corresponds to original work in a variety of
disciplines.

As seen in the diagram below, each level of language (1, 2, 3) can have
different orientations (A, B, C).

	Group Oriented A	Humanities Oriented B	Pure Sciences Oriented C
NON-NARRATIVE PROSE (dialectic) 1. Learned 2. Refined 3. Popular			

It is highly possible that dialectic prose might pertain only to the given
speech community for a long period of time (A); and only later will it spread
beyond this subject topic to the humanities (B) and then to the pure sciences
(C).

We have also established a fourth division in our study, that of *Bible
translations*. These are mostly narrative (the Gospels, the Acts of the
Apostles, the Book of Revelation, and the Pentateuch). However, there are
also non-narrative writings within the narrative sections (Kloss 1978: 45). In
Western Europe, the use of Bible translations could be indicative of *whether a
particular form of speech is considered a distinct language*. However, speech
forms such as those of Bavaria, Thuringia, Swabia and Rhineland are not used
as independent channels of the Christian word, despite literacy production of
a high quality (Hoffman and Berlinger 1978).

In carrying out our study, we have been guided by notions related to those
developed by Bourdieu, Petrella, Rokkan, Fishman, and especially, Kloss.
What follows is our theoretical position for inclusion in the information file

of written regional and minority languages in the States of the Council of Europe and a description of how our survey was carried out.

3. Theoretical Delimitations of the Information File

Our description of written regional and minority language use is not based upon a narrow linguistic approach, but is rather a sociological one. And thus, our questionnaire asked about the number of *non-narrative prose, literature, religious practices, periodicals and mass media* in regional and minority languages. Often these were part of personal and private collections. In Occidental democracies, small linguistic groups are able to use freely and openly their own means of expression. And if a group does not choose to use its language, it is not generally because of restrictions or conflicts, but simply because it is not interested in doing so. Thus, the use of regional and minority languages shows the importance of community initiative for free expression in a manner that does not conflict with, but rather, complements the other existing language(s).

Our questionnaire also aimed to determine the level of State assistance to the regional and minority languages in the form of grants or direct or indirect assistance. Thus, it covered the use of minority language usage in *administration, law* and *education*. The diversification of language use supposes a certain amount of official bilingualism. Inclusion in our inventory was based on whether *there were written publication in the language*. Because of inadequate linguistic censuses in Europe, it is not easy to locate works published in the various languages. We, therefore, had to depend on the bibliographical sources and statistics found in Kloss and McConnell (1984).

Our study divided written works into measurable levels or units rather than merely distinguishing between language and dialect, an impossible task. In drawing the difference between language and dialect, the general public often negatively judges dialects as lacking unity. But no language is strictly homogeneous; they are all susceptible to a variety of changes and, therefore, are polynomial to varying degrees. Standardization is a relatively recent phenomenon and can be instated in varying degrees; thus, German is less standardized than French, if we consider the number and importance of its regional variants. In addition, different standards can exist simultaneously, for example, Portuguese of Portugal and Brazilian Portuguese.

4. The Process of Developing the Information File

In an effort to obtain our data, regional authorities, organizations supporting each language and a number of recognized experts were contacted. The Council of Europe has been instrumental in this effort.

In addition to our written survey, we visited the majority of the indigenous groups studied. We usually obtained several replies per language, and in the few cases when these were contradictory, we made further contacts. If unanimity was not possible, we included all of the replies that we received.

As often as possible, we verified our information in independent parallel works, such as Linet (1989), *Minorités linguistiques* ... (1986), Rokkan and Urwin (1983), and Touret (1973). At times, encyclopaedic works such as those of Kern (1989) and Straka (1970) had to be consulted.

Verifying the literary production was relatively easy. But verification of non-narrative prose, the most original part of our work, has been most difficult.

Before analyzing the list of languages we came up with (section 5), we should keep in mind that we have included all languages for which we received replies through the Council of Europe, even though some languages are very close linguistically. What was important to us was that a *speech community recognizes itself as different from a neighbouring community*.

It is important to justify some exclusions from our list and some inclusions. The language of immigrants was a major problem in our study. Many of these immigrants, such as Masurians (Polish) in the Rhineland or Italians everywhere in Western Europe, arrived decades ago. And many of these people still make use of their language of origin. But we were forced to exclude these languages from our study because the Secretary of the SCLRA did not wish to include immigrant languages.

We did not treat Gascon, Monegasque and Provençal as distinct languages, although Kloss-McConnel (1984) had listed them apart from Occitan. Because, whenever possible, we stayed within larger language units, we included Valencian with Catalan and Surselvian with Rhaeto-Romance. We were not able to obtain information concerning Oriental Frisian (Sater). This is thus the reason for not including these six languages on our list, even though they do appear in the Kloss and McConnell index (1984).

Yet, we were able to add twenty-one written languages to the Kloss and McConnell index (1984). We received replies from regional and local authorities on the following languages: Brabantic, Brusselese, Gaumais, Limburgian and Picard in Belgium; Greenlandic in Denmark; Aragonese and Aranese in Spain; Auvergnat, Lothringer Platt, Norman and Picard in France; Catalan-Alghero, Greek, Venetian and Walser in Italy; Drenthese, Groningese, Twents and Zealandic in the Netherlands; and Kurdish in Turkey, which Kloss and McConnell rightly considered an Asian language, but which we include here because Turkey is a member of the Council of Europe. These languages meet our basic selection criterion since they possess a significant written production.

Upon the request of the ICRB, we also included Irish, Luxemburgian and Maltese in our list of indigenous regional and minority languages. Although official, these three languages are limited *de facto or de jure* in their roles. And they all must extensively share domains of usage with one or two other international languages.

Finally, because of replies from defense organizations of French in the north of Belgium and because of the promotion of Dutch in the south of the same country, we included these as being minority languages in Flanders and Wallony.

5. The Information File: Written Minority Languages in Countries that Are Members of the Council of Europe

Austria: Croatian, Czech, Hungarian, Slovenian.

Belgium: Brabantic, Brusselese, Dutch (south of the linguistic border), French (north of the linguistic border), Gaumais, German, Limburgian, Low German, Luxemburgian, Picard, West Flemish, Walloon.

Confederation, Swiss: Rhaeto-Romance, Swiss German.

Denmark: German, Greenlandic, Faroese.

France: Alsatian, Auvergnat, Basque, Breton, Catalan, Corsican, Frankish, Franco-Provençal, Lothringer Platt, Norman, Occitan, Picard, West Flemish.

Germany: Danish, Low Saxon, North Frisian.

Great Britain: Cornish, French, Gaelic, Jersey (Norman), Manx, Scots, Welsh.

Greece:	Arumenian, Turkish.
Iceland:	(No regional languages.)
Ireland:	Irish.
Italy:	Albanese, Catalan-Alghero, Cimbrian, Croatian, French, Franco-Provençal, Friulian, German, Grecanico (Greek), Ladin, Piemontese, Romani, Sardinian, Slovenian, Venitian, Walser.
Liechtenstein: (principality)	(No regional languages.)
Luxemburg:	Luxemburgian.
Malta:	Maltese.
Norway:	Landsmål.
Netherlands: (Holland)	Drenthese, Groningese, Limburgian, Twents, West Frisian, Zealandic.
Portugal:	(No regional languages.)
Spain:	Aragonese, Aranese, Asturian, Basque, Catalan, Galician.
Sweden:	Finnish, Sami.
Turkey:	Armenian, Greek, Hebrew, Kurdish.

6. Publications in the Regional and Minority Languages

Different kinds of publications have been located for the different regional and minority languages listed in section 5.

1. *Periodicals* seems to exist in all of the regional languages, except in Italy for Catalan-Alghero, Cimbrian and Croatian; in Sweden for Sami; and in Turkey for Greek and Hebrew.

2. *Non-narrative, or dialectic prose* had fewer positive replies than the *narrative prose* category, but the presence of each type of writing varies from language to language.

a. Quality post-secondary or *learned prose*, with the exclusion of books published in that language in a neighbouring country (e.g. Hungarian books published in Hungary and used in Austria), are only found in the following regional languages : German in Italy; Aragonese, Asturian, Basque and Catalan in Spain; Gaelic and Welsh in Great Britain; Irish in Ireland; Sami in Sweden; Luxemburgian in Luxemburg; and Occitan in France. Only Basque and Catalan in Spain have a large quantity of truly *learned prose*.

b. Secondary level or *refined prose*, exists in the following languages: Low Saxon in Germany; Armenian and Greek in Turkey; Frisian and Groningese in the Netherlands; Faroese, Greenlandic and German in Denmark; Corsican, Alsatian, Frankish, Picard and Basque in France; Friulian, Piemontese, Ladin, German, Albanian, Greek, Venetian, Walser and Slovenian in Italy; Gaelic, Cornish, Manx and Jersey in Great Britain; Gaumais and Brabantic in Belgium; Drenthese in the Netherlands; and the languages mentioned in a. Many readers of regional languages use refined prose published in a neighbouring State, where there is a larger group of speakers of the same language. Only Faroese has a relatively important production in *refined prose*.

c. Elementary level, or *popular prose*, exists in the languages mentioned in a and b, as well as in Rhaeto-Romance, Breton and Frisian.

3. *Bible translations* exist in almost all of the regional languages, except Auvergnat, Gaumese and Picard. Translations of non-narrative books are still missing in Walloon (Belgium), Low Saxon and Frisian (Germany), in Occitan (France), in Franco-Provençal, Romani and Walser (Italy).

7. Schooling in the Regional and Minority Languages

Regional languages corresponding to an official language in a neighbouring country are used more frequently in education than those which have no such advantage. Usually these minority language schools can obtain textbooks from the country where that language is in full possession of its rights. This is particularly the case for: Hungarian and Czech in Austria, German in Belgium, Danish in Germany, German in Denmark and in France, Turkish in Greece, and Catalan-Alghero and Greek in Italy.

In cases where this is not possible, textbooks have to be published. Therefore, *secondary level texts* are only found in Rhaeto-Romance in Switzerland; Luxemburgian in Luxemburg; Maltese in Malta; Low Saxon and Frisian in Germany; Faroese, Greenlandic and German in Denmark; Asturian, Basque, Galician and Catalan in Spain; Auvergnat, Breton, Corsican, Franco-Provençal and Occitan in France; Gaelic and Cornish in Great Britain; Friulian, Albanian, German, Slovenian, Ladin, Piemontese in Italy; and Drenthese, Frisian, Groningese and Zealandic in the Netherlands. *Elementary level texts* can be found in the aforementioned languages, as well as in: Picard in Belgium; Aragonese and Aranese in Spain; French and Sardinian in Italy; Kurdish in Turkey; Sami in Sweden; Landsmål in Norway; and West Flemish and Basque in France.

If there are no textbooks, there are usually no schools that use that language or teach it as a subject. This is why we have not found any elementary or secondary schools where the following languages are either *used* or *taught*: Romani, Sardinian, Walser, Catalan-Alghero in Italy; and Arumanian in Greece. And, contrary to agreement, there are no Croatian secondary schools in Austria. Romani in Italy encounters the problem of its dispersion all over the country.

We have found a growing number of special schools (night and weekend) for the following languages: Low Saxon and Frisian in Germany; German and Greenlandic in Denmark; Occitan and Corsican in France; Irish in Ireland; Basque in Spain; Cornish, Manx and Welsh in Great Britain; Sami in Sweden; Frisian in the Netherlands; and German, Friulian and, in a more modest measure, Piemontese in Italy. This is an encouraging phenomenon.

All in all, one should not stress too much the advantages of a minority whose language corresponds to that of a neighboring country as opposed to minorities without a linguistic counterpart outside their own country. A State is always afraid of a foreign country helping a group of the same language by means of education material. Moreover, an attempt at political integration is now underway in Europe. This aims to surpass all Nation-States and to establish a broader unit that would be open to the demands of today's minority speech communities.

8. Conclusion

The theoretical concepts of *diglossia* and of *Ausbausprache* (or language development) have enabled us to show clearly the level(s) attained by each of the languages in writing and schooling.This is the first time that such an approach has been used in Europe and it could later serve as a basis of comparison with research carried out on other continents (see McConnell-Gendron 1988).

When bilingual education is contemplated, linguists and psychologists are often the only persons approached. They naturally have a role to play. But sociologists should also be consulted. Their help is vital in defining the regional linguistic and social landscape, particularly the place held by the minority languages. Should the minority languages be included or, at least, admitted in the school? The answer to this question depends on a number of issues. The availability of teachers and of teaching material are important issues to consider in answering this question. And linguistic and psychological tests might provide some of the answer. But, as the issue involves more than the individual, these tests are not enough.

As a sociologist I think that the choice of using the minority language in education must be the result of taking stock regularly with the local community. This is my most important conclusion, and it explains why schooling constitutes the crown (section 7) rather than the central framework of this paper.

As sociologists, we believe that bilingual education has only limited potential. It may even be said that in a number of cases pressures for bilingual schooling are stronger where the regional language is socially weaker. But given the role that the written word plays in schooling, we have been able to demonstrate that the absence or the poverty of printed texts in a language is at the basis of a negative prognosis in the use of this language in textbooks, and thus in education.

As a follow up to our research project, a list of oral domains where the minority languages are used should be established. This would give us a better indication of the chances for survival of the minority language and its potential for use in schooling. A good illustration of this more complete approach has been followed in the Grand Duchy of Luxembourg (see Baetens Beardsmore, this volume). It is possible to verify there how the more oral than written regional language obtains only a limited role in this country's school system.

In general, the blossoming of regional languages in education will not change the domains of use of the minority language. It will only confirm an already existing decentralisation of linguistic choices.

Bilingual education enters the picture to save Little Red Riding Hood from the Big Bad Wolf.

Joshua A. Fishman, 1976a: 33

Language in Education: A Comparative Study of the Situation in Tanzania, Ethiopia and Somalia

M.H. Abdulaziz

University of Nairobi

1. Introduction

The issue of language in education in African countries has a crucial bearing on the cultural, economic, political and linguistic development of these nations. As it is well known, most African countries did not exist within their present boundaries before the colonial period, as they are a result of arbitrary partition of the continent by European colonial powers. With the notable exception of some, many countries comprise multi-ethnic and multilingual communities that challenge the very concept of the legitimacy of these geographical entities as comprising nation-states.

The question of language in education involves decisions on what languages are to be used as medium of instruction in schools at the various levels: nursery, primary, secondary and tertiary stages, and which ones will be taught as subjects in the various phases of the education system.

In Africa, on the one extreme, there are countries where the medium of instruction throughout the primary and secondary schools is the indigenous national/official language. This is true, for example, of the Arabic speaking countries of the North. On the other extreme are African countries that use a European language throughout the education system. Examples are some of the Francophone and Portuguese speaking countries. In between are varieties of language educational policies. The most common policy is to use the mother tongue in the lower primary classes, one to three, in conformity with the UNESCO recommendation of 1951, and from then on to use a European language.

Tanzania, Ethiopia and Somalia provide interesting case studies of educational language policies. The three countries have different historical, demographic, cultural and political backgrounds, and yet their language policies follow similar patterns. The three countries promote their indigenous African languages as national/official and they share an approach to the question of language in education.

This paper attempts to survey in a comparative manner the development of language in education in these three East African countries in the light of their national, cultural and economic aspirations.

2. Tanzania: The Demographic, Historical and Linguistic Situation

Tanzania is 362,688 square miles in area, with a population of about 25 million. The country is mostly open savanna and sparsely populated, except for a few regions with high-density habitation. Tanzania is said to have over one hundred languages, ninety percent of which belong to the Bantu family, languages that are very closely related at all linguistic levels. This fact must have contributed to the easy acceptance of Swahili as the national language. None of the language groups is big enough to assert itself against others.

Since the beginning of the 19th century, Swahili began to establish itself as the trade language along the trading routes from the coastal towns to the great lakes to the West and South. During German rule in the late 19th century up to the First World War, Swahili was further entrenched by being made an important language of administration and education. Junior administrative officers, policemen, soldiers, teachers were all expected and actually compelled to know Swahili before they were employed. This fact made Swahili worthwhile to learn, while giving it a sense of prestige as an important language of the protectorate, quite early in the history of its development and spread. This policy of extensive use of Swahili in administration and education was continued during British rule which lasted from the end of the Second World War to independence in 1960.

Another group that played a significant role in the development of Swahili in Tanganyika were the various Christian missions operating in the country since the late nineteenth century. For example, the Universities Mission to Central Africa (UMCA) started using Swahili as far back as the 1890s as the language of their liturgical books and hymns. They were also responsible for running the first newspaper in Swahili called *Habari ya Mwezi* (*News of the Month*) in 1895 and for the preparation of a Swahili-English dictionary. The Lutheran Church too used Swahili in its churches and schools throughout the country. The German Benedictine Church was particuarly influential over the whole of Southern Tanzania (Abdulaziz 1971), where the White Fathers encouraged the use of Swahili in their churches especially in areas near Lakes Tanganyika and Malawi. In the Lake Victoria provinces however, their policy was to use vernacular languages. The result has been that people around the Lake in Bukoba, Mwanza and Musoma have been among the less fluent speakers of Swahili until recent times.

It is said that more than fifty percent of the population in Tanzania are Muslim by religion. Muslim Africans in East Africa have always adopted Swahili as a strong second language, if not the other mother-tongue, since it is through this language that their religious and communal identity is mostly manifested. The presence of such a large proportion of Muslim population in Tanzania has undoubtedly contributed to the wide acceptance that Swahili enjoys.

Another extremely important factor that has contributed to the acceptance, spread, and development of Swahili is that it has always been the mainstay of Tanzanian political and other national movements. Its integrative characteristic was observed very early in the modern history of Tanzanian political struggle. For example, during the Maji-Maji War of 1905-1907 against German rule, Swahili provided an important rallying force, the movement itself (*Vita vya Maji*) bearing a Swahili name. The first wholly political movement, the Tanganyika African Association, the forerunner of the Tanganyika African National Union, endorsed Swahili as the only language of their political organization in 1947.

The ruling party after independence has pushed the idea of one-language-one-nation so hard that it has given a tremendous boost to the prestige of Swahili. The party stand has always been that Swahili is to be developed as an essential component of Tanzania's identity and as a base for its national culture.

The elevation of Swahili to the status of national language has required the development of necessary institutions for its promotion and growth. In August 1967, the government of Tanzania established by Act of Parliament the National Swahili Council. The function of the Council is to promote and develop Swahili as a strong, working official and national language of Tanzania.

There are other bodies concerned with the development of Swahili. Among these is the well-staffed Institute of Kiswahili Research at the University of Dar es Salaam. The Institute is charged with producing a Swahili-Swahili dictionary and new Swahili-English and English-Swahili dictionaries. The Institute has plans to translate great works of literature from classical and modern languages, to produce a Swahili grammar in Swahili and to produce periodically word-lists and glossaries that are in immediate demand. The Institute also publishes twice a year a journal, *Kiswahili* and its supplement, *Mulika* which acts as a guide to teachers of Swahili. Other services of the Institute include translating material for government and parastatals, translating of Swahili material originally in Arabic characters, compiling and editing Swahili poems, and maintaining a radio programme on the growth and development of Swahili.

Other private or sponsored bodies are equally busy. One of them, UKUTA (Swahili Writers and Poets Association) promotes literary forms in Swahili. UKUTA has produced an interesting form of dramatic poetry called "Ngonjera" which are plays in poetic form. These are very popular, especially in schools.

At the University there is a full Department of Swahili apart from that of Linguistics and Foreign Languages. The Department of Swahili conducts both undergraduate and graduate courses in Swahili. An interesting feature of this Department is that it has developed technical terminology for the theoretical and descriptive teaching of Swahili phonology and grammar. The same is being done for the teaching of literature and literary criticism.

Swahili is now used extensively in the country. It is the language of instruction and command in the armed forces, the police, the national youth movements and the national militia. The language is used in all political organization from the ten-cell level up to the ruling party's top executive committee. It is the language of Parliamentary debates, the Lower courts, mass media, creative activities like literary writing, plays and drama. It is the language of national identity and participation.

2.1 *Language in Education in Tanzania*

Swahili is the only medium of instruction in primary schools. In secondary schools Swahili is only used for certain subjects such as Political Education and Civics. The rest of the subjects both in secondary schools and university are taught in English.

The function of school, and especially of the primary level Swahili-medium education has been outlined in a government pamphlet, *Education for Self Reliance*:

> For the majority of our people the thing which matters is that they should be able to read and write fluently in Swahili, that they should have an ability to do arithmetic, and that they should know something of history, values, and working of their country and their government, and that they should acquire the skills necessary to earn a living.... Things like health-science, geography and the beginning of English are also important, especially so that the people who wish may be able to learn more themselves in later life. But most important of all is that our primary school graduates should be able to fit into, and to serve, the communities from which they come. (Abdulaziz 1971: 70)

It is also because of this vision that literacy and adult education classes in Tanzania are conducted wholly in Swahili; neither English nor the mother tongues are used.

The Institute of Education at Dar es Salaam University was responsible for the development of Swahili equivalents for English concepts and terms in various subjects in the late sixties and seventies. And appropriate Swahili primary school books and texts were produced. Swahili material for the teaching of mathematics, science, geography and nature study is now readily available. But little has been done at the secondary level.

Originally it was proposed that language developers in the Ministry of Education, Institute of Kiswahili Research and the Tanzanian National Language Council cooperate to produce Swahili glossaries for concepts to be used at the secondary level. It was envisaged that by the mid-1970s Swahili would be introduced as the medium of instruction at the secondary level. But this objective has never been realized. No adequate Swahili books were written and teachers were not trained to teach the various secondary subjects in this language.

Turning now to English, it is clear that English is considered very important and is taught as a subject throughout primary school level. As we said before, English is the medium of education for the fifteen percent who go on to secondary schools and university. There are also English courses for adults in order to improve their English proficiency. However, there is conscious discouragement by the ruling party of the entrenchment of elites whose main distinguishing characteristic is the possession of an European language and Western type of education.

In recent years the acquisition of English, especially among school children, has declined. Despite the ruling party's mistrust of English-speaking elites, it has been recommended that action be taken to improve the teaching of English in schools and the level of proficiency acquired by the students. The British Council is assisting with books, teachers, and English teacher training.

One of the major educational language problems encountered in Tanzania has to do with the transfer of children from Swahili-medium primary schools to English-medium secondary schools. Children who go to secondary schools have very little working knowledge of English and no special provisions have been made for remedial English courses. The result has been that educational standards at the secondary level have deteriorated. This is even more serious for the few who go to university, where everything except Civics and Swahili is taught through the medium of English (Batibo 1986, Schmied 1989).

Despite Tanzania's educational language policy of Swahili in primary school and English in secondary school, Tanzanians continue to speak their own mother-tongues with members of their language groups. However, there is no place for these mother tongues in the school curriculum. It is felt that it would be too expensive for a poor country to provide materials and teachers for over 100 languages. It is also felt that teaching in the other mother tongues might have a negative effect on the policy of national integration and a common political culture.

Although the mother tongues have not entered the Tanzanian schools, there are a number of postgraduate linguistic university students who are engaged in writing modern descriptions of their own mother tongues.

Many Tanzanians are now looking with skepticism at their educational language policy in view of the noticeable drop in the standard of education at the secondary and university levels.

The government is now ambivalent about the introduction of Swahili as the medium of instruction above the primary level because of a paucity of books and qualified teachers. A great deal of preparation is still needed if Swahili is to be successfully used at the secondary and tertiary levels.

At the same time, English, the language of science, technology and international communication must be taught efficiently at all levels, and particularly in primary and secondary schools. Attitude towards English is becoming more positive. All these factors will be important in the reshaping of Tanzania's educational language policy.

3. Ethiopia: The Demographic, Historical and Linguistic Situation

Ethiopia is also located in North-East Africa. It is bounded by Kenya to the South, Somalia to the South-East, the Red Sea to the North-East, Sudan to the North and West and Djibouti to the East.

The population of Ethiopia is currently estimated to be over 40 million made up of diverse races who speak Ethno-Semitic, Cushitic, Omotic and Nilo-Saharan languages (Bender et al. 1976). Ethiopians are of various racial types including Negro, Bushman, Caucasoid, Pygmoid and Mongoloid. Ethnic groups like the Amhara and Oromo constitute the largest groups.

About forty to fifty percent of Ethiopians are Christians, mostly of the Ethiopian Orthodox Church. Thirty to forty percent of Ethiopians are Muslims, and fifteen to twenty-five percent follow traditional African religions (Bender et al. 1976).

Ethiopia was linked through trade and immigration to the Arab Peninsula many centuries before the advent of Christianity. There also seems to have been contact with the peoples in the Nile Valley region, such as the Ancient Egyptians, the Cushitic and the Nilotic.

Early records show the capital of Ethiopia as Aksum in the Province of Tigre, with Ge'ez, the ancient classical language, as the language of the kingdom. The Aksum Kingdom, famous in the 4th Century, was later broken up by local neighbouring invaders as well as the Persians, Turks and Arabs, the latter introducing Islam (Bender et al. 1976). In the 19th century, Menelik II is credited with having unified Ethiopia and introducing modernism.

Modernization of all aspects of life continued strongly during the reign of Emperor Haile Selasie who became King in 1928 and Emperor in 1930. Ethiopia was invaded and occupied by Fascist Italians between 1936-1941.

Eritrea was federated to Ethiopia in 1952. In the period of the Federation between Ethiopia and Eritrea (1952-1962), Amharic was the national/official language of Ethiopia, while the official languages of Eritrea under the Eritrean constitution were Arabic and Tigrinya. However, the Revised Constitution of Ethiopia (Proclamation 149 of 1955, Article 125) declared Amharic the official language of the Empire (Cooper in Bender et al. 1976).

In 1974 Emperor Haile Selassie was overthrown, ushering the Marxist-Leninist military regime of Mengistu Haile Mariam. The emphasis of the marxist revolution was on granting equal rights to all ethnic communities within the State. Article 5 of the 1974 "National Democratic Revolution Programme of Socialist Ethiopia" states: "Within its environs (those of a nationality), [each nationality] has the right to determine the contents, its political, economic and social life, *use its own language*". (Emphasis added.)

There was also need for overcoming the high illiteracy, the strengthening of mass communication for socialist development, and the process of political and ideological education of the masses. Fifteen major languages were singled out for literacy programmes, and were designated nationality languages. In the period 1974-1977 a massive campaign was launched to prepare literacy materials in a number of Ethiopian languages. University and secondary school students were used to spread literacy in the rural areas. However, Amharic has continued to be the *de facto* official language and *lingua franca*.

Amharic is widely spoken and is well standardized with its own indigenous writing system going back many centuries. Tigrinya, spoken mostly in Eritrea has also a well developed standard variety and is regularly written. Ge'ez is still the classical language of the Ethiopian Church and classical literature. It is not a mother-tongue of any speaker, but is used extensively in church services and by a few traditional scholars in literary works. Ge'ez today is one of the main sources for the modernization of Amharic.

The Marxist/Leninist government of Ethiopia has paid a lot of attention to the development of Amharic. An Institute of Language Studies was set up at the University of Addis Ababa in 1977 to study Linguistics, Ethiopian languages, English, other European Languages and Theatre Arts. In 1981 the new Ethiopian Language Academy was set up within the Ministry of Culture and Sports.

Amharic seems to be gaining strength in Ethiopia. On the other hand, development of other Ethiopian languages, in spite of an apparent liberal linguistic policy, has been slow.

3.1 *Language in Education in Ethiopia*

Christianity was introduced in Ethiopia in the fourth century. Imparting education then was the purview of the Orthodox Church. The few who managed to learn under priests were introduced to reading and writing in Ge'ez (Dagne in Cooper 1976).

Among Muslims Ethiopians, reading and writing and the recitation of the Quran was done in Madrassas or Quranic schools which also taught aspects of classical Arabic.

At present, Amharic is the sole language of primary education, with English taught as a subject, as in the Tanzanian case. At the secondary and tertiary levels, however, especially English, but also French and Italian are the media of instruction. English is rapidly replacing French and Italian as Ethiopia's language of higher education. In Quranic schools, Arabic is also used as the language of religious practices and an Islamic education.

In recent years the Ethiopian Language Academy has been working vigorously to produce Amharic glossaries in all branches of science and technology with the hope that Amharic will eventually be used as the language of instruction in the secondary and tertiary levels.

The policy to introduce Amharic as the language of instruction at the secondary and tertiary levels is a difficult one to implement. It would need appropriate texts and well-trained teachers. The balance of Amharic with English also needs to be taken into consideration.

4. Somalia: The Demographic, Historical and Linguistic Situation

Somalia proper is in the Horn of Africa and is bounded by Kenya to the West and South, Ethiopia to the North, and the Red Sea and Indian Ocean to the East. Big communities of Somali people are also found in the Ogaden region of Ethiopia, the North-Eastern areas of Kenya and in Djibouti.

The Somalis are remarkably homogeneous with respect to ethnicity, language and culture (Leitin 1977). Most of Somaliland is arid or desert land and the majority of its inhabitants are very poor. Ethnically speaking, Somalis belong to the dark Cushitic speaking people of the region that includes Ethiopia, Sudan and Kenya. They tend to be tall, have acquiline features and non-negroid hair, facial characteristics that distinguish them from other racial and ethnic groups in the world. Their main occupation is camel herding.

Somalia is one of the few African countries which are to a large extent monolingual, the others being Ruanda, Burundi, Botswana, Leshoto, Swazi and some of the Arab countries to the north of the continent.

In this century, the linguistic situation in Somalia has been one of sustained contact between the Somali language on the one hand, and Italian,

English and Arabic on the other. Italian in the South and English in the North were the languages of the two colonizing powers. Contact with Islam and Arabic goes back many centuries, with Somali itself written mostly in Arabic script before 1969, when the Roman alphabet was officially decreed for Somalia. Many Somalis claim Arab descent.

In more modern times the Egyptians under Khedixe Ismail had a strong presence in Somaliland between 1877 and 1882. In the early fifties, with the Egyptian revolution, contact between Egypt and Somalia intensified. Nasser had strong pan-Arab, pan-Islam and pan-African aspirations. Many Somali students were awarded scholarships to study in Egypt. In Somali itself there were a good number of Arabic primary and secondary schools, even before Somalia attained independence. All this resulted in the Arabic language posing as a strong second language. Today a large proportion of Somalis know some Arabic and some know it very well.

In the decades including the trusteeship period (1950-1960) and the first ten years of independence (1960-1970) the problems of the national script for Somali and the official language for the country were among the most hotly debated national issues. The issue of the national orthography was debated by the national assembly, government councils, commissions, and the press, but no firm decision was made because of the deeply political nature of the problem. There were groups that supported the adoption of modified forms of the Arabic script on the grounds that it would reinforce the common Islamic identity of the Somali nation. Those against the Arabic script indicated the technical deficiency of this form of writing for Somali. There was also a strong nationalist lobby which advocated the adoption of a unique indigenous Somali script.

As the indecision as to the proper script for Somali continued, Arabic, English and Italian continued to be considered official languages after independence. In October 1969, when the Somali Revolutionary Council took over, it decided to resolve the language question. A committee was set up in 1971 to come up with a recommendation. In 1972 the SRC decreed:

> The Somali language will be adopted, starting from today, as the only official language of the country. After careful study it has been decided to adopt the Latin alphabet as the script of our language. (Leitin 1977)

Since then, because of the commitment of individuals and members of the Somali Language Academy, the language is being rapidly promoted and new terminologies in the social, political, technological, scientific and cultural field have been developed. Besides being the medium of education as we will see below, Somali is the official language of the civil service, the armed forces, and the judiciary.

4.1 *Language in Education in Somalia*

The Italian colonial administration which started officialy in 1905 did very little to educate the Somalis. There were few Somali students in primary school and post-primary education was only open to Italians, mulattoes and other non-African people.

During the trusteeship period (1950-1960) the Italian government made a commitment to provide a quality education that would prepare Somalis in the Southern territory for self-rule in 1960. Elementary and secondary schools were opened and a good number of Somali students from the Southern parts were enrolled. In spite of the haphazard nature of Italian education, the Italian language was fairly well known among the Western educated Somalis from the South at independence.

Up to the second World War there was very little English-based education in the Northern part of Somalia, ruled then by the British. A number of elementary schools teaching English were opened in the forties. But schools served mostly the elite.

At present Somali is used as the medium of instruction in primary and secondary institutions. Somalia is the only country south of the Sahara that uses its own national/official language as medium at the secondary school level. School books in mathematics and science have been written in Somali. At the secondary level, Arabic and English are also taught.

Although Somali is also used as a medium at the tertiary level, careers in some fields are limited to Italian and/or English. Italian is the medium of instruction in scientific subjects, medicine, and engineering, since the Italian government has provided the physical facilities and staff to teach these subjects. Teacher training is conducted in English.

In order to ease the language transition, university students undergo two years of intensive studying of Italian and/or English depending upon the faculties they join. The first year is used to teach the general aspects of the language, whereas the second year focuses on the use of the languages in their professional field.

There is also a separate university in Somalia for Arabic studies. Students from Arabic schools often attend this university.

Somalia has been using Somali for the entire school system for nearly twenty years now. However, there are still some problems with language transition for those who join the university.

5. Conclusion

This paper describes in comparative perspective, language use in education in three Eastern African countries. Tanzania, Ethiopia and Somalia have been fostering socialist ideologies that desire to mobilize the masses for production. All three countries wish to eliminate the elitism as manifested by possession of a colonial European language. Each one of them aims at creating a national, egalitarian culture through the language of the people. All these countries have strong nationalist fervour.

The policy of using the national language as medium of instruction is working quite well at primary levels, as it is relatively simple to produce school texts and teachers for these levels. Problems still remain at the secondary level. Tanzania has not implemented the 1970 policy of using Swahili as the medium for secondary school work. Ethiopia has only declared its intention to use Amharic in the future. And although Somalia has been using Somali at the secondary level, problems of language transition remain for those who go on to the university level.

It would be interesting to see if new shifts in ideology away from Marxism and radical Socialism to more liberal "market" forms of economy would in some ways affect the language in education policy in Tanzania, Ethiopia and Somalia.

Brotherhood does not mean uniformity.

Joshua A. Fishman, 1981b: 526

Bilingual Education in India

Kamal K. Sridhar

State University of New York

1. Introduction

The question of bilingual education in India cannot be discussed in isolation without referring to the sociolinguistic scene. Educational policy must take into account the interests, motivations, and aspirations of the people in the community, whether they be speakers of majority or minority languages. This paper presents the linguistic profile of India and provides necessary background information to make the discussion of language issues in Indian education understandable. A discussion of language policy issues in education then follows. Three salient issues are covered: the number of languages to be taught; the medium of instruction; and the educational policy toward minority groups (at the grade school level only). For lack of space, the question of university education is only briefly discussed. Two more sections are then devoted to bilingual education in India and to a report of an attitudinal survey involving the teaching of minority languages in the Indian school system conducted by the present author.

2. A Linguistic Profile of India

Any attempt to evaluate the language planning efforts in Indian education must start with an appreciation of the unique nature of multilingualism in India. In particular, it is necessary to keep in mind (a) the number of languages; (b) the geographical distribution of their speakers; and (c) their sociocultural functions. Within the scope and space of this paper only a sketchy description of the extremely complex case of India can be offered. For a more detailed description, see Emeneau 1974; Kachru and Sridhar 1978; Khubchandani 1983; Pandit 1977; Pattanayak 1981; Sridhar 1985, 1989; and Srivastava 1988.

2.1 *Number of Languages*

One hundred and seven mother tongues were reported in India in the 1981 Census (Krishnamurti 1989). However, this figure is not reliable because in the 1961 Census, 1,652 mother tongues were reported (Pattanayak 1971, Srivastava 1988). The figures vary for a number of reasons: a given language may be reported under as many as forty-seven different names reflecting the returnee's ethnic, professional, attitudinal, and other affiliations; several varieties of the same language exist, some are mutually intelligible, others are not. Counting only languages reported by more than 1,000 persons and excluding foreign mother tongues, we get approximately four hundred languages used in India. These belong to four different language families, namely, Indo-Aryan, Dravidian, Sino-Tibetan, and Austro-Asiatic.

2.2 *Official Recognition*

Of all the languages used in India, only fifteen major languages are recognized as major languages by the VIIIth Schedule of the Constitution. Table 1 gives the list of major languages and the percentage of the total population who speak them.

All of these languages have rich literary traditions, and are spoken by large segments of population in well-defined geographical areas. The exceptions are Sindhi, Urdu, and Sanskrit. Sanskrit is not spoken any more for ordinary purposes, but it is an important part of pan-Indian cultural heritage. Hindi and Urdu are ethnic languages whose speakers are distributed throughout India. In addition, the Constitution recognizes Hindi as the Official language of India, and English as the associate official language, to be eventually replaced by Hindi.

Thus, the linguistic profile of India consists of the official language of the country, Hindi; the associate official language, English; the fifteen major languages recognized by the VIIIth Schedule of the Constitution, most of which are also dominant state languages; and a number of minority languages, tribal and non-tribal, not given official status by the Constitution.

Table 1

Languages listed in the VIIIth schedule of the Constitution
(Figures are from the 1981 Census)

Language	No. of speakers (in millions)	Percentage of total population
1. Hindi	264.18	39.94
2. Telugu	54.23	8.20
3. Bengali	51.50	7.79
4. Marathi	49.62	7.50
5. Tamil	44.73	6.76
6. Urdu	35.32	5.34
7. Gujarati	33.19	5.02
8. Kannada	26.89	4.06
9. Malayalam	25.95	3.92
10. Oriya	22.88	3.46
11. Punjabi	18.59	2.81
12. Kashmiri	3.17	0.48
13. Sindhi	1.95	0.29
14. Assamese*	0.07	0.01
15. Sanskrit	0.003	N

* No Census was taken in Assam.

2.3 *Linguistic Minorities*

No single mother-tongue emerges as the dominant numeric majority language of the country. Even Hindi-Urdu, which is the single largest group, is spoken and understood by only 45 percent of the population. Thus, it seems fair to say that, strictly speaking, India is a nation composed of numerical linguistic minorities.

The geographic distribution of languages reveals interesting complexities. First of all, proficient use of Hindi-Urdu is confined largely to the Hindi-speaking belt, i.e. the northern states in India. Second, while it is true that most of the states in the country have one dominant language spoken in that region, it is equally true that every state and every district is multilingual. Finally, there are a number of tribal languages, some with no writing systems.

Some others are literary languages whose speakers are either distributed over several states (e.g. Konkani) or do not form the dominant language in their region (e.g. Tulu), or are foreign languages spoken in border areas (e.g. Nepali), or in erstwhile colonies (e.g. French and Portuguese).

3. Language Policy in Education

The current language policy in the Indian educational system is in part a legacy of the colonial British government, and in part a product of a series of deliberate efforts by the government to meet the national goals of an independent developing country. Limitation of space does not permit a lengthy discussion of language policy during the colonial rule, or the policies formulated soon after India became independent in 1947. For a detailed discussion, see Kachru (1983), Kanungo (1962), Nurrulah and Nayak (1964), Sridhar (1977, 1989).

From the point of view of education, we need to recognize the following typology of languages in India: (1) the classical languages; (2) the regional languages; (3) the mother tongues other than the regional languages; (4) English; and (5) Hindi.

In order to accomodate the above languages, the three-language policy recommended by the Education Commission (also known as the Kothari Commission) is currently in use. According to this policy, the mother-tongue or regional language is taught as a compulsory language, from Grades 1 to 10. A second language, either Hindi or English is taught as a compulsory language, from Grades 5 through 10. A third language, either Hindi or English (whichever was not studied in the previous stage) is taught as a compulsory language from Grades 8 through 10. Thus, the first, second, and third languages are mandatory for 10, 6, and 3 years respectively. No language is mandatory at the university level (Kothari 1970).

The three language formula is a result of several compromises to accommodate the interests of various pressure groups. Although it is regarded as a reasonable compromise, it is by no means a perfect solution to a complex problem. The commission recommended that students in the Hindi-speaking regions should learn a modern Indian language, particularly from the South, in order to equalize the 3 languages that students in non-Hindi areas had to learn. While the official patronage by the federal government and its compulsory status in the curriculum obliges the non-Hindi students to learn Hindi, the Hindi students do not find the corresponding motivation to learn a South Indian language. This non-reciprocal agreement is resented in the South Indian states, specially in Tamil Nadu.

The complicated series of choices (in the 3 language formula) is summarized by Nadkarni (1977: 101) in Table 2.

Table 2

Modified and graduated 3-language formula

Educational level	*Languages as subjects of study*
Lower Primary (grades -IV)	(1) Mother tongue (Regional language)
Higher Primary	(1) Mother tongue (Regional language) (2) English
Lower Secondary	(1) Mother tongue (Regional language) (2) Hindi in non-Hindi areas and a modern Indian language in Hindi area (3) English
Higher Secondary	Any two from *Group A* or *Group B* (A) (1) Mother tongue (Regional language) (2) Hindi in non-Hindi areas and a modern Indian language in Hindi area (3) English (B) (1) A modern Indian language (2) A modern foreign language (3) A classical language, Indian or foreign
University	No language compulsory

3.1 *Medium of Instruction*

The choice of the medium of instruction at various levels and in different fields is a major language issue in Indian education, and it generates a good deal of debate. Two main questions relating to the medium of teaching are raised: (1) What should be the medium for minority language speakers at the early stage; and (2) For how long should English continue to be the medium at the university level?

The government of India, as well as all the state governments subscribe to the principle of using the mother tongue as the medium of instruction at least in initial stages, ideally throughout the educational career. In the case of speakers of the major national languages of the country (covering approximately eighty-seven percent of the population), there has been no serious problem in implementing this policy, except in small towns and rural areas where teachers may not be available for small numbers of children of migrants. The real problem is the choice of medium of instruction for the minorities who speak one of the unrecognized (tribal or other) languages. Many of these languages are (i) not cultivated, and (ii) do not enjoy official recognition for administrative purposes. Therefore, the main reason for using them as subjects and/or media is to affirm the student's linguistic identity and to aid the learning of basic skills such as literacy and arithmetic. Beyond this stage, it is felt that many of these languages are of little practical value to the child, if only because there is little written material available in these languages. The policy has been to provide two types of schools: (i) Where the "principal" medium is the official language of the state (the majority of schools are of this type) and (ii) Where a minority language is used as the medium of instruction whenever there are at least ten students in a given class who request it. Tribal languages are used as media usually only up to the end of the primary grades (hence referred to as "subordinate" media) at which point the state languages become the chief medium. This has been referred to as "mainstreaming". When the minority language is one of the recognized national languages (e.g. Kannada in Andhra Pradesh), it is allowed to be used throughout the school years. Although the states and union territories have their own state official language as the major medium of instruction, other languages and some unrecognized tribal languages are allowed to be used as subordinate media in the primary grades (Chaturvedi and Mohale 1976: 46).

In a well researched survey, Chaturvedi and Singh (1981) demonstrate that compared to the number of mother tongues, the number of languages taught as subjects or used as media of instruction is small. According to the above authors, fifty-eight languages are studied and used as media of instruction in the states and union territories at present. The following 21 languages are considered cultivated literary languages (with the exception of Khasi and

Mizo), are also recognized official languages, and are used as first, second, or third languages: Arabic, Assamese, Bengali, English, Frency, Gujarati, Hindi, Kannada, Khasi, Konkani, Malayalam, Manipuri, Marathi, Mizo, Oriya, Persian, Punjabi, Sanskrit, Tamil, Telugu, Urdu. Eleven languages, most of which are tribal languages, except for Sindhi, Nepali, and Tibetan, are either used as media of instruction or are studied as second or third languages. These are: Angami, Ao, Chokri, Garo, Karen, Konyak, Lotha, Nepali, Sema, Sindhi, Tibetan. The remaining twenty-six languages are studied only as subjects, as second or third languages. None are used as media of instruction. These are: Bodhi, Bodo, Chakma, Ghang, Dogri, German, Hmar, Kashmiri, Keiemnunger, Kuki, Lai, Lakher, Latin, Nicobaree, Pali, Pawi, Phom, Purtuguese, Rengma, Sangatam, Santhali, Syriac, Tripuri, Yimchunger, Zeliang (Chaturvedi and Singh 1981: 37-38).

3.2 Medium of Instruction at the University Level

At the university level, replacing English as the medium of instruction has proved to be problematic. English is valued as a "neutral" language among rival native languages, and it is regarded as a language of international acceptability which can also be used nation-wide. There are certain advantages to having English as the medium of instruction: it has no territorial restrictions, and it is more developed in vocabulary and registers in the areas of science, engineering and medicine. On the other hand, fear of provincialization and retrogression in an age of rapid mobility and technological innovations, plus the delay in giving official recognition to the regional languages in such domains as administration and law contribute to the perception that the regional languages have limited value in higher education.

Thus, while policy-makers recognize the need to promote all mother tongues, there are several problems encountered in its implementation. Even when the language is offered as medium of instruction in a school or university, it is not a popular choice among the students or the instructors. Krishnamurti (1979: 44) cites several reasons for the popularity of English. Pragmatically, education through the medium of English provides nationwide mobility, while education through the regional languages is perceived as a restrictive force. The sheer prestige of English as a symbol of power, knowledge, and sophistication is undoubtedly a factor in itself.

A survey conducted by the present author seems to provide empirical support for points listed above. The survey was conducted in the state of Karnataka among 299 B.A. level students. Sixty-eight percent of the students indicated that they opted for English as a medium of instruction even when mother-tongue instruction had been available at the high-school level. The reason for their choice becomes apparent in their response to a question which asked about employment opportunities if their education was through (1) English, (2) Hindi-Urdu, (3) mother-tongue, and (4) the State language. Fifty-two percent of the students said that their job prospects would be excellent if their education was through the English medium. The mother tongue comes out as a very distant second, supported by only sixteen percent of the students. Finally, as much as eighteen percent thought that their job prospects were none with Hindi-Urdu (Sridhar 1982: 145).

4. Bilingual Education in India

If bilingual education is defined as "the use of two languages as media of instruction for a child or a group of children in part or all of the school curriculum" (Cohen 1975), a good part of the Indian educational system may be said to involve bilingual education. Two models of bilingual education are found in India, in addition to the monolingual pattern. One model may be termed *sequential* bilingual instruction in which students study all the subjects through the mother-tongue or the regional language up to a certain grade level, and then switch over to another medium for the rest of their education. This model is quite widespread and the switch usually comes at the end of the secondary school or tenth grade level. Another model may be termed *concurrent* bilingual instruction. This involves study of some subjects through one language and others through a second language all through the curriculum. This model is also widespread, the science subjects especially being taught through English in many schools. In the case of the Central schools, that is, schools for children of Federal Government employees, and in many universities, this is established practice. A third model does not strictly belong in the domain of bilingual education, but involves the use of a language other than the mother-tongue as the medium of instruction. This is the case with the linguistic minorities in India. A student whose mother-tongue is a minority language may learn his mother-tongue as a subject but may have to study the rest of the curriculum through the dominant regional language or English. It may be argued that this pattern also belongs in the domain of bilingual education since the language of instruction is different from the student's mother-tongue.

A vast segment of the Indian student population receive their education in a language other than their mother-tongue, either because of choice (the prestige of English, the inadequacy of the regional languages as media of instruction in science subjects, being cited as reasons) or because of necessity (when the mother-tongue is a tribal or non-literate language or if the students belong to too small a linguistic minority in the state). The consequence of such instruction through a second language has not been systematically investigated. The same is true of the other two models of bilingual education mentioned above. The few studies which are available on these topics will be discussed below.

Ghosh (1980) presents two very brief reports on the Indian experience regarding bilingual education. The first report covers the case of New Delhi, where the use of two languages as media of instruction has been operative in 156 Central schools run by the Union government. The children of transferable Union government employees attend these schools. English and Hindi, the two link languages of the country are used as media of instruction in all these schools irrespective of their location. Social Studies, i.e. History, Geography, and Civics, are taught in Hindi, and the rest of the curriculum – Science, Mathematics, etc., in English. Although empirical studies on the effectiveness of this method have not been conducted, it is generally felt that instruction in the Central Schools is better than that in regular schools. An important drawback of the program, however, is that children from non-Hindi backgrounds do not study their mother-tongues. Hindi is more or less imposed on all children whose parents hold transferable jobs.

Another study investigated the effect of bilingual education on the learning of English as a second language (David 1978). In this study, the bilingual model consisted of the regional language and English. A select group of seventh grade children in a Telugu medium school were provided instruction in History and Geography through the medium of English. The rest of the school subjects were taught in Telugu. David concluded that, (1) bilingual education improved students' proficiency in English slightly, without causing any subject-matter deficiency; (2) a certain level of English language proficiency was a pre-requisite to the successful participation in a bilingual education program; (3) especially prepared materials were necessary to teach effectively the selected school subjects in English. David summed up her report by saying that this was a viable strategy for improved teaching of English without any loss of subject content learning.

The well-researched and documented work of Annamalai (1980), entitled *Bilingualism and Achievement in School* is one of the very first empirical studies of the effects of bilingualism on language achievement, overall achievement in school, and the correlation between achievement in languages and other school subjects. The study was conducted in five schools in Mysore city. The data is based on a total of four hundred and twenty-seven students in those five schools. The students were divided into two groups, monolingual and bilingual, on the basis of their answers to items in a questionnaire. The scores for each student for all school subjects was collected for two consecutive years, for grades 8th and 9th. The results indicated that in language achievement the bilinguals scored higher than the monolinguals. The overall performance of bilinguals and monolinguals did not differ significantly, although the bilinguals who opted for a language other than the mother-tongue as the medium of instruction showed better performance than the monolinguals. Annamalai concluded that bilingualism does not lead to any form of mental retardation, nor does it hamper the progress in other school subjects.

One of the arguments used by the promoters of regional languages in India is that students learn better when taught through their mother-tongue. The use of English as the medium of instruction has generally been blamed for the low educational standards prevailing in the country. In this context, another study by Annamalai, is extremely interesting. The study included two groups of students – one group for whom the mother tongue and the medium of instruction was Kannada, and a second group for whom the medium of instruction was not the mother-tongue (i.e. English). The two groups of students were matched for achievement, intelligence, and creative abilities, and all were from the 8th grade level. They were tested on all school subjects. In addition, their results on the final examinations (at the end of the academic year) were also taken into consideration. The results indicated that students who were instructed in English did significantly better on all the tests. The higher socioeconomic background of the students in the English medium schools and the better qualifications of their teachers may have contributed to their success. Nevertheless, in the absence of evidence to the contrary, it does seem that instruction through a second language is not detrimental to learning, and may even be positively beneficial.

As the foregoing discussion indicates, bilingual education in India usually involves primary instruction through the regional language and English. The popularity of instruction in English is largely a consequence of the lack of modernization of many Indian languages, the non-availability of instructional materials and trained teachers in those languages, and of course, of the privileged sociolinguistic status of English in India. In this context, a recently published news item is worth noting. In the city of Pune (Maharashtra) which has 94,000 telephone subscribers, very few Marathi directories have been sold, while there are long ques for the English language directory. One of the reasons for this preference is that not all Marathi speakers know the Devanagari alphabet (which has 56 characters, as opposed to 26 of English). It has even been requested that Marathi be written in the Roman script to obviate difficulties (New Language Planning Newsletter 1989).

In education, the trend seems to be toward replacing English with modern Indian languages. However, this impression is misleading for two reasons. Professional training at the university level, and especially at the post-baccalaureate level in fields such as the Sciences, Engineering, Medicine, Law and Computer Science, is largely done through English at present and is likely to continue in the foreseeable future. Secondly, as more and more speakers of minority languages get mobilized and demand instruction through their mother tongue, bilingual education will probably become more attractive as a means to maintain the ethnic identity and culture.

5. Minority Languages in Education: An Attitudinal Survey

In light of what has been said above, it would be interesting to examine some of the empirical evidence on the attitudes to the teaching of minority languages (especially tribal languages). The evidence is from a survey conducted by the present author during the summer of 1987 in the state of Bihar. According to the 1981 Census, Bihar (along with Orissa) has the third largest concentration of speakers of tribal languages in India (5.9 million each) after Madhya Pradesh (12 million), although Hindi is the regional language.

The survey elicited information through means of a questionnaire given to fifty-six faculty members teaching in schools and colleges in various towns and cities in Bihar, e.g. Ranchi, Chas, Dhanbad, Lohardagga, and Jhumritillaya. Eighty-nine percent of the faculty persons claimed Hindi as their mother tongue, and forty-seven percent claimed bilingualism in Hindi and a tribal language (e.g. Oraon, Mundari, Kurux, Kharia, Ho, Adivasi, etc.). Most of the respondents were highly educated, with ninety-one percent possessing bachelors degrees and beyond. About forty-five percent of the faculty members stated that they had students from various minority language back-grounds (above-mentioned languages). Asked if they had a say in choosing the medium of instruction, ninety-three percent acknowledged they did, and chose Hindi as the medium of instruction. The reasons for that choice became apparent when they answered that their students felt most comfortable in Hindi. Thus, for tribal speakers, the regional language Hindi is preferable to their mother tongue or English.

The faculty members were also asked questions related to the three language formula, summarized in Table 3.

Table 3
Reasons for studying various languages, according to teachers

English should be studied because it is:	
an international language	67.8%
language of tourism	16.1%
language of higher education	7.1%
an easy and concise language	11.1%
Hindi should be studied because it is:	
our national language and for national integration	58.9%
our mother tongue	26.8%
easy to understand; / our language	7.1%
Tribal language should be studied:	
for regional/cultural development	73.2%
only in the primary stages	26.8%

The respondents were very supportive of the three language formula. They were also asked about the level of competence that should be expected in each of the three languages. Their responses were the following:

Hindi : Full command (understand, speak, read, write);
English: Only read and write;
Tribal : Understand and speak.

The data, though limited, suggests that economic and cultural pressures are forcing tribal languages to perform most L functions (Ferguson 1959). This awareness among the educated minority may eventually help Hindi fulfill the prophecy of being the "replacive language".

6. Conclusion

In this paper, I have tried to show how a huge developing country like India is trying to come to grips with a complex language situation in formulating educational policy. The educational system has to deal with mass illiteracy as well as space age technology; it has to reconcile the understandable nationalistic pull toward the indigenous languages with the realistic need for continued reliance on the colonial language; it has to ensure national mobility without offending regional linguistic interests. Against this background, the government and the experts have forged a compromise – one that institutionalizes multilingualism by actively promoting the study of three languages. The minorities in India are slowly becoming aware of their rights. The three language formula policy, together with the massive literacy campaign constitutes one of the greatest experiments in language education that mankind has ever seen. Developments in the next few years will determine whether major languages such as Hindi or English will continue to be "replacive" or whether the mother tongue will be successfully used to educate minority language speakers. Bilingual education in India is still in the making.

SECTION III:

"MULTILINGUALISM FOR MINNOWS AND WHALES"

Languages in Education: Policies and Implementation in an International Context

In a multilingual world it is obviously more efficient and rational to be multilingual than not, and that truism increasingly applies to the whales, as well as to the minnows.

Joshua A. Fishman, 1978b: 47

Trilingual Education
in the Grand Duchy of Luxembourg*

Hugo Baetens Beardsmore and Nathalie Lebrun

Université Libre de Bruxelles

1. Introduction

The Grand Duchy of Luxembourg represents a unique example of a western nation where the entire school population undergoes a fully developed education transiting through three different languages as media of instruction. As such, it is a prime counter example to the assumptions, castigated by Pattanayak (1986), which relate multilingualism to under-development, inadequate educational achievement and problematic language planning issues. The Grand Duchy has an indigenous population that is almost 100% trilingual and uses Luxemburger (Letzeburgesch), German and French.

The Luxemburger is by birth monolingual in Luxemburger and becomes trilingual through education. Knowledge of three languages is felt necessary for several reasons: the small size of the country, the need to develop close ties with neighbouring countries, and the cosmopolitan status of the capital, Luxembourg City, which is the seat of several European institutions and a major banking and financial centre.

Luxemburger is the symbol of national identity and represents what Smolicz (1979) has termed a "core value" of culture, as is clear from the celebration of the country's 150 years of independence in 1989 when the Prime Minister stressed its function as the only symbol to distinguish the citizens from its neighbours (*L'Avenir du Luxembourg* 1988). The language has been a compulsory element of the primary school programme since 1912 when an official spelling and textbook were produced. In 1938 naturalization was made dependent on knowledge of Luxemburger. It was declared the national language in 1983 and the Luxembourg constitution states that citizens may address the authorities in Luxemburger, French or German and should, where possible, receive official responses in the language of the citizen's choice.

Luxemburger is a Germanic language related to Low German. According to Siguán and Mackey (1987: 115) it can be classified as a "partially standardized language", while for Spolsky (1977b: 6) it is a "local vernacular" because of its lack of technological vocabulary and limited register variants. The language uses many loanwords from French and German and has only a limited written tradition. Fishman (1976a: 75) refers to Luxemburger as a "neglected minority mother tongue", partially because it fits into a group of countries characterized by "very faint, if present at all, rumblings of recognition for minority mother tongues (in bilingual education)".

It is difficult to clearly define the status of Luxemburger, one of the problems being what is meant by "recognition". Although the language is only taught for 125 hours of the whole school curriculum, it is nevertheless present, informally, in all levels of education and represents the vehicular language for oral communication for all social categories. Luxemburger has official recognition at the national level and will occur sporadically in all levels of communication, ranging from parliamentary debates and the media to informal interaction. Yet its absence as the major medium of instruction means that it is not a fully developed language on a par with French and German.

A survey published in 1986 (*Enquête* etc.) revealed that Luxemburger is the language most frequently used for oral exchanges in the private sphere, as claimed by 77% of the sample, though only 53% of respondents claimed to use it exclusively in interactions with relatives and friends. Consequently, code-switching prevails in the Grand Duchy, with certain patterns of "preferred language" (Dodson 1981) according to the nature of the interaction. The survey revealed that in private oral communication the order of preference of languages was Luxemburger, French, German, while in written private communication the order of frequency of use was German, French, Luxemburger. In official or public life the order may vary. Debates in parliament, for instance, may be conducted in any of the three languages, though predominantly in French or Luxemburger, but are printed in German and distributed free of charge to every householder in the country. Government documents, on the other hand, are published in French. More than 50% of the population always write in French to the administration or in business, but in oral contacts with the same bodies 62% use Luxemburger, 20% prefer French, while 18% use German (*Enquête* etc. 1986).

Luxembourg's two national newspapers publish predominantly in German but also contain French material and occasional texts in Luxemburger. Television is available in French or German on the national channels, with two hours on Sunday afternoon in Luxemburger.

Problems arise when one attempts to classify the relationship between diglossia and bilingualism according to Fishman's (1989b) schematic categorization. Both trilingualism and diglossia (or more accurately, *terglossia*) obtain throughout the Grand Duchy since all the languages are widespread and institutionally buttressed. However, the three are not separable along clearly demarcated High/Low dimensions since the compartmentalization which normally defines such distinctions is "leaky". Although there is some degree of *normative functional complementarity* (Fishman 1989b: 186) in that the education system goes through a clearly demarcated language switch and official instances use different languages in different circumstances, it is also true that any of the three languages involved *may* occur in most circumstance with any category of speaker. Moreover, in spite of its restricted role in education, Luxemburger is in no way a minority language dependent on societal rewards for its survival, nor is it under threat from the two languages of wider impact, French and German. One could classify it as a Low language as far as institutionalized support and functional limitations are concerned but as a High language on a par with the other two, thanks to its role as national identity marker, its prevalence in all walks of life, and its use by all social categories, from the head of state to the humblest citizen.

2. The Education System and Trilingualism

Trilingualism is achieved through the education system as a complex, long-term process. In nursery schools and the first year of primary education Luxemburger is the sole medium of education. But Luxemburger is progressively replaced by German. German is taught as a subject during the first year of primary school and by the end of grade six the transition to the exclusive use of German as a medium of instruction must be completed. In grade two of primary school French is introduced as a subject in preparation for its use as a medium in secondary education. In the first three grades of secondary education most classes are taught through the medium of German, except for mathematics and French language which are now taught through the medium of French. The further the pupil progresses in secondary education the more subjects are taught through the medium of French, with German gradually disappearing as a medium, except for language classes. This complex system operates on the principle of introducing the child to schooling by means of the home L1, rapid transition to a genetically related L2, German, and a gradual switch to a genetically unrelated L3, French. Throughout the programme German and French are the focus of attention as subject matter at the same time that they are used as medium of instruction, which may well have implications for the quality of the outcome in terms of productive accuracy. Table 1 indicates the number of contact hours per language for the entire curriculum in Luxembourg for children following the standard programme from age 6-18, ignoring variations due to course options and specialized type of education.

Table 1
Number of contact hours per language for the entire curriculum

Language	Primary	Secondary	Total
Luxemburger subject	72	54	126
Luxemburger medium	?	–	?
German subject	1224	720-990	1944-2214
German medium	?	1331-2159	?
French subject	1080	954-1350	2034-2430
French medium	–	2106-3744	2106-3744

N.b.   ? indicates it is not possible to give valid statistics for the actual usage of the language in question as a medium, due to great individual variation within schools. In cases where a range of figures are given these reflect course options within different orientations in the curriculum.

For illustrative purposes Table 2 indicates the amount of time in the secondary standard curriculum devoted to each language, expressed in percentages. As such it reflects the step-wise nature of the transition from one major language of instruction to another and is merely a continuation of a similar transition in primary education but where the shift occurs from Luxemburger to German. Variations in percentages in Table 2 depend on course options selected by pupils, but whatever the options at least one fifth of the time in school is devoted to the study of languages as a subject, a very different picture from standard Canadian immersion programmes where apparently very little time is devoted to the study of the language per se.

Table 2

Amount of time in the standard secondary curriculum
devoted to each language, expressed in percentages

LANGUAGE	GRADES						
	1	2	3	4	5	6	7
Lux. subject	3%	–	–	–	–	–	–
Lux. medium	–	–	–	–	–	–	–
German subject	13%	13%	10%	10-13%	10-13%	10%	0-17%
German medium	50%	36%	36%	0-13%	0-13%	0-20%	0-27%
French subject	20%	20%	15%	13-16%	10-16%	10-16%	0-17%
French medium	13%	10-30%	26%	40-60%	40-60%	43-70%	38-83%
Other languages	May use French, German or the target languages						

N.b. Variations in percentages depend on options taken by pupils.

According to Fishman (1976a) most bilingual education programmes are designed to produce one of three outcomes: language maintenance (in the case of small and threatened languages), transition to a different language (in the case of temporary bilingual education until proficiency in the second language is considered adequate), or enrichment (when a second language is added in education but at no cost to development of the first language). In Luxembourg the education system is a combination of all three. Although Luxemburger is rapidly eliminated from the curriculum, this does not lead to language shift given its role in the nation. The stepwise nature of the introduction and replacement of each language as pupils get older is obviously an example of a transitional system. But the programme is also of the enrichment type in that competence in two languages (German and French) is pushed to a maximum, enabling their full usage where required.

Fishman's (1976a) frame of reference also distinguished between partial or full biliterate bilingualism on the one hand, and monoliterate bilingualism on the other, as potential outcomes of a given programme. In the latter, literacy is developed in the majority language of the out-of-school environment while oral skills are developed both in the school and in interaction with a minority community; such programmes represent an intermediate position between language maintenance and language shift policies. The school programme in the Grand Duchy develops biliterate trilingualism, where oral skills are developed in the three languages involved whereas literacy skills are developed in German and French. The reality of language usage in the country, however, means that the school programme does not fit concisely into Fishman's categorization. This is because the L1, Luxemburger, although only minimally taught, is a majority language used by the entire population. Moreover, when literacy skills are developed in German in primary school there is a transfer of literacy from German to Luxemburger, facilitated by the genetic relationship between the two languages. Hence the programme subsumes Cummins' (1984) Common Underlying Proficiency Hypothesis which accounts for the successful transfer of literacy skills from one language to another. It is the nature of the language as a small, partially standardised language, which impedes its development for literacy programmes. It is its genetic relationship to German which makes this partially unnecessary and which facilitates transfer once literacy has been attained. It is its status as a national language which accounts for the transfer actually taking place.

3. Evaluating the Success of the Educational Program in the Grand Duchy of Luxembourg

Of all pupils who completed the standard secondary school programme in the 1985-1986 school year, 70% succeeded in final examinations leading to higher education (*Statistiques, Année Scolaire 1985-1986*) indicating that trilingual education can have a high success rate, irrespective of social class, selection or other variables so often considered as conducive to a satisfactory outcome. This is not to deny the significance of other variables, particularly attitudinal and motivation factors and opportunities for use, but does reveal that trilingual education as such is a perfectly feasible operation for mass education, as is further borne out by the European School system described by Housen and Baetens Beardsmore (1987) which is an adaptation of the Luxembourg programme.

In order to assess the outcome of bilingual education programmes it is necessary to make comparisons which have some validity. On the assumption that bilingualism should not be compared with unilingualism (Baetens Beardsmore 1986; Hamers and Blanc 1989; Romaine 1989) but should be examined along criteria specific to the bilingual nature of the population in question, it is useful to compare the Luxembourg system with that of other populations undergoing bilingual education, but in a different context. To this end a comparison was made with the Canadian immersion experience on the one hand, and with the outcome of multilingual education as provided in the European School network on the other.

Given that the Canadian immersion system has the most substantive research experience behind it (Swain and Lapkin 1982), a set of tests designed to measure proficiency in French for Canadian English-speakers undergoing immersion was used as a comparison. The same tests had been used in a comparative analysis between Canadian immersion pupils and European School children (Baetens Beardsmore and Swain 1985).

The Canadian tests had been designed for 13+ year olds and were particularly significant for this age group in that 13 represents a turning point in the curriculum both in Luxembourg and the European School network (Baetens Beardsmore and Kohls 1988), when French (or an alternate L2 in a European School) becomes a significant vehicle of instruction as the language begins to operate in cognitively-demanding and context-reduced scholastic activities (Cummins 1984). Prior to this, French had functioned as a medium predominantly in cognitively undemanding and context-embedded circumstances, both in Luxembourg and the European School network, though with considerable support in lessons of French as a subject.

The three tests administered had been designed "to identify a number of real-life situations in which immersion students might have contact with French speakers, and to measure their understanding of the French used in each situation" (Swain and Lapkin 1982: 20).

The tests consisted of:

1. A 22 item multiple-choice test of written comprehension based on newspaper extracts, advertisements, television programmes, prose fiction, etc.

2. A 22 item multiple-choice test of auditory comprehension based on Canadian broadcasts, including news, weather forecasts, radio drama, chatshows, etc.

3. A 41 item cloze test designed to measure global language knowledge.

The tests were accompanied by a modified form of a Canadian questionnaire, adapted to take into account the multilingual circumstances in both Luxembourg and the European School network.

All tests contained a cultural bias in favour of the Canadians, in content, which was specifically Canadian, in certain lexical and syntactic structures, and for the auditory comprehension test, in accent. Since this bias had not adversely affected results in a previous comparison with European School children, it was not considered a disturbing factor in the Luxembourg investigation.

The enquiry in Luxembourg covered 14% of the total secondary school population in the second grade (N = 179) taken from four locations. One school in the capital was used since it was prestigious and drew its intake from a cosmopolitan environment where there was ample opportunity to use French outside the classroom. A second school was in Esch-sur-Alzette, an industrial town centred on the steel industry, a few kilometers from the French border; pupils were of a lower socio-economic status than in the capital and comprised a large proportion of foreigners. The third school was in Diekirch in the north of the country with a predominantly agricultural intake and less strongly influenced by an immediate out-of-school French environment. The fourth school was in Echternach, separated from Germany by a river representing the international frontier, and likely to have the least French influence in the environment but a strong German one.

Table 3 provides results on the tests comparing Luxembourg, the European Schools and Canadian immersion, revealing similar scores in spite of widely diverging programmes and contexts.

The similarity in scores between the three populations can only be explained by reference to responses on the questionnaires. Both the Luxemburgers and the European School pupils revealed that the multilingual out-of-school environment and their use of the target language outside the classroom differed significantly from circumstances in Canada.

In Luxembourg the parent's knowledge of French constitutes an important background feature which distinguishes them from parents of Canadian immersion pupils; the same is true for European School parents. Almost 70%

Table 3

Achievement scores on three standardised tests for
the Grand Duchy of Luxembourg (Lux.), the European School (ES)
and Canadian immersion pupils

	Lux. N = 179	Stand. dev.	ES N = 80	Stand. dev.	Canada N = 80	Stand. dev.
Total class contact hours	1450	–	1325	–	4450	
Written comprehension max. = 22	15.26	3.4	15.6	2.9	14.6	4.2
Auditory comprehension max. = 22	14.84	3.5	17.7	3	14.9	3.7
Cloze max. = 44	21.3	4.3	21.95	4.8	19.9	4.3

N.b. Luxembourg scores compared with European and Canadian scores published
in Baetens Beardsmore & Swain (1985).

of Luxembourg parents are fluent in French and use it regularly, as is the case
with almost 60% of European School parents, whereas most immersion
parents are Anglophones with little knowledge or use of French.

A second point revealed by the questionnaires concerned self-initiated use
of French, both inside and outside school. In immersion programmes few
pupils have the opportunity to use French outside the classroom, and as the
majority are Anglophones few initiate exchanges in French among peers.
Similar conditions prevail in Luxembourg where all pupils have Luxemburger
as a first language. Yet in Luxembourg 93% of respondents claimed they used
French at least sometimes outside school and only 10% claimed they never
used it in shops. Similar trends were found with the European School population in Brussels (Baetens Beardsmore and Swain 1985: 12). Thus, although
there is no absolute necessity to use the target language outside school, its
prevalence in the environment makes it naturally occur in some interaction.

Another significant point which may account for the results concerns the use of French media. Canadian pupils reported minimal use of French radio, television, newspapers and magazines, despite their prevalence. Since there is little media provision in Luxemburger, French and German media must be taken up. Fifty-three percent of Luxemburgers claimed they sometimes read newsprint in French, and 19% claimed they often did, though the scores were lower in locations nearer German influence. Similarly, 37% of European School pupils claimed to read newsprint in French and 35% watched French television for more than six hours per week.

Such differences in responses indicate that the target language has greater *immediate pertinence* (Baetens Beardsmore and Kohls 1988) in both Luxembourg and the European School investigated, probably accounting for the similarity in test scores in spite of great disparities in classroom contact hours. The amount of time devoted to the language as a subject in Luxembourg and the European School may also represent a compensatory effect for the fewer contact hours, when compared with the immersion programme (cf. Table 3).

Differences in geographical location and in socio-economic background did account for slightly diverging global test score results within the Grand Duchy (cf. Table 4). The highest scores were obtained in the capital of Luxembourg City, where there were more upper socio-economic group pupils and French was used more often than elsewhere outside school. Lower global scores were obtained in Echternach, where the German influence was predicted to be strong, but these did not differ significantly from scores obtained in Esch-sur-Alzette and Diekirch, indicating that the educational programme itself must play an important role in accounting for the scores on tests with an in-built bias against the Luxembourg population.

4. Reappraising Bilingual Models of Analysis in the Light of the Luxembourg Case

The success of the education program in the Grand Duchy of Luxembourg leads one to turn to Fishman's (1977c) analysis of the necessary prerequisites for a successful bilingual programme. Fishman made a distinction between four interrelated dichotomies which are thought to determine the outcome of bilingual education, yet upon examination it appears that the Luxembourg case goes counter to the predictions formulated by the model.

Table 4
Global scores within the Grand Duchy by location

	Luxembourg City N = 48	Esch-sur-Alzette N = 47	Echternach N = 41	Diekirch N = 43
Written comp. max. = 22	17.2	15.6	14.5	14.4
Auditory comp. max. = 22	16.7	15.3	14.2	12.8
Cloze max. = 41	24.6	19.5	19.6	21.5
Father with university degree	50%	17%	12%	19%
French used sometimes at home	25%	19%	12%	34%
French used sometimes in breaks at school	27%	40%	16%	31%
French used sometimes with friends outside school	35%	27%	23%	36%
French used sometimes in shops, etc.	37%	29%	12%	27%

Fishman analysed sixty cases of bilingual education which were rated by twenty specialists for success in terms of the goals with respect to language education. The Luxembourg system does not fit into the theoretical framework predicting success, yet test results, as illustrated, university entrance passes, and the general economic prosperity of the country, clearly indicate that the programme works.

Fishman's arguments are that success is dependent on specific circumstances surrounding the emphasis accorded each language in a programme, based on the following four dichotomies:

1. *Language of primary emphasis versus language of secondary emphasis in education.* If there is more time devoted in school to one language than to

the other then the first language has primary emphasis. In Luxembourg German is given primary emphasis in primary school while French is given primary emphasis in secondary school; Luxemburger is given little emphasis throughout the curriculum. Hence French and German have primary or secondary status according to the pupil's age.

2. *Mother tongue versus other tongue.* Since Luxemburger is the mother tongue, both French and German represent the other tongue in the Grand Duchy.

3. *Minor versus major languages.* By whatever criteria used, Luxemburger must be assessed as a minor language while both French and German can be considered as equal major languages.

4. *Presence or absence of language support via formal, out-of-school institutions.* Although all three languages have official recognition, French enjoys the highest status in formal out-of-school institutions, German is a near equal, while Luxemburger has the least status. Yet in practice Luxemburger may oust the other languages, even in parliamentary debates.

Clustering around the above four dichotomies defining the language circumstances are a further set of variables which Fishman considered as significant for the outcome of a given programme. For example, he felt that greater success is predicted for both languages of primary and of secondary emphasis in cases where *full* bilingualism is the ultimate goal. Since full bilingualism is the ultimate goal in the Grand Duchy, this variable can be considered as influencing the positive results, even though languages of primary and secondary emphasis fluctuate over time. Moreover, there is no negative effect on Luxemburger, the language of tertiary emphasis, in that the major two languages of instruction do not lead to language shift.

A significant variable in determining successful bilingual education, according to Fishman's model, was selectivity. But since trilingual education is compulsory in the Grand Duchy this criterion cannot affect the positive outcome (nor does it operate in the European School system).

A variable said to influence success is the extent to which the languages involved are dependent on school instruction. Success is thought to be lower if the languages of primary or secondary emphasis are school dependent; "School use of language is just not enough" (Fishman 1977c: 102). Both

French and German are partially school dependent but also benefit from out-of-school functions, and therefore fit the prediction. Luxemburger, on the other hand, is not school-dependent but thrives on social interaction, and thus it is in a similar position to the non-codified vernaculars prevalent outside school in many developing nations.

A nationalist or socio-political sentiment with respect to the target languages is also felt to be a criterion for success. Although this may apply to Luxemburger, which plays a minimal role in the curriculum, it cannot be said to apply to French and German.

Fishman's criteria for predicting success in bilingual education, although not watertight for the Luxembourg case, nevertheless clarify significant issues. They reveal that the trilingual education system works because of the following features:

1. Full bilingualism is the avowed goal as far as French and German are concerned.

2. Both languages have strong out-of-school support, in the media and in formal and informal interaction.

3. Luxemburger fulfills the nationalist sentiment which leaves it unthreatened by the other two languages. (Perhaps the fact that *two* languages of wider impact are present in education account for the maintenance of Luxemburger, since although Irish has a similar status in Eire this has not prevented the pressures for language shift to English.)

4. Conclusion

What the Luxembourg case reveals is that a trilingual policy can be successful if certain conditions are met. These include a combination of curricular and extra-curricular features which support all the languages involved. The languages must be perceived as immediately pertinent to the needs of the speakers – only academics and linguistic freaks study languages for their own sake. There is a long-term commitment in the programme operating in Luxembourg and no illusions about quick results, as is so often the case with unrealistic, temporary provision of language education. The programme devotes considerable time to language as a subject as well as language as a medium, which distinguishes it significantly from Canadian immersion programmes.

The Luxembourg case is also significant in that it forces one to rethink about bilingualism in a way which breaks away from dichotomous oppositions. Much western research on bilingualism is based on such dichotomies which are obviously inadequate in the analysis of multilingual entities.

Note

*   The authors wish to thank Merrill Swain of the Ontario Institute for Studies in Education for permission to use the Canadian tests.

Montreal Yiddish intelligentsia fought for a restorative and integrative program that would create a sense of wholeness both within Jewish life and within the fragmented world at large.

5. Through extraordinary self-sacrifice and in the face of bitter in-fighting, this cadre of young ideologues established a network of institutions to embody their bold utopian vision: a Yiddish press, a Jewish public library, a Vaad Ho'ir (the Jewish Community Council), afternoon and dayschools, a teacher's seminary, amateur Yiddish theater groups, summer camps and book stores.

The key to this utopian venture was the word *folk* itself. The word asserted itself in the names of the new institutions and publications alike: *Di yidishe folks-bibliotek, di yidishe folkshuln, Di yidishe folks-entsiklopedye.* When the "Jewish People's Library" finally opened its doors, in rented quarters, on May Day 1914, it amalgamated two earlier collections belonging to the Dorshei Zion and Poale Zion (both Labor Zionist groups). Reuven Brainin, a Hebrew-Yiddish-German publicist of some renown, was invited to preside over the new institution whose motto was "By the People, Through the People, For the People" (Caruso 1989: 53).

The choice of Folkshule was no less programmatic. The Yiddish secular schools were called into being at the Fifth Poalei Zion Convention held in Montreal on the 20th of October 1910. They were to be known as *Natsyonale Radikale shuln* (Entin 1946: 145-146; Kage 1961: 168-172). The Peretz School, founded in 1913 as a Saturday and Sunday school, continued to boast of this pedigree in its official anthem. But ideological differences arose among the Poalei Zion activists over the place of Hebrew in the curriculum and the emphasis on traditional subject matter. With the Peretz School holding out for a more exclusively Yiddish and radical orientation, Yehuda Kaufman broke away to establish the *Folkshule.* His heir and chief disciple, Shloyme Wiseman, would spend forty years of his life trying to preserve the folk character of the Folkshule in the face of attacks from the right and from the left.

The ideology of serving the broadest interests of the "folk" extended even to classical text editions produced in Montreal. Thus, in his Hebrew translation of the Zohar, Yudl Rosenberg only included the exegetical portions connected to the Bible. Replying in the *Keneder odler* to criticism leveled against him by the young Shimshen Dunsky (31 March 1931), Rosenberg argued that one mustn't reveal the esoteric Kabbalah to the simple folk (quoted in Fuks

1980: 277). A dozen years later, Simcha Pietruszka created his *Jewish folk encyclopedia* in order to refamiliarize the Yiddish-speaking masses with the traditional roots of their culture while in his Hebrew-Yiddish *Mishnayes*, Pietruszka (1945: preface) adopted a highly conservative approach to the textual apparatus. Dunsky, now older and wiser, adopted a similar approach to textual emendation in his own *Midrash Rabba*. All these scholars went by the same principle: to speak for the folk meant that one had to respect its boundaries.

The anomaly of Yiddish in Montreal is that a group of "lay Jewish revolutionaries", as David Rome (1975: 61-88) so felicitously calls them, took upon itself the arduous task of guarding Jewish cultural boundaries. To be sure, the ideological foundations of cultural nationalism had been laid elsewhere: by Ahad Ha'am (1858-1927) and Chaim Zhitlowsky (1865-1943), the major theoreticians of the Hebrew and Yiddish revival. By the same token, the postwar treaties negotiated on minority rights and cultural autonomy, not to speak of the Balfour Declaration, had everything to do with Jewish political aspirations in French Canada. But while the roots of the Yiddish cultural revolution in Montreal were decidedly east European, its particular flowering – and the fruits that it ultimately bore – were nowhere else to be found.

To be more specific, it was on this northernmost outpost of the New World that members of the Labor Zionist movement (the Poalei Zion) actualized their party platform. As opposed to those radical Zionists who prepared themselves solely for the rigors of agricultural life in Palestine, the Labor Zionists stressed *Gegenwartsarbeit*, working in the diaspora to raise Jewish productivity and consciousness (Frankel 1981: 281 and *passim*). While the other radical groups had a monolingual policy – the Bund committed only to Yiddish, the Hashomer Hatsair only to Hebrew and the assimilationists only to the coterritorial language – the Labor Zionists fought to maintain an internal Jewish bilingualism. The use of both Hebrew and Yiddish had become a matter of ideology precisely because Jewish culture was no longer unified and internally coherent. Whereas once, before the Emancipation, Jews could move effortlessly back and forth between Yiddish and *Loshn koydesh* (the Holy Tongue, Hebrew) simply on the basis of utility, now an ideological bulwark was needed to keep Humpty Dumpty from falling down. If east European Jewish writers wished to address the entire Jewish body politic, they had to write the *same work* in both Hebrew and Yiddish – or pay to get it translated. The act of self-translation that was so characteristic of secular Jewish culture in eastern Europe prior to World War I was an act of will, a last ditch effort to reimpose a sense of cohesion onto an ever more fragmented reality. Internal Jewish bilingualism was an ideological tactic for combatting the centrifugal forces at work politically, socially and geographically (cf. Even-Zohar 1978, Miron 1987).

Adopting this bilingual scheme to the exigencies of the New World, the lay Jewish revolutionaries of Poalei Zion discovered a special place for Yiddish. Yiddish would evoke memories of Paradise Lost; would be a vehicle for revolutionary action; would be a bulwark against assimilation. Yiddish, the language of the immigrant community, of the "generation of the wilderness", would cut across all classes and all ideological sectors. Yiddish would be the key to history and to *lebns-shteyger* (folkways). Yiddish would be the bridge to Loshn-koydesh and to modern Hebrew.

This utopian experiment could only be carried out on virgin soil, because everywhere else the battle lines had already been drawn. As early as 1907, Yitzhak Ben Zvi was forced to close *Der onfang*, the official organ of Poalei Zion in Erets Yisroel, and Hebrew was adopted as the language of the party (Pilovsky 1986: ch. 1). Then came Czernowitz a year later at which the resolution to proclaim Yiddish as the national Jewish language was only narrowly defeated (Fishman 1981a: 369-394; Goldsmith 1976: ch. 8). Meanwhile, the Yiddish press in the United States, regardless of its ideological stripe, was successfully promoting the process of Americanization (Soltes 1925). Against this backdrop of language wars and rapid acculturation, a Yiddish-Hebrew ideological program with an overlay of folksiness was more than merely a radical alternative. It was a full-fledged eschatology.

At this point, armchair sociologists will counter that the qualitative differences of Montreal Jewry were not a function of ideology, much less, of eschatology. External factors alone can explain the differences: the ethnic makeup of Quebec, with Jews caught between two inhospitable groups (the French-speaking Roman Catholic and the English-speaking Protestants); the parochial school system; the later immigration; the climate. There is even the Litvak Connection. With so many of the founding fathers – Brainin, Wiseman, Dunsky, Rabinovitsh, and David Rome – hailing from Lithuania, is it any wonder that education and culture loomed so large?

Environment or pedigree do very little, however, to explain how a tiny group of recent immigrants with no political clout and with no traditional sources of authority to fall back on, how these lay Jewish revolutionaries took their case for a separate Jewish school panel all the way to the Privy Council of England; how, when their legislative efforts failed, they created the very first dayschools in Montreal, which were also the first *Yiddish* dayschools anywhere in North America, and while they were at it organized the Vaad Ho'ir to oversee the sale of kosher meat for the sake of their Orthodox brethren. Indeed, it was in the Jewish School Question that raged in Montreal from 1923-1931 that the Labor Zionists took their stand and became – despite their lack of Canadian roots – a major integrative force in the community.

To prepare for battle, the secular revolutionaries led by the Poalei Zion established the Vaad Ho'ir, also known as the Jewish Community Council. Included in this Council, according to David Rome (1975: 69), were 66 labor unions, Zionist groups, mutual and sick benefit societies, fraternal groups, synagogues, Yiddish schools, rabbis, journalists and scholars. In addition to rationalizing the distribution of kosher meat, this unlikely coalition of bearded rabbis, atheist socialists, Zionists and anti-Zionists, were to lobby the Canadian government for a separate Jewish school system under the provisions of the British North America Act. Needless to say, there was no unanimity among the members of the labor caucus about the necessity of separate Jewish schools, especially if it involved collaborating with the Orthodox. The party line was finally hammered out at a series of labor conferences, one of which, at Communist insistence, met on Yom Kippur, at Yizkor time. The Orthodox, for their part, had made their opposition to the secular Yiddishists eminently clear as far back as July 5, 1916. In a protest resolution published in the *Keneder odler* they had accused the National Radical Schools and the Folkshule of replacing the sacred Torah with Yiddish songs (rpt. in Zipper 1938: 104-105). Let the education of the young, they pleaded, remain in the same hands as before. A more powerful opposition emanated from the Uptown Jews. A certain Rabbi Corcos articulated the horror with which the Jews of Westmount viewed the prospects of a separate Jewish school panel:

> The originators of this mad scheme, whoever they may be, are not only enemies of God ... but they are also the worst enemies of their country, since nothing but calamity and misfortune can come to a country that is divided against itself.... They would mean the creation of a state within a state. They would mean the revival of a ghetto and the return of the dark ages of ignorance and superstition; they would mean the perpetuation of their horrid jargon known as Yiddish, and thus the province of Quebec will become a veritable tower of Babel with so many confused dialects. (Quoted in Rome 1975: 79)

And so, for one very powerful group of Montreal Jews, Yiddish represented a return to the Dark Ages, to poverty, superstition and segregation, whereas for the Orthodox, it meant precisely the opposite: the dangers of subversion from within. Given the Yom Yippur caucuses, their fears were certainly not unfounded.

What, then, did Yiddish and yidishkayt mean to that tiny group of ideologues led by Yehudah Kaufman, Simon Belkin, Moshe Dickstein and Shloyme Wiseman? It was Wiseman who, on that Yom Kippur day in 1923, had to rush off from shul to confront the Jewish communists and other radical leftists. It was he, on the strength of his graduate degree from McGill, who was called upon to defend the the Yiddish-speaking Downtown Jews in the pages of the Montreal Star. It was he, in a remarkable series of analytic and programmatic essays written in the 1940s, who became the chief theoretician of the Yiddish secular schools in North America. In his classic essay "The Jewish Holidays and Jewish Education", first published in the massive *Shulpinkes* (Wiseman 1948a: 216-252) and later reprinted in the *Shloyme Wiseman bukh* (Dunsky 1961: 107-144), he argued for the place of yidishkayt in the Yiddish cultural revival. The reason this culture had to be reinvented, he explained in a rare outburst of passion, was that everything of value had already been destroyed.

> We of the old generation will never feel at home in the new American yidishkayt. We will always feel that it "just isn't it". We will keep right on running from one synagogue to another; no shul will truly satisfy. We will eternally seek the echo of the chords that long since resounded but were never forgotten. Sounds, melodies, smells and memories. What we actually seek is both our irrevocably lost childhood and that total yidishkayt that was possible under certain conditions once prevalent in the small *shtetlekh* but that cannot be reproduced here in the metropolitan American exile. But that longing and unhappiness is an important pyschic factor in our lives. It can become a constructive force if it stimulates us in our protest against the pale and anemic yidishkayt in America to create those maximal conditions for improvement and strengthening that are still possible even under our unfavorable conditions. (pp. 224; 115)

The brave new world of Yiddish and yidishkayt, he revealed in this extraordinary passage, was built on the ruins of traditional Jewish life. The real destruction, the irrevocable loss, had occurred the moment these young men and women left the organic communities of eastern Europe. There was no going back to that world of wholeness. Forever would their generation wander from shul to old-style shtibl trying to recapture the lost sounds and smells. Out of their unrequited longing, however, they would establish a new Jewish calendar, making the old festivals yield new meaning. In a cynical age of minimalism they would dedicate every ounce of their energy to creating a *maximalist* culture of yidishkayt.

That invented-yidishkayt, Wiseman went on to argue, however insufficient it might seem to themselves, would be real and existentially compelling to their students. The native born generation would have no other measure of authentic yidishkayt. Besides, it would be the task of Jewish educators to keep alive the longing for a more total and more beautiful yidishkayt. When the students grew up, they would then be motivated to work towards that restorative vision.

Insofar as Yiddish was a key to *lebns-shteyger*; insofar as Yiddish literature extolled the beauty of Jewish holidays; insofar as Yiddish was symbiotically tied to Loshn-koydesh; insofar as Yiddish was the living link to a living people – Yiddish would be the crucible of past, present and future. Insofar as the new cultural institutions embodied this integrative vision, Yiddish would become the embodiment of yidishkayt.

A new brand of diaspora nationalism was thus created by Wiseman and his fellow Labor Zionists, designed to combat the fragmentation within and the seductions from without. Wiseman spelled out the nationalist agenda in no uncertain terms. Our purpose, he wrote at the beginning of the same essay, is to condition our students so that they couldn't live *other than as Jews*. To achieve this end one must create a total environment, both within the school and without – by teaching them to live in two Jewish languages; by celebrating all the holidays in a meaningful way; by instilling within them a sense of responsibility for Jewish history and Jewish destiny. What a sophisticated educational philosophy! What a utopian, and at the same time, pragmatic vision!

In practice, however, things didn't turn out quite so well. The first thing to go, as Wiseman was to recall in his unfinished memoirs (1982: 391-392), was spoken Yiddish. It was simply impossible to enforce Yiddish speaking among the students themselves. The best that could be hoped for was that students and teachers would communicate solely in that language.

Besides, the 1920s and 30s were a time of competing utopian visions. Many were the forces vying for the souls of Jewish youth, especially those who were already committed. For the longest time, Wiseman recalled in that same memoir, the Folkshule *klubn* were kept separate from Habonim, the youth movement of the Labor Zionist Federation because Habonim honored only Hebrew. More painful still – and Wiseman was not one to forget or forgive – were the rebellious group of Shule graduates who, in flyers they circulated in 1933, repudiated the yidishkayt curriculum as so much petty bourgeois apologetics (rpt. in Wiseman 1982: 391-392). They called instead for workers' solidarity and for a more positive attitude to their Soviet brethren.

But ideologies came and went. What Wiseman and his cohort understood is that only institutions, or what the Israelis would later call "creating facts", would insure the transmission of their integrationist lifestyle. Small wonder then that it was they and not the leaders of the Talmud Torah who pioneered the Jewish dayschool in Montreal – in 1928. Only the dayschool, Wiseman argued in an essay devoted specifically to that topic (1948b: 45-52), with its integrated curriculum, could counteract the dualism of goles (the diaspora). Only the dayschool could make yidishkayt central to the students' experience, rather than an ocassional late afternoon appendage. Only the dayschool could forge a Jewish elite that would someday assume leadership positions in the community.

The first graduating class of the Folkshule graduated in 1940, only one year after the Shule finally received full accreditation from the Protestant School Board. The Shule occupied its new building on Waverly Street in 1941. At about that time, a teacher from the Folkshule named Chaim Pripstein set up a summer camp where the Yiddish-Hebrew curriculum shifted towards sports and waterfront activities but was maintained nonetheless. In 1946, a Jewish Teachers' Seminary was established that ran in two parallel tracks: one in Yiddish-Hebrew and the other in Hebrew only. Eventually the two were combined. Later still, in 1956, Dora Wasserman organized a Yiddish Drama Group under Folkshule auspices. A large part of its repertoire would be translated and adapted from Hebrew by teachers from the Shule. This institutional growth spell, this coming of age of the Montreal integrationist utopia, coincided with the collapse of Yiddish cultural life almost everywhere else on the globe.

3. A Generation Later. Montreal Yiddish Culture

Now the durability of a utopian experiment is never really tested until at least one generation after its founding. In our case, the new generation came of age just as the world of east European Jewry was totally destroyed and dispersed. Of course there would be an influx of refugees and survivors – my own parents among them – who replenished Montreal Yiddish culture from its native soil, but if the institutional and ideological foundations had not been sound to begin with, no amount of transplantation would have saved the day. Many great Jewish movements collapsed under the weight of history: Territorialism, the Jewish Labor Bund and the Jewish Section of the Communist Party. That the Yiddish-Hebrew-and-yidishkayt equation of the founding fathers weathered the storm is, I think, its ultimate vindication.

The Montreal Yiddish-Hebrew intelligentsia was prepared for the Holocaust because, as Shloyme Wiseman revealed in that remarkable passage, the destruction of their world had already happened. Destruction and loss were the very stuff that Jewish dreams were made of. Because there was no going back to a world of orthodox faith and communal autonomy, they invented a surrogate yidishkayt embodied in an all-encompassing network of cultural institutions. They came as close as one could to establishing the "state within a state" that Rabbi Corcos was so afraid of. The actual, physical destruction of Jewish eastern Europe only intensified the longing for a more whole and beautiful *yidishkayt* that had long ago become part of the hidden curriculum.

If the vast bloodletting in Europe could be turned into a source of creative longing for the past, there was even greater scope in the Zionist vision of the future. In a wonderfully evocative essay called "A Goles Education", my sister Ruth Wisse (1977: 28, 62) recalls how she and her fellow students in the Folkshule vicariously experienced every act in the drama of Israel's independence. "I was startled", she writes, "when an Israeli friend said to me, about her education in Rehavia, 'You would never have known that we were living through the most memorable period in Jewish history.' As for us, we were never in doubt."

Yet the very success of the Zionist revolution might have overwhelmed the modest achievements of the mini-utopia on North American soil. As committed Zionists, the Yiddish-Hebrew intellectuals of Montreal had to acknowledge, as Wiseman did in an essay written in December 1943, that only in Erets-Yisroel could Jews fulfill themselves (*oyslebn zikh*) as Jews national-ly and spiritually (1943: 78). And indeed, other Zionist ideologues viewed with scorn any attempt to instill a sense of belonging to North America. But North America, Wiseman countered, offered something else: the unique opportunity to *integrate* one's yidishkayt within a multi-ethnic and culturally diverse American lifestyle (1943: 78).[2] That, according to Wiseman, was the challenge facing Jewish educators in the latter half of the twentieth century. He now openly lamented that the exclusive emphasis on Yiddish and Hebrew had made for an elitist attitude towards English-speaking Jews and denigration of North America. American Jewry was finally coming of age and who could tell what spiritual forces that new-found independence might unleash? Yiddish, then, was invaluable as an integrative force, as a means of holding the diverse parts of the culture together. The claims of the immediate severed past could best be made through Yiddish in conjunction with Loshn-koydesh. The drama of a people reclaiming its ancient homeland could be conveyed in Yiddish, in conjunction with Hebrew. And as for America, the story of that miraculous new haven of east European Jewry had already been played out primarily in Yiddish, and could now be retold in conjunction with English.

4. Conclusion

The Yiddish glue did not put Humpty together again. The integrationist ideology fell apart when faced with renewed fragmentation from within and the totally unexpected challenge of French Canadian ethnic supremacy from without. The east European Jewish past, the North American present and the Zionist future have gone their separate ways. Still, there is much to be learned from that brief sojourn in utopia.

First, that all Jews live after the *hurban beit hamidrash*, the destruction of traditional faith, but out of that loss, a new and viable culture can be reinvented. Just as alienated intellectuals looking to reinvent themselves as traditional Jews gave Yiddish literature its most compelling vision of the east European Jewish past (Roskies 1986), the radical educators built a cradle-to-grave alternative to the old way of life with the Yiddish dayschool inheriting the place of the synagogue.

Second, that a community cannot be built without an ideology, without a collective vision that somehow integrates past, present and future. Those who believe the Marxist canard that ideologies are tools of the ruling class are fated to be ruled by their own lack of vision.

Third, that some ideologies are better than others. The radical secularists who tried to tear Yiddish completely away from yidishkayt, who believed that a humanist-socialist faith could be totally self-sustaining, could never adopt to the profoundly religious character of both Judaism and North America. The young Jewish rebels of the late 1960s, in contrast, who tried to establish monastic orders of neohasidic mystics, disbanded once their apocalyptic fervor waned and the war in Vietnam was over.

The lay Jewish revolutionaries in Montreal succeeded beyond one generation because they were collectivists with a restorative, neoclassical bent who operated in the public domain. They organized, they fought, they lobbied, they built institutions from the bottom up, they went from house to house collecting the 50 cents a month tuition for the afternoon school. Their ideology was predicated on peoplehood, not prophecy; on language not divorced from the liturgy; on getting their hands dirty in the nitty gritty of communal and, when need be, of national politics.

Yiddish in their scheme was never an end in itself; it was a means towards achieving cultural integration: of reuniting east and west, the folk and the intelligentsia, the *frume* and the *fraye*. Yiddish was to be the vehicle of national liberation.

Notes

1. An earlier version of this paper appeared in *Everyday Miracle: Yiddish Culture* in Montreal (Montreal: Véhicule Press).

2. Horace Kallen's writings on cultural pluralism seem to have greatly influenced Wiseman's thinking.

SECTION IV:

"YES, VIRGINIA,
WE TOO HAVE LANGUAGE PROBLEMS"

Languages in Education: US Policies

Yes, Virginia, we too have language problems. And now, as if to add insult to injury, Philistines have been admitted into the temple: that devil known as Bilingual Education has sullied the sanctum sanctorum *of American English, the public school, by conducting instruction in some seventy foreign languages.*

Joshua A. Fishman, 1981c: 34

Bilingual Education: Politics or Pedagogy?

Ursula Casanova

Arizona State University

1. Introduction

My first contact with bilingual education in the United States came in 1971, only three years after the passage of the first Bilingual Education Act, when I assumed a position as assistant principal for instruction in an urban elementary school. One of my major responsibilities was the supervision of the school's bilingual program.

My professional experience previous to bilingual education was similar to that of many Hispanics at the time. I had been a teacher of Spanish as a foreign language for five years. A veteran of one of the many blips in the US educational landscape: the foreign language in elementary schools (FLES) program implemented during the sixties. When bilingual education came upon the scene, everyone assumed that if you could teach a foreign language, or even if you were only a competent speaker of one, then you knew how to teach students in bilingual education. It was soon evident that we had much to learn.

In 1971 bilingual education was little more than an idea, a step-child of the Civil Rights Act. Bilingual programs were being implemented much quicker than materials were made available or teachers trained. And a knowledge base to support the instructional activities being initiated was practically non-existent. We operated more out of instinct than anything else, and everyone worked exceedingly hard trying to keep ahead of the demands presented by their classes. With characteristic bluntness Fishman and Lovas (1970) called attention to those very lacks in bilingual education: lack of funds, lack of trained personnel, and lack of evaluated programs.

The next few years were accompanied by growth in all areas of bilingual education. Early experimental efforts culminated in the passage of the 1974 Bilingual Education Act, the first one accompanied by a respectable budget, and consciously targeted to the needs of non-English speaking students. By that time moneys for training had been made available and publishers were producing materials more or less suited to the needs of our students. The mood was optimistic, the energy level high. Barely four years later, and not too surprisingly, those early tentative efforts would be negatively evaluated in the AIR report which will be discussed below.

It is useful to remember that the late sixties and early seventies were a time of ferment for bilingual education when politicians spoke passionately about their hopes for children. Bilingual education was a friendly concept then. But it was also a time of struggle for those of us in the schools. Although bilingual education had existed in various guises throughout the country's history, and was alive and well in many parts of the world, we had no maps. (For a review of that history, see, for example, Heath 1981, Keller and Van Hooft 1982.) Our energy and commitment made up for our ignorance as we invented programs and curricula to respond to the new legislation. Under the current attacks from US English we tend to forget the hope and promise of those years. But the past remembered serves as context for the present. And understanding the historical context is particularly important in an area as young and conflicted as bilingual education.

In this chapter I will attempt to shed light on the persistent conflict over bilingual education through a comparison of the evolution of bilingual education policy at the federal level against the knowledge base on bilingualism and bilingual education. My focus will be on the relationship between these two strands of influence on bilingual education.

2.   Bilingual Education: Policy

2.1   *The Early Years*

Perhaps the most important characteristic to remember about the 1968 Bilingual Education Act is what it was not. It was not a pedagogical response to a previously documented problem but rather the result of political strategies designed to funnel federal poverty funds to the Southwest. This is not to say that children lacking English skills were not failing in the schools, but while the need existed, there was no great demand for the type of federal political intervention represented by the Bilingual Education Act. The problem remained at the local school and district levels.

In 1965 the Johnson administration, besieged by urban riots, sought to direct Federal funds to the poor in US cities. With the passage of the Elementary and Secondary Act (ESEA) of 1965 Johnson succeeded not only in targeting money to the poor, but also in overcoming historical opposition to federal aid to education. Title I of the ESEA was the first attempt by Congress to pledge money for children of low-income families (Schneider 1976).

The sweetener tossed for Hispanics into the 1968 Title VII Amendments to ESEA was not based on knowledge about language learning or bilingualism. The move has been attributed to Sen. Yarborough's (Democrat from Texas) interest in funneling a portion of the federal anti-poverty funds to the Southwest. He, and those who joined him in the effort, appealed to the needs of Mexican-Americans who were described as the second largest minority, very poor, and with a language deficiency (descriptors that unfortunately continue to haunt the program). Hispanic leaders were recruited to testify and they also described the great injustices suffered by this newly discovered "culturally disadvantaged" group. A few experts were also called to testify, among them Joshua Fishman. Their combined effort resulted in the Title VII Amendments, the first categorical Federal law authorizing bilingual-bicultural educational programs (Betances et al. 1981).

Other pressures also contributed to the acceptance of the Title VII Amendments. One was the presence of hundreds of immigrants from Cuba who saw themselves as only temporary residents of the United States. They were ready to leave as soon as Castro was chased away and were therefore eager to maintain their culture and their children's Spanish language skills. In 1963 the Ford Foundation had already helped Cuban refugees to set up an experimental program in bilingual education. The program was considered a success and provided a viable model for later efforts. Unlike later government funded programs, the Dade County program was oriented toward enrichment instead of remediation (Hakuta 1986).

The Civil Rights movement was also beginnning to inspire demands for equal educational opportunity from other linguistic minorities, including Native Americans. Those pressures contributed to the extension of bilingual education beyond the original Hispanic target group. And from Alaska to the

Mexico border, poor children from homes where English was not the dominant language became the beneficiaries. The nation's newspapers proclaimed
that Public Law 90-247 would establish "bilingual education programs for
children of Indian, Puerto Rican and Mexican descent" (Schneider 1976).

From its conception then, bilingual education was a political artifact; born
not of knowledge, or even of expressed need, but of political maneuvering
perhaps heavily laced with a sense of social responsibility. Such serendipitous
beginnings had unintended consequences. Bilingual education rapidly became
a rallying point for Hispanics. It was a cause that could, and did, unite
Hispanic people across the country, across cultural, educational, and even
class barriers. As a result, the political climate surrounding the Education
Amendments of 1974 was drastically different.

2.2 *Legal Support*

In 1974 the Supreme Court of the United States handed down its decision in
the landmark Lau vs. Nichols case. In this decision the Court ruled that students were being denied equal educational opportunity when school officials
took no steps whatever to help speakers of other languages (SOLs)[1] participate meaningfully in the school program. The decision came at a fortuitous
time, in the midst of congressional hearings about bilingual education.
Through this ruling the Court legitimized the need for bilingual instruction:
"... there is no equality of treatment merely by providing students with the
same facilities, textbooks, teachers, and curriculum; for students who do not
understand English are certain to find their classroom experiences wholly in-
comprehensible and in no way meaningful" (Lau vs. Nichols 1974). Thus,
through the Court's commonsensical decision Congress' previous political
actions were translated into a pedagogical need.

The importance of this ruling was not lost on members of Congress who
could now see themselves as being on the side of the law, and perhaps even
ahead of it. It is likely that the court's resolute statement encouraged legislators to accept a requirement for native language instruction in the legislation.
In addition, eligibility was broadened through elimination of the poverty
requirement. For Hispanics the court's decision provided needed encouragement. Schneider (1976) found that non-English dominant populations exerted
a significant influence in the passage of the 1974 Bilingual Education Act.
They did this directly as lobbysts and active participants in the drafting of the

legislation, and indirectly as constituents to senators such as Edward Kennedy of Massachusetts and Alan Cranston of California, both from states with large SOLs populations and, therefore, strong advocates of the legislation. In contrast, Schneider found that public opinion had little influence on the passage of the law. But once again, four years later the climate was vastly different.

By 1978, the next reauthorization cycle, research on bilingual education had begun to accumulate and the findings were generally supportive of the programs (see, for example, Dulay and Burt 1978 and Troike 1978). Bolstered by this research, reauthorization should have been easily accomplished. However, critics had also found their voice and the 1978 hearings gave them a national forum. Noel Epstein's *Language, Ethnicity and the Schools* became a much cited source in the attacks on bilingual education. As a reporter for *The Washington Post*, Mr. Epstein's opinion was assured wide dissemination, even though his position was sharply criticized by some of the very people he had cited in his support. Fishman, for example, called it "an ignorant critique ... heaps bias upon bias, suspicion upon suspicion, misinterpretation upon misinterpretation..." (Fishman 1978a: 16). Albert Shanker, then president of the American Federation of Teachers, also had a ready soap-box from which to promulgate his opposition through his editorials and position papers, and he used them often to attack bilingual education.

The Congressional committee heard more substantial criticism from Malcolm Danoff, of the American Institute of Research (AIR). Under his direction, this organization had conducted a study which less than four years after its uncertain beginnings had concluded that Title VII did not appear to have a significant impact in meeting the goals of the legislation. Although the study was severely criticized on methodological grounds by O'Malley (1978) and others, the findings received wide publicity from the press and became a rallying point for the opposition during the 1978 hearings. In spite of this formidable opposition, bilingual education was retained in language close to the original legislation.

This temporary reprieve masked the gradual erosion of support for bilingual education. The program, and its sister programs in the Great Society collective were not well received by politicians. Their political power depended on the disbursement of federal funds to their constituents. By circumventing traditional relationships through direct assignment of funds to the barrios and ghettos, the Great Society offended these politicians and generated hostility toward the programs (Piven and Cloward 1971).

The Lau decision was followed by the creation of Lau Centers to provide technical assistance and support to school districts. These centers applied the Lau Guidelines which did not have the force of law but were implemented through the Department of Health, Education and Welfare's (now the Department of Education) monitoring responsibilities. The Lau Guidelines encouraged the use of the native language in the bilingual/bicultural education for SOLs. In 1980 the Guidelines were reviewed by the newly created Department of Education and its first Secretary, Shirley Hufstedler. Formal regulations, mandating bilingual instruction in any public school enrolling 20 or more speakers of a given language emerged from that review but were never implemented. They were withdrawn soon after President Reagan took office in 1980. His election also led to the softening of the government's advocacy role in civil rights and, therefore, the weakening of Title VI, the Equal Educational Opportunity Act of 1974, which had provided legislative support for the Bilingual Education Act.

The drastic change in climate was heralded in an early address by President Reagan to the National League of Cities where he characterized bilingual programs as "absolutely wrong and un-American" (Reagan, March 2, 1981). Instead of demands for compliance, the Reagan White House engaged in activities directed at discrediting bilingual education. In September 1981 the Baker/de Kanter report was issued to the press in draft form and before formal review. Although the authors claimed to have conducted an independent study, they acknowledged that it had been initiated "at the request of the White House Regulatory Analysis and Review Group for an assessment on the effectiveness of bilingual education" (Seidner and Seidner 1982).

The report was roundly criticized on methodological grounds by many researchers, nonetheless it succeeded in gaining the attention of the media.

2.3 *Increased Opposition*

The Bilingual Education Act was reauthorized most recently in 1988. Conflict over the relative emphasis on native-language instruction has been continuous since, in spite of its name, the Act did not originally require "bilingual" instruction. In addition, although transitional goals have been emphasized, the possibility for other instructional programs has never been excluded. The requirement for native language instruction has nonetheless been maintained throughout, although lately portions of bilingual education funds have been set-aside for the implementation of competing instructional strategies advocated by its opponents.

Previous to the 1988 reauthorization, William Bennett, then Secretary of Education attempted to remove the specific reservation of funds for programs using the students' native language from the law altogether. His department cited the supposed ambiguity in research and evaluation reports as the reason to oppose continuation of that requirement. In an effort to clarify the issues, the House Committee on Education and Labor requested the Government Accounting Office (GAO) to conduct an independent review of the research evidence in bilingual education. Their review culminated in the GAO's *Bilingual Education: A New Look at the Research Evidence* (1987). In their summary analysis the GAO reports that:

> The experts' view on the official statements ... indicate that the department interpreted the research differently in several major ways. First, only 2 of the 10 experts agree with the department that there is insufficient evidence to support the law's requirement of the use of native language to the extent necessary to reach the objective of learning English. Second, 7 of the 10 believe that the department is incorrect in characterizing the evidence as showing the promise of teaching methods [such as immersion] that do not use native languages. Few agree with the department's suggestions that long-term school problems experienced by Hispanic youths are associated with native-language instruction. Few agree with the department's general interpretation that evidence in this field is too ambiguous to permit conclusions. (GAO 1987: 3)

Thus, the GAO comparison of statements by Department of Education officials with the research evidence suggests either that department officials were unfamiliar with or misinterpreted the evidence, or that, for their own reasons, they chose to misquote and misuse it. Mr. Bennett, and other Reagan administration officials, succeeded, nevertheless, in shifting the policy debate. Discussions about the preferred goal for bilingual education pre-1980 addressed the relative value of maintaining the native language alongside English instruction vs. using the native language purely as a transitional stage (see, for example, Gonzalez 1978, and Trueba 1979). The debate has now shifted.

Immersion programs conducted solely in English for SOLs were endorsed particularly by William Bennett during his tenure as Secretary of Education (1985-1988). And although Canadian researchers had warned against the transfer of successful immersion Canadian programs to the different US context (Tucker 1980), the 1988 BEA increased the funding set-aside for "Special Alternative Instructional Programs" under which immersion programs are categorized. In addition, and perhaps most damaging, the 1988 Act required students to exit from BEA funded instructional programs at the end of three years, and under no circumstances may a student continue to be enrolled in such programs for more than five years.

Under the threat of total loss of support for bilingual education, the possibility of maintenance is no longer discussed, we now speak of immersion vs. transitional. Ironically, this shift has occurred while the proposed evidence supporting positive efects for both bilingualism and bilingual instruction continues to mount.

It is this contrast between public policies on bilingual education, and the research evidence that is of interest to this writer. In the following pages I will cite selected findings to document the evolving evidence favoring bilingual education and bilingualism against the policy backdrop of the last twenty-one years discussed above.

3. Bilingual Education: The Research

The research I will cite falls across three categories: research about bilingualism, research about bilingual education, and research about the effects of bilingual education. The questions that guide me are: Is bilingualism an asset or a handicap? If an asset, is there reason to believe that bilingual education is an appropriate vehicle for instruction? If so, how do we know? This is not intended to be a full review of the literature regarding these broad topics that task has been accomplished elsewhere (see, for example, Larter and Cheng 1984). The purpose is, instead, to contrast the robustness of positive research findings against eroding government support.

3.1 *Bilingualism: An Asset or a Handicap?*

Most of the research conducted until the early sixties concluded that bilingualism was a language handicap. This research was sharply questioned in 1962 by Peal and Lambert. They reported that bilingual children performed better than monolinguals in a series of cognitive tests, when sex, age, and socioeconomic status were appropriately controlled. These researchers attributed the negative findings of earlier studies to the failure to differentiate degrees of bilingualism and to control for socioeconomic status.

Diaz (1985: 72) in a well-substantiated review intended as a plea of support for bilingual education in the Southwest United States lists a number of studies which show the advantages of bilingualism: "... in measures of conceptual development (Bain 1974, Liedtke and Nelson 1968), creativity (Torrance et al. 1970), metalinguistic awareness (Cummins 1978), semantic development (Ianco-Worrall 1972) and analytical skills ... (Ben-Zeev 1977)". Diaz (1985: 72) also reports that children with higher levels of bilingual proficiency perform at a higher level than their peers on measures of analogical reasoning and tests of spatial relations.

Kessler and Quinn (1987) have compared the performance of 6th grade bilingual children in a southwestern barrio school to private school Anglo children in the same grade in the northeast in the solution of science problems. In spite of the Anglo children's superior reading level (7.38 compared to 3.0) children from the barrios of San Antonio achieved higher scores in their ability to generate more (1,945 to 579) and higher quality (176 to 53) scientific hypotheses, to use more complex metaphors (26 to 19), and to produce more syntactically complex statements (182 to 130) while attempting to solve science problems.

3.2 *Is Bilingual Education Effective?*

Assessing the effectiveness of bilingual education will always be a problem. The term "bilingual education" has no specific definition. It tends to be applied to any program directed at SOLs. Some of these programs may use the native language very little, if at all. In addition, the transitional nature of bilingual schooling ensures frequent turn-over in student population and the accumulation, especially as students move up the grades, of students who may require a longer period of native language support. Those are also the students who are least likely to perform well in standardized tests.

Both the AIR study of 1974 and the Baker/de Kanter report of 1981 were criticized for the researchers' lack of discrimination among various programs purporting to be "bilingual education". Rigorous assessment of instruction would require careful attention to program content and structure, as well as to student population. But this has not been the case in most assessments of bilingual education.

Willig (1985) has conducted a "partial replication" of the Baker/de Kanter review by using all but five of the original set of studies. The excluded studies were conducted on programs outside of the US or, in one case, outside of a regular public school setting. Willig also controlled for methodological inadequacies such as initial group differences in language dominance, in environmental language exposure, in need for the bilingual program, inappropriate comparisons with "graduates" of bilingual programs, and differences, due to exiting of successful students and addition of newcomers, between pre- and post-test population. Willig found that participation in bilingual programs consistently produced small to moderate differences favoring bilingual education. Willig concluded that the predominance of inadequate research designs, and inappropriate comparisons of children in bilingual programs to children who were dissimilar in many crucial aspects, has done a disservice to bilingual education: "In every instance where there did not appear to be crucial inequalities between experimental and comparison groups, children in bilingual programs averaged higher than the comparison children on criterion instruments" (Willig 1985: 312).

Researchers have also been criticized for limiting their criteria to those easily measured through standardized achievement tests. Paulston (1980a), for example, noted that the 1976 dropout rate for Native Americans in Chicago public schools was 95% while it was only 11% in the bilingual-bicultural Litle Big Horn School in Chicago. She argued for the use of broader criteria and longitudinal studies to determine a program's success. Also excluded from the criteria used to evaluate bilingual education is the value of bilingual competence which is added to an individual's linguistic repertoire. In studies of 4th and 5th grade bilingual children, Hakuta (forthcoming) found that the translation skills of these young students were comparable to those of foreign language adult students. Hakuta suggests that the students' translation skills are related to a variety of metalinguistic skills.

In spite of the scarcity of rigorous, comprehensive studies, the experts judging the available data for the GAO report did conclude that the data favored programs using native language instruction. They were also clear in stating that there were no data to support the assertion that bilingual education was impeding the educational progress of Hispanic students.

3.3 *Is there Evidence for Positive Outcomes?*

The notion that bilingualism impedes the educational achievement of Hispanic students is also belied by data from the National Center of Education Statistics' "High School and Beyond" study. Fernández and Nielsen (1986) found that exposure to Spanish during upbringing was not a handicap but an asset, greater Spanish proficiency was associated with greater achievement in both verbal and nonverbal tests.

Data is also available regarding differences in aspirations. One might infer that students with higher aspirations are likely to also achieve at a higher level. This was the position taken by Nielsen and Lerner (1982) in an analysis of language skills as they affected the school achievement of high school seniors. These researchers considered three measures of school achievement: educational aspirations, grade point average, and age. They found ability and socioeconomic status to be the strongest determinants for achievement, effects that are well substantiated in the literature. However, they also found that Hispanicity was the third strongest determinant of aspirations. That is, among the group of bilinguals, those who used Spanish more often also had higher aspirations. Conversely, English proficiency had no significant effect on these students' aspirations.

Along a similar vein, García (1981) also found positive associations with bilingualism among Latinos. He found that when Spanish dominant homes enhanced the Spanish fluency of children, the offspring developed higher levels of self-esteem, more ambitious economic plans, greater assuredness of achieving such plans, greater locus of control, and higher grades in college.

The research evidence thus tends to favor Spanish language maintenance. The benefits of bilingualism are now widely recognized and they appear to accrue not just to advantaged populations, but also to the children of the barrio. Over and over we find that native language competence appears to contribute, rather than detract, from academic achievement. There does not appear to be any evidence to the contrary.

So, how has this recent, and consistently positive research knowledge influenced policy-makers? Not much.

4. Social Science Research and Government Policy

Hakuta notes that "bilingual education has received a disproportionate amount of public horn-locking by politicians, educators, and ordinary citizens alike" (1986: 206). This has been true even though in its richest year (1984) the bilingual education budget was less than one percent of the total United

States federal education budget. He ascribes this mismatch between funding level and the amount of controversy generated to the emotional loading of the issues represented by bilingual education.

And this is the real battle for bilingual education advocates. After 21 years we now have the research to support our instinctive beliefs. We can now argue with a measure of confidence about the benefits of bilingual education. Through the years we have become more knowledgeable about effective instructional strategies and even about language assessment, although we still have much to learn about both. In spite of all this progress, the battle has become more, rather than less, difficult.

The conflictive situation of bilingual education contrasts sharply with the easy acceptance of educational funding for other federal programs, for example, for the gifted and talented. The allocation of special funding for this population was probably as much a creature of the political climate as was the original allocation of moneys for bilingual education. However, unlike bilingual education, programs for the gifted and talented have never received judicial support or the support of research in the social sciences resulting in the positive findings reviewed above, nor do programs for the gifted and talented have the obvious potential for satisfying a national need such as that for increased language fluency. Programs targeted for the gifted and talented have not been proven effective against any criteria. And yet, funding for these programs continues to be accepted by the public and our legislators without question.

It is ironic that the conflict over bilingual education occurs side by side a gathering tide of concern over US students' lack of competence in foreign languages. In November of 1980 the Presidential Commission on Foreign Languages and International Studies, appointed by President Carter, described the national state of incompetence in foreign languages as "scandalous". The need for foreign language education appears to be a cause everyone can comfortably espouse. Even the former Secretary of Education, William Bennett, in spite of his aversion to bilingual education, included two years of foreign language in his proposed model high school.

What are we to make of these conflicting positions? Steve Muller, commenting on the Presidential Commission's report, notes that bilingualism in the US has seldom been a learned achievement, more often it has been a stigma of recent immigration. He argues that inspiring greater national receptivity to the languages of other people will require a persistent asault on the

American consciousness (Muller 1980). But resistance to foreign languages is selective.

Lambert and Taylor (1986) found that citizens of the majority culture tend to be favorably disposed towards the maintenance of heritage cultures and languages for all ethnic groups. But their generosity stops at the schoolhouse door since they also consider instruction in languages other than English inappropriate in the public school setting. However, this same group of parents considers bilingualism developed through schooling as a social, intellectual, and career advantage for their own children. They want their children to achieve skills in another language and become bilingual, but they do not endorse native language instruction for language minority students. These students, they believe, should be taught in English, though they might want to maintain their language in informal settings. The less successful white, working class parents, tend to reject the preservation of heritage cultures and languages in or out of school. However, they also see advantages for their children if their children become bilingual.

The negative associations that tend to accompany bilingual education may also reflect early identification of the program with poverty and educational deficiency. Those labels served a convenient purpose, they made the program possible, but they have also contributed to the confusion of language difference with language deficiency. Students who may, in fact, be competent in two languages, continue to be described as language deficient.

These conflicting values are reflected in public policy. In Arizona, for example, bilingual education programs are at best, transitional. SOLs are expected to receive only minimal instruction in their native language before being mainstreamed into English only classrooms. While these children are being encouraged to forget their mother tongue, recent legislation demands that other Arizona children begin to learn a second language in the elementary school. Thus we may shortly find classrooms where students are being alienated from their native language adjacent to those where their age-mates are struggling to learn a second language.

Hakuta (1986) argues for dissolution of this paradox of admiration for school-attained bilingualism on the one hand, and scorn and shame for home-brewed immigrant bilingualism on the other. He proposes the development of all students, including monolingual English-speakers, as functional bilinguals by substituting linguistic, cognitive, and enrichment purposes for current compensatory goals. This writer shares his opinion that there are only two possible solutions to the conflict over bilingual education. Advocates will either have to convince the general public of the pedagogical value of bilingualism, or they must manage to dilute the identification of bilingual education with ethnicity, poverty and compensatory education. This could be achieved through programs that integrate monolingual English speakers with SOLs in mutually productive instructional relationships.

The intimate connection between bilingual education and foreign language competence has also been noted by prestigious organizations: the Carnegie Corporation, through its *Presidential Report* (Pifer 1979), and in a joint report, the Academy for Educational Development and the Hazen Foundation (AED & E.W. Hazen Foundation 1982). All have endorsed the value of bilingual education, and its potential for complementing a national effort at advancing foreign language competence in the nation.

In spite of such strong and prestigious endorsement, and of the commonsensical notion of connecting two national issues of pedagogical significance, bilingual education continues to be treated as a threat. The lack of influence of relevant scientific data to the debate is particularly surprising in a country that prides itself on its positivism.

The contrast between the scientific/pedagogical argument and public policies puts in question the relevance of the social sciences to the conduct of public policy. In so doing the question of how to preserve the benefits of bilingual education for the increasing number of SOLs remains. The pedagogical avenue appears to be weak in relation to the emotional loading of the concept. If so, only the political avenue remains. This will require a united flexing of the emerging minority voting muscle and appeals to the interests of liberal monolingual populations. Bilingual education as a remedial program will not survive. Its only hope is in the embracing of those who understand that language competence of whatever variety is not a deficiency but an advantage.

Note

1. I consider the acronym LEP offensive because "limited" puts a negative cast on the linguistic skills of these students and it calls to mind a historically oppressed population. I have therefore adopted "speakers of other languages" as a more descriptive and accurate way to identify these children. The phrase results in a much more positive acronym as well: SOLs.

The Bilingual Education Act of 1968 ... is a classical case of 'damned if you do; damned if you don't'... It has always been a 'heads, I win: tails, you lose'... We find Bilingual Education in the usual schizophrenic double-bind.

Joshua A. Fishman, 1978a: 14

The Politics of Paranoia:
Reflections on the Bilingual Education Debate

Jim Cummins

Ontario Institute for Studies in Education

1. Introduction

The debate about the merits or otherwise of bilingual education has preoccupied educators, politicians, the media and occasionally the general public in the United States for more than twenty years. Many commentators have warned that bilingual education is not only educationally ill-advised, it also threatens the social and political stability of what is often referred to as "the most powerful nation on earth". Newspaper editorials across the country have detailed a catastrophic scenario of Hispanic "activists" demanding ever more intensive bilingual education as a ploy both to prevent minority children from learning English and to fuel Hispanic separatism, resulting ultimately in the disintegration of the United States.

If such arguments were not taken seriously by so many North Americans, they would be laughable. In fact, this line of "reasoning" has been effective in emasculating bilingual education throughout the seventies and eighties such that only "quick-exit" transitional bilingual programs have been tolerated in most jurisdictions. I have chosen to examine this debate because it is one to which Joshua Fishman has made immense contributions, both with respect to theory and research and in both popular and academic publications. From the beginning of officially sanctioned bilingual education in the U.S., he has been an ardent critic of its compensatory character; he has pointed again and again to the obvious fact that "bilingualism" is not a deficiency to be remediated, as assumed by most transitional programs, but rather an intellectual and educational enrichment for the individual and society. There are some indications that this message is finally being heard in the 1990s as "two-way" or developmental bilingual programs involving both English- and non-English-background students are increasingly being implemented. This progress is in no small measure the result of Joshua Fishman's intellectual leadership in the field and his tireless advocacy for equity and justice for all children.

In the first section I cite some prominent examples of the popular debate to illustrate the shrillness of the opposition to bilingual education and the palpable threat that it appears to represent to many commentators. I then examine the arguments advanced by some academics against bilingual education. One might assume that any academic who comments on an area of public policy such as bilingual education, where policy decisions affect the lives of so many children, would take seriously their ethical responsibility to inform themselves about the relevant research and to critically evaluate this research. In fact, for the most part, this is not the case. Academic critics of bilingual education in the United States tend to demonstrate as little concern for the research and theory underlying bilingual education as do the media commentators. I argue that a deliberate process of disinformation is underway aimed at, in Noam Chomsky's (1987) terms, "invalidating the threat of a good example". In other words, enrichment or "empowering" forms of bilingual education are seen as representing a threat to the societal power structure in that they institutionalize and valorize languages and cultures other than those of the dominant group. They are also considerably less likely to reproduce what Tove Skutnabb-Kangas (1981) has termed "the caste of assembly-line workers". If this is, in fact the motivation behind much of the opposition to bilingual education, it carries important implications for researchers who have tended to assume a rational model of the relation between research and policy; in other words, they have assumed that positive results of bilingual programs will increase the likelihood of these programs being accepted and implemented more extensively. In fact, the argument that I will propose suggests that the more empirical evidence is produced that certain types of programs result in personal and academic growth among minority students, the more vehement will be the denial of this evidence and rejection of these programs by those sectors of the dominant group who are committed to maintaining the societal status quo.

2. The Evolution of the Policy Debate

Initially, as Troike (1978) has observed, bilingual education was instituted in the late sixties on the basis of what appeared to be a self-evident rationale, namely that "the best medium for teaching a child is his or her mother tongue", but with relatively little hard evidence to back up this rationale. The reaction of many press commentators in the initial years of this experiment was one of "wait-and-see"; they didn't particularly like the idea but were willing to give it a chance to prove its potential for reducing educational inequities. Some were concerned, however, that bilingual education might have the opposite effect, namely of preventing Spanish-speaking students from entering the mainstream of English-speaking America, and also that it might give rise to the divisiveness that appeared to be associated with bilingualism in Canada. However, in general, this first phase (1967-1976) of the modern bilingual education debate was marked by tolerance for the educational potential of bilingual education and, although doubts were certainly raised, its rationale was not disputed in any sustained or systematic way.

Since the mid-seventies the bilingual education debate has become considerably more volatile. The concern with political divisiveness resulting from bilingual education was articulated clearly in a *New York Times* editorial entitled "Bilingual Danger" on November 22, 1976:

> The disconcerting strength gathered by separatism in Canada contains a relevant lesson for the United States and its approach to bilingual education.... it is no exaggeration to warn that the present encouragement given to making [Spanish-speaking] enclaves permanent, in the mistaken view that they are an expression of positive pluralism, points the road to cultural, economic and political divisiveness. The reason why such a warning appears appropriate is that political splinter groups within the Spanish-speaking community, and among educators, are misinterpreting the goals of bilingual education in New York as a means of creating a Spanish-speaking power base.... Without exaggerating the threat to America's nationhood now that English has prevailed, it nevertheless remains pertinent to warn against a misguided linguistic separatism that, while it may seem to promise its advocates limited political and ideological power, can only have the effect of condemning to permanent economic and social disadvantage those who cut themselves off from the majority culture. (Quoted in *The Linguistic Reporter*, January 1977: 1,7)

Although his reply was not printed in the *New York Times*, Joshua Fishman refuted the arguments of this editorial as follows:

The *New York Times* seems to fear that something divisive ... might grow
out of bilingual education in the USA. Having spent many years studying
bilingual education throughout the world ... I consider this to be highly
unlikely, both because ethno-cultural divisiveness, where it obtains, is far
too deeply imbedded in a pervasive socioeconomic matrix to be "caused"
by any kind of education, as well as because bilingual education per se is
unfailingly unifying rather than divisive. The hallmark of all bilingual
education (including its compensatory USA variant) is that it includes a
unifying supra-ethnic language of wider communication (in our case:
English...). Indeed, if any educational pattern can be said to typify Quebec
it is the absence (historically as well as currently) of bilingual education
(education via two media of instruction), rather than its presence. All of
which is not to say that there is no striving for "a Spanish-speaking power
base in the USA", or that such strivings may not be justified.... What
might counteract such strivings would be genuine opportunity for
Hispanic participation in "political power" and a genuine end to the "economic and social disadvantage" of Hispanics in the USA, all of the foregoing having been promised in theory and so obviously denied in practice
by the monolingual English establishment. If Hispanic (or rather minority)
"divisiveness" increases in the USA, it will be because of the long tradition of English-dominated inequality, such as that long practiced in Quebec, rather than because of bilingual education which functions to link
together populations that might otherwise be totally estranged. (*The Linguistic Reporter*, January 1977: 7)

As the debate evolved, the sociopolitical concerns of many commentators
were backed up by psychoeducational arguments against bilingual education
and in favor of all-English "immersion" programs. The usual argument in
favor of bilingual education, namely, that "children can't learn in a language
they don't understand", was no longer regarded as self-evident in view of the
fact that findings from French immersion programs in Canada showed that
English-background children who were taught initially through French in
order to develop fluent bilingual skills did not suffer academically as a result
of this home-school language switch (see Cummins and Swain 1986; Swain
and Lapkin 1982). To many commentators in the United States, these results
suggested that English immersion programs were a plausible educational alternative to bilingual programs.[1] Furthermore, immersion programs appeared
to avoid the potential divisiveness associated with the recognition and institutionalization of Spanish.[2]

The intense opposition to bilingual programs during the 1980s is well
summed up in the following three quotations which vividly outline the con-

cerns of many Americans about the increasing penetration of Spanish into mainstream institutions such as the educational system:

> Bilingual education is an idea that appeals to teachers of Spanish and other tongues, but also to those who never did think that another idea, the United States of America, was a particularly good one to begin with, and that the sooner it is restored to its component 'ethnic' parts the better off we shall all be. Such people have been welcomed with open arms into the upper reaches of the federal government in recent years, giving rise to the suspicion of a death wish. (Bethell 1979: 30)

President Reagan also joined the fray in early March 1981, arguing that:

> It is absolutely wrong and against American concepts to have a bilingual education program that is now openly, admittedly dedicated to preserving students' native language and never getting them adequate in English so they can go out into the job market and participate. (*Democrat-Chronicle,* Rochester, March 3, 1981, p. 2A)

The incompatibility that is implied in President Reagan's remark between preserving the native languages of minority students and the learning of English is a theme that occurs frequently in the opposition to bilingual programs. This assumed incompatibility is made explicit in the following excerpt from a *New York Times* editorial (October 10, 1981):

> The Department of Education is analyzing new evidence that expensive bilingual education programs don't work ... Teaching non-English speaking children in their native language during much of their school day constructs a roadblock on their journey into English. A language is best learned through immersion in it, particularly by children ... Neither society nor its children will be well served if bilingualism continues to be used to keep thousands of children from quickly learning the one language needed to succeed in America.

The general line of argument against bilingual education is clear: such programs are a threat to national unity and furthermore they are ineffective in teaching English to minority students since the primary language, rather than English, is used for a considerable amount of instruction in the early grades. The bilingual approach appears to imply a counter-intuitive "less equals more" rationale in which *less* English instruction is assumed to lead to *more* English achievement. It appears more logical to many opponents of bilingual education to argue that if children are deficient in English then they need instruction in English, not their native language (L1). School failure is caused by *insufficient exposure* to English (at home) and it makes no sense to further dilute the amount of English to which minority students are exposed by instructing them through their L1 at school. Unless such students are immersed in English at school, they will not learn English and consequently will be prevented from participating in the mainstream of American society.

This line of argument was continued by former Secretary of Education William J. Bennett who, in the fall of 1985, described bilingual education as "a failed path" and emphasized the need to provide flexibility to local school districts to decide which instructional approach to follow. As reported in *FORUM*, the Newsletter of the National Clearinghouse for Bilingual Education:

> Bennett stressed that learning English is the key to equal educational opportunity and is the unifying bond for the diverse population of the United States. Proficiency in English should thus be the primary objective of special instructional programs for LEP [limited-English-proficient] students, the secretary declared. According to Bennett, federal policy has lost sight of this goal by its emphasis on bilingual education as a means to enhance the students' knowledge of their native language and culture ... The secretary cited research studies, the below-average performance of Hispanics, and the high Hispanic dropout rate as indications that bilingual education programs have not been effective and that federal policy needs adjustment. (Volume 8, number 5, p. 1, October/November 1985)

During the 1980s, the U.S. English organization coordinated much of the opposition to bilingual education, initiating and passing referenda in several States to make English the official language (see Crawford [1989] for an analysis of the U.S. English movement). Several of the academic critics of bilingual education are consultants to the U.S. English organization. The arguments of academic critics are considered in the next section.

3. The Academic Critics of Bilingual Education

I argue in this section that a systematic process of disinformation has been promoted by certain groups opposed to bilingual education. The term "disinformation" refers to the spreading of false information in order to confuse and disorient the opposition. For present purposes, we can distinguish two broad types of disinformation: first, the deliberate spreading of false information for political ends where those who are spreading the information know that the information is false; the second, and in the bilingual education situation, more common type of disinformation is where the false information is genuinely believed by those spreading it. This second phenomenon merits the pejorative term "disinformation" in cases where there is no excuse for being ignorant and/or misinformed since the relevant information is readily available. Those in positions of power and influence (e.g. media commentators, politicians, academics) have an ethical responsibility both to inform themselves of the relevant research and to attempt to be logical and rational in the way they interpret this research.

This second type of disinformation involves not so much a conscious "conspiracy" as a selective inattention to awkward facts and questions. Thus, in the 1920s and 1930s, researchers were very quick to attribute differences they observed between minority bilingual and majority monolingual children to the debilitating effects of bilingualism, despite the fact that so many obvious variables were confounded with bilingualism (e.g. socioeconomic status, language of testing, violence against minority children in schools, etc). They also did not consider the obvious question of why bilingualism appeared to exert no adverse effects on children of the rich and powerful. In short, the process involved abdicating logic and the scientific method in order to screen out potential explanations that might compete with the preconceived and societally-approved explanation; in other words, the explanation that contributed to the preservation of the societal power structure.

The same type of disinformation process appears to be operating today with respect to the effects of bilingual education. The data on bilingual education are both clear and abundant (see Cummins 1989; Fishman 1988b; Krashen and Biber 1988), yet the myth has been perpetuated that there are few data and what there are do not have any value.

A first observation in reviewing the academic literature on bilingual education is that the vast bulk of this literature in both the United States and internationally is supportive of the educational merits of bilingual programs for both majority and minority students. Within the United States, despite the largely negative media coverage of bilingual programs, there are only a few academics who have argued against the educational validity of bilingual education. Most of the arguments reduce to the following: there is minimal evidence that bilingual education is effective in comparison to alternative programs, and English-only immersion programs represent a more promising alternative supported empirically by the results of Canadian immersion research.

This line of argument was first articulated by Noel Epstein (1977) but its elaboration into a coherent position was carried out by Keith Baker and Adriana de Kanter (1981) in their detailed review of research evidence on bilingual education. Much of the initial scepticism regarding the effectiveness of bilingual education derived from the findings of the American Institutes for Research (AIR) report (Danoff et al. 1977, 1978) that transitional bilingual programs appeared to be no more effective than English-only programs in promoting academic development among minority students. Claims of empirical support for English immersion programs have been made by Russell Gersten and John Woodward (1985a, 1985b). A monograph by Lloyd Dunn (1987), an article by Nathan Glazer (Glazer and Cummins 1985), literature reviews by Christine Rossell (e.g. Rosell 1990) and printed comments by both Diane Ravitch and Herbert Walberg (United States General Accounting Office 1987) have all supported English immersion over bilingual education. I will take just three examples of the opposition to bilingual education to illustrate the shallowness of the arguments used and the cavalier attitude that frequently obtains in relation to the research data.

4. Gersten and Woodward: A Case for Structured Immersion

Gersten and Woodward (1985a) claim to have found empirical evidence that structured immersion that uses the "direct instruction model" (i.e. DISTAR) produces large academic gains among minority students. Their initial discussion of the rationale for immersion programs reveals a truly incredible ignorance of the Canadian research upon which they base their arguments. For example, they note the fact that Baker and de Kanter

> called public attention to the promising research findings from Canada on *structured immersion* (emphasis original). With structured immersion, all instruction is done in the commonly used language of the school (English in the U.S., French in Canada).... Difficult new words are pretaught, sometimes using the child's native language.... Santiago, in the March 2, 1983, *Education Week*, said that 'the immersion method has only been tried with middle class children'. His statement is not accurate; the bulk of the Canadian research was with low-income students. (1985a: 75-76)

There has been a vast amount of research on French immersion programs in Canada and this research has been reported extensively in many academic journals and books. It is therefore astonishing to see statements such as those above. First, in French immersion programs, children's L1 (English) is usually introduced about grade 2 or 3 and its use increased as children go up the grades so that by grade 5 about half the instructional time is spent through English. Thus to say that all instruction is done in French is totally inaccurate.

Second, French immersion programs are based explicitly on the premise that language is acquired through *use* not through explicit instruction out of the context of meaningful communication. Vocabulary is virtually never pre-taught, any more than it is in the process of children acquiring their first language.

Third, although researchers have argued that French immersion programs are appropriate for low-income students and should not be restricted only to middle-class children (e.g. Cummins 1984; Genesee 1987; Swain and Lapkin 1982), the vast majority of children in French immersion programs come from middle-class backgrounds and very little research data are available on the performance of working-class children in these programs. Gersten and Woodward (1985b) reiterate their claim that Canadian immersion programs involved predominantly working-class students in their response to Santiago's (1985) rebuttal of their original article, stating that

> there were four studies other than the St. Lambert study, all of which involved children from working-class families. The results of structured immersion with these students were comparable to those found with the middle-class children in the St. Lambert study. (1985b: 83)

Gersten and Woodward seem to believe that only five studies of French immersion have been carried out in Canada, and four of these involved working-class students. In fact, Swain and Lapkin's (1982) bibliography in their book on immersion contains more than five hundred citations, most of these empirical studies, and that number has probably doubled since 1982.

How convincing are the empirical data presented by Gersten and Woodward? They describe results of two programs that used DISTAR with minority students, one group of Hispanic origin near the Mexican Border in Texas (Uvalde), and the other predominantly of Asian origin in California (Pacific City). In the Uvalde evaluation no comparison group was available and thus the evaluation data would be dismissed according to the criteria set up by

Baker and de Kanter (see Santiago 1985). When tested at the end of grade 3, after three years of DISTAR, the children were reported to be performing close to national norms on the language (i.e. usage, tense, punctuation, etc) and math subtests of the Metropolitan Achievement Test. However, scores on the reading subtest were considerably lower, at the thirty-fourth percentile, just slightly above the median district score in previous years (thirtieth percentile). Becker and Gersten (1982) report total reading percentiles of 31 for the Uvalde group at the end of grade three but this declines to the sixteenth percentile by grades five and six. This decline in reading comprehension scores as children advance through the elementary grades is the opposite of what happens in well-implemented bilingual programs where students' percentile scores tend to progressively approach national norms as grade level increases (Krashen and Biber 1988).

Gersten (1985) reports longitudinal data from the Pacific City program that suggests better progress in English in the early grades for minority students in a DISTAR-based immersion program than for students in a transitional bilingual program. However, the numbers of students involved in this evaluation were extremely small; the first cohort involved only twelve immersion program students and nine bilingual program students while the second involved only 16 and seven in each group. These numbers scarcely constitute an adequate sample upon which to base national educational policy, especially since DISTAR-type drills are likely to be much more similar to standardized test content than the program to which the comparison group was exposed.

A final point in relation to the Gersten and Woodward article concerns their reduction of the framework of discourse to "structured immersion versus transitional bilingual education", as in the Baker/de Kanter report. For example, in reviewing Lambert's injunction against English immersion for minority students, they note that

> He claims that typical compensatory education models will not work. The only salvation is transitional bilingual education, involving introduction of a 'separate English language instructional component when it is certain that the child's home language has taken root and it is a secure base for starting the buildup of English, a stage that may not be reached until a child enters the 2nd or 3rd grade'. (Gersten and Woodward 1985a: 76)

To anybody familiar with bilingual education research and policy, it is clear that what Lambert is discussing is a "reverse immersion" or two-way bilingual program where minority children are "immersed" in their L1. The goal is additive bilingualism involving high levels of both English and L1 literacy. To label this type of program as "transitional bilingual education" is a travesty of what Lambert has eloquently argued for on many occasions (e.g. Lambert 1975) which is directly opposed to the monolingual monocultural goals of transitional bilingual education. However, when the issues are conceptualized within this framework, educational enrichment of minority students does not become a policy option for open discussion.

5. Glazer: Stirring the Melting Pot

Nathan Glazer's views on bilingual education were outlined in a journal called *Equity and Choice* which asked both him and me to respond to a series of questions on bilingual education (Glazer and Cummins 1985). While admitting a role for "taking cognizance of native language, using it for part of the school day [and] continuing it after transition to English for purposes of maintaining facility", he expresses concern that some bilingual programs are "keeping children in classes conducted primarily in their native language as long as possible" (p. 47).

In response to a question on the best methodology for teaching English as a second language, Glazer responded as follows:

> I don't think (probably) there is one 'best' way. But all our experience shows that the most extended and steady exposure to the spoken language is the best way of learning any language. (1985: 48)

Glazer here abdicates his academic (and ethical) responsibility to examine and rationally interpret the research evidence rather than remaining at the level of assumption and "common sense". A vast amount of data overwhelmingly support the fact that there is no direct relationship between amount of exposure to English and development of English academic skills among minority students, obviously given a certain minimum amount of exposure to English. In fact, in many cases there is an inverse relation between exposure to English instruction and achievement in English (see Cummins 1989).

Glazer's answer to the the subsequent question regarding how long it takes for children to achieve sufficient proficiency in English for them to be able to learn school subjects successfully through English instruction similarly reveals a total ignorance of the research. This, however, did not stop him from articulating his opinion:

> How long? It depends. But one year of intensive immersion seems to be enough to permit most children to transfer to English-language classes. (p. 48)

The data, in fact, show that on the average it takes *at least* four to five years for ESL students to attain grade-appropriate levels in English cognitive/ academic skills (Collier 1987, 1989; Cummins 1981) although fluency in conversational skills may develop considerably sooner.

The point I wish to make here is that even those posing as "experts" in the field appear to have little hesitation in making pronouncements regarding bilingual education that are totally at variance with the research data but are consistent with their sociopolitical concerns; in Glazer's case, as with many other commentators, these sociopolitical concerns relate to the dangers of creating a separate Hispanic enclave in American society (1985: 51). Regardless of the legitimacy or otherwise of these concerns, the reality is that they are spreading disinformation by avoiding abundant opportunities to inform themselves about what the research on bilingual children's development is actually saying.

6. Rossell: Deconstructing Structured Immersion

Christine Rossell's (1989, 1990) analyses of the bilingual education data suffer from most of the inadequacies of both the Baker/de Kanter report and the Gersten/Woodward papers, albeit in a more sophisticated way. She accepts the Gersten studies together with Canadian French immersion data as the primary evidence in favor of structured immersion over "transitional bilingual education". The Baker/de Kanter review is cited as showing that "transitional bilingual education" works no better than English-only programs. Willig's (1985) meta-analysis of the Baker/de Kanter database that reported positive effects of bilingual education is dismissed as using statistically invalid procedures (an opinion obviously not shared by the editors of the *Review of Educational Research*). I will comment here only on one aspect of her analysis, namely, the argument that Canadian French immersion data constitute evidence in favor of structured immersion for minority students.

Rossell's case for structured immersion is stated as follows:

> No study has found transitional bilingual education to be superior to structured immersion and the only one to show no difference between the two in second language learning was conducted 17 years ago in the Phillipines.... All studies comparing bilingual education to structured immersion since then have found the latter to produce greater achievement in the second language than the former. All the studies conducted in Canada of immersion and bilingual education (partial French immersion) have shown that the middle class and working class English speaking students who were immersed in French in kindergarten and grade 1 were almost the equal of native speaking French students until the curriculum became bilingual in grade 2, at which point their French ability declined and continued to decline as English was increased. (1989: 16)

This description is so confused as to be almost uninterpretable. In the first place, what is meant by "structured immersion"? If Gersten and Woodward's description is intended (i.e. vocabulary pretaught using only the target language) then this bears little resemblance either to the Phillipine program cited (Ramos, Aguila and Sibayan 1967) or to French immersion programs in which the target language is learned through interaction. Rossell's understanding of French immersion programs is bizarre. For example, she implies that a substantial number of working class children were/are involved in French immersion. This is simply not the case; the two studies (out of several hundred) conducted with so-called working class students were not continued past grade two and the students in these studies were far from low-income inner-city or migrant students typical of bilingual programs in the U.S. (Genesee 1987).

The assertion that students in French immersion were "almost the equal of native speaking French students until the curriculum became bilingual in grade 2" is totally inaccurate. There are major differences in French achievement between native speakers of French and immersion students at the grade 2 level and beyond. Immersion students may *approach* native speaker levels in some receptive skills by grade 6 but major differences in expressive skills (speaking and writing) continue regardless of the grade at which English (L1) skills are introduced.

Rossell also argues that "time-on-task" is the major predictor of achievement in second language programs. While instructional time through the target language is undoubtedly important in that a language cannot be learned without exposure to it, the argument that maximum exposure to the target language is a central component of successful programs is refuted by virtually all the research data, whether from so-called "immersion" or bilingual education programs. In the first place, in French immersion programs, students in intensive late immersion programs (starting L2 immersion at grade 7) catch up to their colleagues in early immersion within about three years (grade 9) in almost all aspects of French proficiency despite considerably less instructional time through French (Harley, Allen, Cummins and Swain 1990). Secondly, in French immersion programs there is clearly no relationship between achievement in English and instructional time spent through English in that students taught for substantial amounts of time though French do not suffer in English academic growth. Exactly the same phenomenon is reported with respect to bilingual programs for minority students in that students taught through a minority language do not experience negative consequences with respect to achievement in the majority language (see Cummins 1989).

All of these fallacies in Rossell's position boil down to the misrepresentation of French immersion programs as "structured immersion". The logic in Rossell's position is to argue for a monolingual English-only program, taught largely by monolingual teachers, and aimed at producing monolingualism, on the basis of the success of a program involving full bilingual instruction, taught by bilingual teachers, whose explicit goal is to produce full bilingualism and biliteracy.

7. The Goal of Disinformation: to Invalidate the Threat of a Good Example

Chomsky (1987) has identified three processes whereby powerful nations or groups counteract what he calls the "threat of a good example"; in the present context the threat of a good example is the possibility that enrichment or empowerment bilingual programs might demonstrate effectiveness in promoting high levels of academic achievement among minority students. These processes are:

* limiting the framework of discourse;
* denying/distorting empirically documented counter examples;
* ignoring logical inconsistences in the positions being advocated.

These three processes are very much in evidence in the arguments proposed by the academic critics of bilingual education reviewed above. For example, despite the fact that virtually all researchers who have evaluated Canadian French immersion programs as well as the most prominent bilingualism researchers in the U.S. (particularly Joshua Fishman) have consistently criticized transitional bilingual education as inferior to full enrichment (or additive) programs designed to develop bilingualism and biliteracy, critics always frame the issues in terms of "transitional bilingual education" versus "structured immersion". Thus, any successful enrichment program is likely to be classified as either transitional bilingual education or structured immersion (or both as in the case of Legaretta's [1979] 50/50 Spanish-English program in the Baker/de Kanter report). Thus, in reviewing the data the positive results of enrichment programs can be aggregated out of existence in the midst of mediocre results from emasculated quick-exit transitional programs.

The most significant way in which empirically documented counterexamples are either dismissed or ignored is through the refusal to examine the research evidence with respect to its consistency with the theoretical assumptions underlying policy. This refusal permits opponents of bilingual education to ignore the fact that virtually all the data they review is inconsistent with the assumptions underlying structured immersion but consistent with those underlying enrichment bilingual programs. Thus, structured immersion assumes that there is a direct linear relationship between amount of instruction in English and achievement in English despite the fact that all the data from both majority (e.g. French immersion) and minority programs refutes this assumption.

The logical inconsistencies ignored by critics of bilingual education range from the argument for monolingual programs (structured immersion) on the basis of the success of bilingual programs (French immersion) to the insistence that minority children's first languages be eradicated as a prelude to teaching these same languages as "foreign languages" at the high school level (see Cummins 1989).

8. Conclusion

The psychoeducational arguments against bilingual education are so bereft of empirical support and devoid of theoretical coherence that they themselves require explanation. The most obvious explanation is that they constitute part of a process of disinformation designed both to prevent the institutionalization of Spanish and other languages and to deny equality of educational opportunity to minority children. Many of the arguments proposed against bilingual education are based on interpretations of the research data that are truly bizarre (e.g. Gersten and Woodward's suggestion that only five studies have been conducted on French immersion and four of these involved working-class students). One is forced to conclude that what is important for the opposition is not the truth or falsity of the arguments proposed but rather that there be a counter argument against bilingual education that obfuscates the issues. In this way, policy-makers are likely to conclude that "the experts disagree" and act on the basis of political expediency rather than research evidence.

Thus, the process of maintaining the societal power structure over the past decade has involved paying lip-service to the rhetoric of educational equity by funding various forms of compensatory programs while ensuring that potentially empowering pedagogical programs (i.e. those that challenge institutional racism in schools, e.g. two-way bilingual programs) do not qualify for funding. Thus, the intervention goals are defined narrowly in terms of learning English and, as far as possible, only programs that pose little threat to the power structure get implemented (namely, emasculated quick-exit transitional programs). However, since it has transpired that even these programs have affected the power structure in providing jobs for Hispanics and other minorities (even though for the most part they have not reversed minority students' school failure), it is regarded as desirable to eliminate them; this becomes an urgent priority in view of the changing demographics which potentially pose a real threat within a democratic country. Thus, the next step must be to demonstrate that these programs (not surprisingly) do not work very well and should therefore be eliminated in order to help minority children succeed academically. Thus, the status quo (submersion under the label of "structured immersion") can be reinstated while preserving the myth that minority students' needs are being met. This analysis suggests that the more convincing the evidence for the effectiveness of certain kinds of bilingual education the more vehement will be the rejection of this evidence by the academic critics of bilingual education.

Notes

1. As documented below, many United States commentators who use the Canadian immersion programs to argue for "English immersion" for minority students fail to realize that French immersion programs are fully bilingual in that they are taught by bilingual teachers, the goal is bilingualism and biliteracy, and children's first language (L1) is strongly promoted after the initial grades so that about half the instruction is through L1 in grades 4-6.

2. Noel Epstein (1977) was the first to point to Canadian French immersion programs as a counter-argument to the psychoeducational rationale underlying transitional bilingual education. His monograph entitled "Language, Ethnicity and the Schools" evoked a stinging rebuke from Fishman (1978a).

Research operations in education are never-ending, for their value resides in their provocativeness and in their fruitfulness with respect to future research.

Joshua A. Fishman, 1959: 62

What Bilingual Education Has Taught
the Experimental Psychologist:
A Capsule Account in Honor of Joshua A. Fishman

Kenji Hakuta

Stanford University

1. Introduction

In the fall of 1979, shortly after receiving my doctorate in Experimental Psychology from the hallowed halls of William James Hall at Harvard (home of B.F. Skinner, S.S. Stevens, and others trying to make physics out of psychology), I found myself with a job in the Psychology Department at Yale University wishing to build on the research trajectory set by my dissertation on the burning issue of word order and relative clause processing in Japanese children. Now a little over a decade later, I frequently find myself in the heart of the policy debate over bilingual education in the United States. How did I go wrong/right? What have I learned?

This piece is admittedly narcissistic, and I speak as a novice to the field of bilingual education when compared to the other contributors to this volume, many of whom were publishing on the issue before I had ever heard of the term. My contribution concerns my transformation into an academic whose burning question has become something having to do with the real world.

I felt that a brief account such as this might be fitting as a tribute to Joshua Fishman because of his record as an intellectual omnivore, a model to which I aspire. Further, I wished to document the aspects of research and researcher development that have little to do with the idealized textbook model of research (someone who, on the basis of theory and previous research, sets up hypotheses tested by critical studies,which lead to progressive approximations of truth through the elimination of alternative hypotheses). If you will, that idealized researcher is analogous to Chomskyan competence, and this chapter is about performance. In the course of this account, I also wish to capture a bit of history of the interaction between research and politics that have marred the landscape of bilingual education. Joshua Fishman has, of course, been central in the formation of this landscape throughout.

2. Science

The greatest legacy of the psycholinguistics movement of the 1960s was in impressing the value of formal description in advancing our knowledge about human behavior. Undoubtedly, we spent a lot of time finding out what we were not, e.g. that we do not follow the operations of such and such a version of Chomsky's transformational grammar when we process sentences. But at least this approach took us out of a purely inductive process towards our language behavior, an approach whose epistemological status was strongly refuted by Chomsky.

In 1979, as I was emerging out of the cocoon having shown that a few esoteric linguistic theories were inapplicable to children acquiring Japanese syntactic structures, a finding that was noted by at least ten individuals (including my mother, but excluding my wife), I wanted to keep doing this kind of mapping between formal theory and behavior until my TIAA-CREF retirement fund would reach maturity.

Several factors intervened in my continued progress. First, formal linguistics was becoming increasingly abstract and required an inordinate amount of time to keep up with. I had been warned by my mentor (who tolerated the focus of my dissertation). The awful truth about chasing those purple mimeo manuscripts was that formal linguists can disassemble theories overnight, far more quickly than experimental psychologists trying to test these theories can construct an experiment. In any event, like most psycholinguists, at about Chomsky's Government and Binding theory, I lost motivation to keep reading the formal stuff.

A second major factor had to do with the nature of the students at Yale's psychology department. My predecessor there was Katherine Nelson, a developmental psychologist specializing in language but who never really had bought into what formal linguistics had to offer. So the graduate students I found waiting for me at Yale were primarily those who saw language development from a traditional cognitive developmental perspective. Although several bright undergraduates found this esoterica interesting (I still have a few of those once in a while), most graduate students were too wise to get into something that was seen as a strange preoccupation centered around Cambridge, Massachusetts, and rapidly diminishing in value as one moved away (with notable oases). In any event, it became quickly evident that force-feeding my papers or even those by Steve Pinker would win few converts (see Pinker 1979 for an example of his work on learnability theory).

3. Money

Another influential force was the fundamental fact of life in a university. Without funding, you are nobody. About a month after my arrival at Yale, my senior colleague Bill Kessen plopped on my desk a grant application packet for the National Science Foundation's Applied Behavioral Sciences Program. Not being totally stupid, I got the message, and I decided to fill it out. The start-up funds of $5000 that I received from Yale was unlikely to pay my bills for long, and with my salary, I was hardly in a position to pay for my own xeroxing and stamps.

4. People

One of my graduate students, Rafael Díaz, introduced me to Aida Comulada, who was the Director of the Bilingual Education Program in the New Haven Public Schools. When they had met at a prior social event, Aida suggested to Rafael that he do some research with the Bilingual Education Program. Aida is an infinitely charming person who clearly saw the significance of encouraging research on bilingual education, and she worked on us to establish a "town-gown" relationship. So Rafael and I decided that we shape a proposal around the Bilingual Program. Rafael made it abundantly clear that he had no interest in pursuing esoteric questions having to do with formal linguistic universals, so we compromised and decided to extend the work on bilingualism and cognitive flexibility, a tradition whose modern beginnings rest with Peal and Lambert (1962). We were funded almost immediately, and we were happy as we merrily went about doing our business of basic science, in the context of a bilingual education program.

5. Politics

We were embarassingly naive about the nature of bilingual education in the United States. Indeed, we were first somewhat surprised to hear that not all children in bilingual programs are bilingual, and indeed, that the goal of the program was to put them in English-only classes. I started reading on the topic, and perhaps the single most useful document to get me grounded was the four-volume series put out by the Center for Applied Linguistics (1977). The volume on the social science perspective by Joshua Fishman painted a profoundly rich document that to this day continues to yield new insights on each re-reading. As we started drawing our conclusions from our research about the positive effects of bilingualism on cognitive ability, we knew that this would have some relevance to bilingual education, but we were not sure quite what.

To reveal how naive I was about the political swirls that buffeted (and continue to buffet) bilingual education, in June of 1981, I received a call from a certain individual from NIE asking me if I would be interested in writing a commissioned paper on the status of bilingual education. Not knowing what I was getting involved in, I innocently replied that maybe I could talk Rafael into doing it with me, since we might learn something about it. Word evidently got around knowledgeable individuals in Washington that I might be doing this. Probably the most merciful phone call of my life came from Tracy Gray at the Center for Applied Linguistics, who knew the exact political motive that lay behind this commission and warned me in no unexplicit terms to stay out. "Now tell me", I vividly recall being asked, "do you know of the Baker/de Kanter document?" To which I innocently replied, "The who document?"

This document, of course, became a famous piece in the bilingual education controversy, having started as an internal memo within the Office of Planning, Budget and Evaluation (OPBE) in the Department of Education. It "reviewed" evaluation studies of bilingual education and concluded that these programs were not effective. There is now wide agreement on the technical limitations of the study (see Willig 1985), and it certainly would not be published in any serious peer-reviewed journal. Indeed, the paper never really made it into print except in the form of a self-serving book edited by the authors of the report (Baker and de Kanter 1983). However, it did fit the anti-bilingual education political agenda of the changing political landscape and the chorus of some high-level (and not-so-high-level) bureaucrats, and even made the rounds in Congress as some members moved to limit Title VII legislation.

What I had been asked to do, evidently by some people in the National Institute of Education and the Office of Bilingual Education and Minority Language Affairs (OBEMLA) who were still politically sympathetic to bilingual education and foresaw the destructive potential of the document, was to offer an antidote document. Obviously, I was not qualified to do this; but even more obviously, such things do not matter in the policy circles where institutional credibility can be more important than substance.

6. Money, Again

As funds from the NSF grant dried up in the end of 1981 (as did the program from which we received funding), I turned to the NIE to help continue our work, which was going well. We had established a reliable way of measuring the relationship between degree of bilingualism and cognitive abilities, and had shown this to be a positive one. We were now set to continue observations over time to look for cause-effect relations.

The NIE was by this time already scaling down, and did not have much funds available. However, they were part of the "Part C Committee" (described later) together with the Office of Bilingual Education and Minority Language Affairs (OBEMLA) and other representatives within the Department of Education (including the Office of Planning, Budget and Evaluation, OPBE) which allocated the research funds under Title VII. And since my study was conducted in the context of a bilingual education program, I was funded for two more years under this program.

The Part C Committee needs to be investigated in greater detail by a future student of the politics of bilingual education. "Part C" refers to Section C of the bilingual education legislation where Congress mandates research activities, including evaluation. Although funds under this section are to be administered by OBEMLA, evidently a variety of conditions led to the establishment of a committee more broadly representative of the department to coordinate research initiatives. As time went along, most certainly by the time my study got funded by Part C, OBEMLA had lost much of the control over the allocation of resources and a number of studies favored by OPBE staff were commissioned (including the study comparing the relative effectiveness of structured immersion and bilingual education programs, still not officially released and entangled in a web of politics thinly disguised as technical problems).

7. Science, Again

We continued to chip away at the problem of bilingualism and cognitive ability. Rafael developed and tested hypotheses about the mechanisms by which bilingualism might lead to improved performance on our measures. I analyzed the longitudinal data and started putting the study in its proper historical and sociolinguistic context.

Throughout this work, I considered it important to invest a good deal of time getting to know the classrooms and came to know many of the teachers quite well. I quickly discovered the extra-linguistic factors that affect the development of children in the programs, including the high rate of mobility (this showed up, for example, in a high rate of sample attrition in the longitudinal study), and the differences in these rates and other indicators of livelihood across the different schools and parts of the city. And I became concerned with the tremendous amount of misunderstanding about bilingual education carried in popular myths and fueled by politicians and the media.

There was a familiar ring to these negative comments about bilingual education. They echoed what I was reading in my explorations into the archival materials on bilingualism and intelligence, where bilingualism was blamed for everything from bad attitude to mental retardation. Indeed, this earlier literature, which was concerned with the problem of bilingualism in "folk bilinguals", stood in stark contrast to the positive assessments made about "elite bilinguals", a contrast that Joshua Fishman has repeatedly emphasized. Thus, the distinction between "good" and "bad" versions of bilingualism and the prejudices that surround this distinction came to be an important theme in my work. I was proud to have found support for the positive effects of bilingualism, not just for its pure scientific value, but for the fact that it demonstrated a parallelism between "good" and "bad" bilinguals.

8. Politics, Again

In August, 1985, I organized a panel with graduate student Bernardo Ferdman for the annual meeting of the American Psychological Association (APA) in Los Angeles on bilingualism. The panel included Donald Taylor, Alexander Guiora, and Robert Gardner. Being in Los Angeles, the APA organizers thought there would be press interest in bilingualism, so they organized a press conference to follow our session.

The panel itself was quite dry, talking about technical aspects of bilingualism and its relationship with cognitive and social variables. It included really dry discussion that only social scientists would have a taste for, such as the question of levels of analysis, and the use of words like "micro versus macro". Indeed, as I recall it, the size of the panel threatened to exceed the number of people in attendance. The press conference following was quite a bit more lively.

We were asked to do what academics more frequently should be asked to do, i.e to summarize our papers in a minute or two. And then we were bombarded by questions about bilingual education. We answered them, saying we felt that bilingual education is a good thing and so forth. Curiously, though, none of our papers was really about bilingual education. Mine was about the closest, having been conducted in the context of a bilingual education program, but never in my wildest dream did I consider it to be a study on the effectiveness of bilingual education. But that's what they all wanted to know about.

Quite a bit of press was generated from this meeting. *The New York Times* ran a headline, "Bilingual pupils said to have edge", and plenty followed suit, along with invitations for talk shows and debates, all having to do with the effectiveness of bilingual education. Another invitation came from Ricardo Martinez of the House Education Committee, who asked if I could come and brief Congressional staff on bilingual education. I told him that I could brief them on basic research on bilingualism. He said fine, I can brief them on bilingual education, and suggested that I come down on September 27th. We confirmed that date later on, and he told me that there was considerable interest in what I would have to say.

The reason why that date turned out to be an odd coincidence was that on the morning of September 26th, Secretary of Education William Bennett launched a well-orchestrated attack on bilingual education. He had most effectively homed in on an issue that would enable him to use his "bully pulpit" and get media attention. The press release circulated in advance of his speech claimed:

> Despite a Federal investment of $1.7 billion over 17 years (currently about $139 million annually), research has not shown transitional bilingual education to be more successful than other methods of instruction in helping non-English speaking children become proficient in English. Therefore, the Department of Education is proposing to give local school districts greater flexibility in choosing instructional methods they believe will be most effective for their limited English proficient students.

As the date approached, I started receiving all kinds of calls from individuals representing interest groups informing me of the importance of my session. Coming on the heels of Bennett, my briefing was seen as a response, something I was hardly equipped to do. "Uh-oh," I thought, "this time I'm really stuck! Tracy, where are you?" I empathized with Bambi in that famous and briefest of films, "Bambi Meets Godzilla".

What I did prepare under fear of total embarrassment was a statement about why evaluation research on bilingual education is seriously flawed and is easily swayed by political winds. That much I knew to be true, having read the history of the Baker/de Kanter debate, its predecessor the AIR report, and other evaluations. Instead, I suggested that it would be more credible to look at basic research on bilingualism to help guide policy, and I prepared a "fact sheet" about basic research on bilingualism. These facts would support the fundamental principles of bilingual education.

I still use these points in speaking to various groups about bilingual education, and reproduce them in modified form in Table 1. They are basic conclusions that have been around for some time, and need to be strengthened and tested as to their limits of generalization. Being very doubtful that evaluation research in bilingual education will ever emerge out of the stranglehold of political forces, it is my strong conviction more than ever that basic research on second language acquisition and the psycho/sociolinguistics of bilingualism must receive priority funding support.

Table 1
Research conclusions about bilingualism and bilingual education

---

* Double standards exist about bilingualism: good for some children, but not for others; expectations about speed of second language learning are different too.

* Evaluation of bilingual education programs is very political; often, it is not clear what is being compared with what – apples with oranges. We have to be very careful about interpreting program evaluations. Instead of looking only at evaluation research, we should be looking at what basic research has to say about bilingualism in children.

* Bilingualism is a good thing for children of all backgrounds – when bilingual children are compared with monolingual children on different kinds of skills, bilingual children are superior.

* To be "proficient", "to be fluent", "to know" a language means many different things: you can have good conversational skills, but that is different from being able to use it in other settings, such as in school. Bilingual children are often informally evaluated in their conversational skills, but not in how they can use English in school.

* The two languages of the bilingual child are interdependent – they do not compete for limited space and resources.

* The stronger the native language of the children, the more efficiently they will learn English.

* Knowledge and skills learned in one language transfer to the other language – they do not have to be re-learned.

* It is a myth that children are like linguistic sponges; they may take anywhere from 2-7 years, especially to master the academic uses of English.

* It is a myth that the younger children are, the faster they learn a second language.

* Bilingual program evaluations, although problematic, suggest that (1) bilingual programs are more effective than alternative programs, and (2) good bilingual classrooms have the same features as any good monolingual classroom.

* When we talk about bilingual education, we are entrapped by myths and labels; we should try not to get worked up about the labels of programs, because the issue becomes primarily political; we know from basic research that a good education in two languages is achievable, that it can have many benefits, and all we need to do is to build the commitment to establish programs that get us out of the imprisoning mentality that the two languages have to be in competition.

9. Science, Again and Again

The study of bilingualism from linguistic, psychological, and sociological perspectives holds an important place in science. Having taken a peek into the world of the politics of bilingual education, I am now even more firmly of the belief that the best role for the student of human mind, behavior and institutions is to continue strengthening the science. The best defense available against politically motivated attacks on the ideals of bilingual education is two-pronged. Obviously, fire must be met with fire, which is to say that advocacy and political activity is essential (I do this poorly, but fortunately there are many others who excel at this). But the other is to have a solid body of theory and research that is not part of special interest groups for particular educational policies. Researchers have their own political opinions that undoubtedly challenge their objectivity and the questions that they ask, but the results and interpretations can at least be questioned and challenged under a set of logic and methods that do not exist in the world of policy.

Besides strengthening my conviction on the need to advance basic knowledge, however, bilingual education has taught me that scientific knowledge can and should be integrated into real world problems without compromising their integrity. The artificial distinction between basic and applied research is a myth that may have served some noble causes, but I believe it is as much a phantom an ideal as is the idealization of progress in research (someone who, on the basis of theory and previous research, sets up hypotheses tested by critical studies, which lead to progressive approximations of truth through the elimination of alternative hypotheses). We researchers are human, and therefore we are opportunistic, serendipitous, greedy and playful; when we are lucky, circumstances combine into a rare configuration that is considered creative. All of us researchers in bilingualism must be thankful to Joshua Fishman for having created so many opportunities in which we can attempt to be academics and pragmatists at the same time.

Bilingual education is a celebration of liberation from provincialism for those who know only English and liberation from self-doubt for those who haven't yet learned English.

AJoshua A. Fishman, 1978c: 1

Extending Enrichment Bilingual Education: Revisiting Typologies and Redirecting Policy[1]

Nancy H. Hornberger

University of Pennsylvania

1. Introduction

The distinction between transitional and maintenance models of bilingual education is well-known, though not necessarily consistently defined, in the scholarly literature. It has also been debated in federal policy and the popular press for at least the last twenty years (see Crawford 1989: 31-49 on the former and Henderson 1974, 1978 for some early examples of the latter). Considerably less attention has been given to a third model identified by Fishman in his writings on bilingual education as the enrichment model (Fishman 1976a: 27-31, 34-36; 1977b: 12; 1982: 22-26). In fact, the transitional/ maintenance/enrichment trichotomy is sometimes collapsed into a dichotomy, where enrichment and maintenance bilingual education are undifferentiated.

This paper calls for more attention in U.S. educational policy and practice to the enrichment model of bilingual education, suggesting that it is the third model which offers the greatest potential benefit not only to language minority speakers but to the national society as a whole (cf. Fishman 1976a: 35; Lyons 1988: 10; Tucker 1987). It argues that both the concept and the practice of enrichment bilingual education need to be extended: the former by revisiting bilingual education typologies and the latter by redirecting bilingual education policy. In the interest of extending the concept of enrichment bilingual education, the paper reviews a spectrum of existing bilingual education typologies; proposes a revised conceptual framework which distinguishes between bilingual education models and program types (cf. Trueba 1979), defining both in terms of specific characteristics and making enrichment bilingual education more salient; and illustrates the framework with description of the Potter Thomas program in Philadelphia. In the interest of extending the practice of enrichment bilingual education, it comments briefly on past and future policy trends affecting this and other enrichment bilingual education programs.

2. Revisiting Bilingual Education Typologies

From the earliest years of federally-funded bilingual education in the United States, typologies have abounded (see Fishman 1977b: 11-17 and Trueba 1979 for early reviews of some of the typologies; and Table 1 for a summary of those reviewed here). These typologies, characterizing bilingual education, or, in some cases, educational programs for language minority children, range from two-type distinctions to Mackey's 90-cell typology (1972 [1970]).

There is considerable inconsistency among the typologies at a number of levels. Most obvious are discrepancies in use of the same term across different typologies. Thus, maintenance bilingual education refers to oral language maintenance in some typologies (Saravia-Shore 1979: 336) and to full biliterate bilingual bicultural maintenance in others (Appel and Muysken 1987; Fishman 1982; Skutnabb-Kangas 1981); it is sometimes distinguished from enrichment bilingual education (Conklin and Lourie 1983; Fishman 1982), but other times subsumed within the enrichment type (Crawford 1989). Similarly, in some typologies, immersion is clearly distinguished from submersion (Appel and Muysken 1987: 67; Crawford 1989; McKay 1988; Ovando and Collier 1985: 43; Skutnabb-Kangas 1981) and from structured immersion (Ovando and Collier 1985), while in others submersion and structured immersion are seen as 'variations' of immersion (GAO 1987). The word shelter appears in two diammetrically opposed terms: sheltered English, which is technically not bilingual education at all (Crawford 1989, GAO 1987) and language shelter, which is another term for mother tongue maintenance bilingual education (Skutnabb-Kangas 1981: 129; 1988: 26).

At the same time, there is a proliferation of different terms for the same type. Thus, Kjolseth's (1972) assimilation/pluralism distinction is equivalent to the transitional/maintenance one (cf. Appel and Muysken 1987); transitional bilingual education is also termed compensatory bilingual education (Crawford 1989; Fishman 1982); maintenance bilingual education is also called language shelter (Skutnabb-Kangas 1981) or developmental bilingual education (Bennett 1988; Crawford 1989; "Department of Education: Bilingual Education Regulations", 1986, p. 22424; Saravia-Shore 1979; Title VII, 1988, sec. 7003); and two-way enrichment bilingual education is also designated utopian bilingual education (Skutnabb-Kangas 1981: 127, 132-133).

A further discrepancy is that while some typologies are strictly concerned with bilingual education proper, that is, education which uses two languages as medium of instruction; other typologies include programs addressed to the education of non-English speaking students but which do not necessarily involve use of the first language as medium of instruction at all; Cazden and Snow (1990) contrast these as technical and popular senses of the term bilingual education, and Table 1 uses this distinction to separate those programs which are properly bilingual education from those which are not. The typologies considered here include replacement (Saravia-Shore 1979: 336); segregation, submersion, and mainstream (Skutnabb-Kangas 1981:125-135; 1988: 22-31); monolingual education (Grosjean 1982: 208-213); English as a Second Language (ESL) (Conklin and Lourie 1983: 234-238; McKay 1988: 342-343); structured immersion (Ovando and Collier 1985); and sheltered English (GAO 1987: 76). Yet neither ESL nor sheltered English, structured immersion nor submersion, segregation nor mainstream, are, technically speaking, bilingual education in any sense.

A mainstream educational program is simply instruction in the majority language for majority children; segregation is its converse, instruction in the minority language for minority children. Submersion refers to the absence of any recognition of language diversity in the school program; it is also known as the 'sink or swim' approach. Structured immersion, despite its name and the tendency to consider it a variation of immersion, has more in common with submersion than immersion. Like submersion, it is a program of monolingual majority language instruction for minority language speakers, with no use or development of the L1; unlike submersion, the teacher uses a "simplified" form of the L2 and may understand and accept contributions from the students in the L1 (cf. Ovando and Collier 1985: 44). To the extent that the teacher actually uses the children's L1 (cf. Baker 1987: 354), structured immersion might be included within bilingual education proper.

Sheltered English and ESL, as their names imply, use only English as medium of instruction. Whereas sheltered English provides content area instruction in English to language minority students, using simplified vocabu-

Table 1: Bilingual education typologies

Cazden & Snow 1990	BE in popular sense	BE in technical sense*			
Kjolseth 1972	Assimilation		Pluralism		Two-type
Spolsky 1974	Salvage the child		Salvage the language		
Gaarder 1976	Folk		Elitist		
Grosjean 1982 outcomes	Linguistic/cultural assimilation		Linguistic/cultural diversification		
Crawford 1989 models	Compensatory		Enrichment		
Fishman 1976		Compensatory	Group-maintenance	Enrichment	Three-type
Fishman 1982		Transitional-compensatory	Maintenance	Enrichment	
Appel & Muysken 1987		Transitional-assimilationist	Maintenance-pluralistic	Immersion	
Fishman & Lovas 1970	Transitional bilingualism	Monoliterate bilingualism	Partial bilingualism	Full biliterate bilingualism	Four-type
Paulston 1978 (1975)	Forced segregation	Voluntary assimilation / Forced assimilation		Autonomy	
Saravia-Shore 1979	Replacement	Transitional	Maintenance	Developmental	
Grosjean 1982 programs	Monolingual	Transitional	Maintenance	Immersion	

Conklin & Lourie 1983	ESL	Transitional	Maintenance	Enrichment
Skutnabb-Kangas 1988	Segregation Submersion		Mother tongue maintenance or language shelter	Immersion
Ovando & Collier 1985	Structured immersion	Transitional	Maintenance	Two-way enrichment Immersion	Five-type
GAO 1987	ESL Sheltered English Structured immersion Submersion	Transitional		Immersion
McKay 1988	Submersion Pull-out ESL	Transitional	Maintenance	Immersion Two-way	Six-type
Crawford 1989 programs	Submersion Structured immersion Alternate immersion (sheltered English)	Transitional program	Maintenance or developmental (including 2-way)	Enrichment immersion
Skutnabb-Kangas 1981	Mainstream Submersion Segregationist	Transition	Language shelter or L1 maintenance	Immersion Utopian bilingual	Seven-type

* This two-way distinction runs all the way through the table.

lary and special methods and materials such as cooperative learning and visual and tactile aids; ESL focuses on instruction of the English language itself.

While any of these six approaches may form all or part of an educational program in a linguistically diverse context, none of them is bilingual education in the technical sense, since none of them uses both languages as medium of instruction. Though most of the authors are careful to distinguish these from bilingual education, the fact that they so often surface in discussion of bilingual education is both a reflection of and a contribution to the direction of bilingual education policy in the U.S. (cf. Rohter 1986); I will return to this point in the concluding section of the paper. For now, I will restrict my discussion to bilingual education in the technical sense.

We have seen that the typologies reveal discrepancies not only in the inclusion of popular as well as technical conceptions of bilingual education, but also in the term-type relationship: the same term is used for different types and different terms are used for the same type. Hidden within these discrepancies is a more profound problem, however: the failure to distinguish, both within and across typologies, between program goals/objectives/intentions, program structure, and contextual factors. Maintenance bilingual education is sometimes defined primarily in terms of its goals: the maintenance of the ethnic language and culture (e.g. Conklin and Lourie 1983: 241; Crawford 1989; Fishman 1982: 24); and sometimes in terms of its program structure: the curricular maintenance of the ethnic language as medium of instruction throughout the years of schooling (Mackey 1972: 418). Yet, a maintenance program structure does not necessarily foster language maintenance if there is no opportunity to use the language outside school (Fishman 1982: 21, 28; Hornberger 1988a; Kjolseth 1972); nor do maintenance goals necessarily ensure a maintenance program structure (Guthrie 1985).

Immersion bilingual education provides an excellent example of this goal/structure/context confusion. A number of the typologies explicitly suggest that immersion offers a third alternative to the transitional and maintenance bilingual education models. Yet, though transitional and maintenance bilingual education are defined primarily in terms of assimilationist vs. pluralistic goals, immersion bilingual education is most often defined in terms of its structure, rather than its goals. For example, from Grosjean:

> Transitional bilingual programs aim to prepare the child as quickly as possible to pursue studies in the majority language, and there is no attempt to

maintain the child's native language or enhance the minority culture.... Maintenance programs ... try to develop and maintain the minority child's cultural heritage as he or she is introduced to the majority culture and help the child become functionally bilingual in the two languages.... [In] immersion programs ... children from a particular language and cultural background are first taught in a second language and then, little by little, their first language is introduced as a second medium of instruction. (1982: 213-217) (Cf. also Appel and Muysken 1987: 65-67; Crawford 1989; GAO 1987.)

Others include contextual factors along with structural ones in defining immersion (McKay 1988: 354). For example, Tucker includes both when he identifies salient attributes of the successful Canadian immersion programs. The structural characteristics he highlights are that children are introduced to formal instruction in their L2 from the beginning by native L2 speakers, but their teachers understand their L1, the L1 is reintroduced by grade 2 or 3, and is used for content area instruction as well; the contextual characteristics are that language majority children of middle socio-economic status participate voluntarily in the programs and that the programs were designed in response to parental pressure and with parental participation (1986: 362-363).

The point here is that what are presented as parallel types are defined by non-parallel criteria. Mackey (1972) attempts to bring order to the complexity of bilingual education types by organizing criteria into parallel sets. He considers the distribution of languages in: 1) the behavior of the bilingual child at home (5 possibilities); 2) the curriculum in the school (5 dichotomies yielding 10 curricular patterns); 3) the community of the immediate area within the nation (9 possibilities); and 4) the status of the languages (1972: 415). This framework has the merit of being comprehensive; however, it is too unwieldy to be practical. What is needed is a framework which minimizes the discrepancies among former typologies, establishes parallel types defined by parallel criteria, and is neither too elaborate to be unwieldy nor too reduced to be simplistic.

3. A New Framework

Fishman foresaw that, with time and experience, the typological systems proposed in the 1970s would need to be collapsed or expanded (1977b: 16).

Here, I will propose a framework which builds from the former typologies (collapsing some, expanding others), and illustrate it with a particular case.

Following Trueba 1979, I distinguish between bilingual education models and program types, the former being broader categories at a higher level of abstraction than the latter. I define models in terms of their goals with respect to language, culture, and society, and program types in terms of characteristics relating to student population, teachers, and program structure (cf. Trueba's 'design'; Cohen 1983). Unlike Trueba, I do not see particular types as subdivisions of particular models; rather, I suggest that any one type may theoretically be implemented within any of the three models, and any model may be implemented via a wide range of types.

Despite the many discrepancies within and among the typologies reviewed here, there are a number of common threads across them, and these will provide the basis for my framework. There is, first of all, agreement as to the existence of transitional bilingual education, characterized by assimilationist goals and compensatory structure; and maintenance bilingual education, characterized by pluralistic goals and a sheltered or developmental structure. Furthermore, there is agreement that a third alternative exists: however, there is both terminological and conceptual confusion as to goals and structures of the third alternative. As to goals, they are largely presented as undifferentiated from maintenance model goals. As to structures, several typologies specify immersion and some include two-way bilingual programs as well (Crawford 1989; McKay 1988; Ovando and Collier 1985); but there is no coherent characterization. My purpose here is to clarify and extend the definition of the third alternative, enrichment bilingual education.

If a transitional model encompasses all those bilingual education program types which aim toward language shift, cultural assimilation, and social incorporation of language minorities in the national society (cf. Spener 1988); and a maintenance model encompasses all those bilingual education program types which aim toward language maintenance, strengthened cultural identity, and the affirmation of ethnic groups' civil rights in the national society; then an enrichment bilingual education model encompasses all those bilingual education program types which aim toward not only maintenance but development and extension of the minority languages, cultural pluralism, and an integrated national society based on autonomy of cultural groups (cf. Fishman 1976a: 34-36; see Table 2).

Table 2
Bilingual education model types

Transitional Model	Maintenance Model	Enrichment Model
language shift	language maintenance	language development
cultural assimilation	strengthened cultural identity	cultural pluralism
social incorporation	civil rights affirmation	social autonomy

Yet, as I suggested above, each model may be implemented via a wide range of program types. While model types are defined by goals, program types are defined by contextual and structural characteristics; that is, parallel types are defined by parallel criteria (see Table 3).

The bilingual education typologies reviewed in the first section of this paper pay varying degrees of attention to contextual characteristics. Kjolseth (1972) argues for the importance of the sociolinguistic context beyond the school; Mackey (1972) addresses the distribution of languages at home, in the community, and in the nation; Paulston (1978) looks at economic or structural integration of the subordinate group with the superordinate group; Skutnabb-Kangas (1981) considers minority vs. majority status, organizational factors, learner-related affective factors, and L1 and L2 related linguistic, cognitive, pedagogical and social factors. Combining these considerations along with the contextual characteristics identified by Tucker above with respect to immersion programs, we find that sociolinguistic and socioeconomic characteristics, voluntary participation, and parental involvement are all significant. Cummins also identifies dominant-dominated relations in the societal context; and in the school context, incorporation of minority students' culture and language and inclusion of minority communities in their children's education, as contributing to the extent to which minority students are empowered or disabled (1986: 24). Here, in the interests of keeping the typology manageable, I formulate these contextual characteristics in terms of student and teacher characteristics which are directly observable in the school (see Table 3: Student Population and Teachers).

Structural characteristics include consideration of the program's place in the school; the treatment of the two languages in the curriculum; and language use in the classroom. A program may be school-wide, involving all stu-

Table 3
Bilingual education program types

	Student population	Selected related references
Contextual characteristics	Numbers	
	Stability (high or low turn-over each year)	
	Participation (voluntary or involuntary)	cf. Skutnabb-Kangas 1988:27-28
	Assessment & placement (advocacy or legitimizing)	Cummins 1986: 24
	Socioeconomic status	cf. Tucker 1986; Cummins 1986
	Minority status (involuntary or immigrant)	Ogbu 1987b
	First language background	
	heterogeneous or homogeneous	cf. Skutnabb-Kangas 1988: 28
	minority or majority	cf. Skutnabb-Kangas 1988: 28
	degree of bilingualism	cf. Mackey 1972: 415-416
	Teachers	
	Ethnic background	cf. Troike & Saville-Troike 1982: 210-212
	Degree of bilingualism	cf. Skutnabb-Kangas 1988: 28
	Training	cf. Troike & Saville-Troike; Skutnabb-Kangas
	Roles (classroom or supplementary teacher, aide, tutor, etc.)	cf. Hamayan 1986
Structural characteristics	*Program in school*	
	School-wide or Targeted	
	One-way or Two-way	cf. Ovando & Collier 1985; Crawford 1989
	Languages in Curriculum	
	Sequencing of languages as mediums of instruction	cf. Mackey 1972: 416-423; Cohen & Laosa 1976
	Oral and literate development	cf. Fishman & Lovas 1972; Cohen & Laosa 1976
	Subject allocation	cf. Mackey 1972: 419; Hamayan 1986
	Classroom language use	
	Patterns	
	alternate: lessons, teachers, days/weeks/am-pm, rooms	
	mixed: codeswitching, concurrent translation, preview-review,	
	new concurrent approach	cf. Jacobson 1979, 1987; Legarretta 1981; Zentella 1981; Fillmore & Valadez 1986
	Functions: speech acts, interactional structures	

dents in the school, or it may be targeted only at certain classrooms or certain students in the school. It may be a one-way program, in which only speakers of language X learn language Y; or it may be a two-way program, in which speakers of X learn Y and speakers of Y learn X.

The treatment of the languages in the curriculum embraces curricular issues of the sequencing of the languages as media of instruction; the degree of oral and literate development of the two languages; and the allocation of the languages by subject or content area. The sequencing of the languages in the curriculum is perhaps the most salient curricular characteristic, and it is from this characteristic that program types may derive their names. There are, logically, four sequencing possibilities for the use of two languages as media of instruction in one educational program (cf. three in Cohen and Laosa 1976):

$$L1 \Rightarrow L2 \qquad \text{(transitional)}$$
$$L1 \Rightarrow L1 + L2 \qquad \text{(maintenance)}$$
$$L2 \Rightarrow L1 + L2 \qquad \text{(immersion)}$$
$$L1 + L2 \qquad \text{(two-way; utopian)}$$

The terms transitional and maintenance, then, refer not only to model types (see above), but also to program types; this is the source of some of the confusion discussed in the first section. On the other hand, immersion and two-way (utopian) bilingual education properly refer only to program type.

Language use in the classroom encompasses both patterns and functions of use. Patterns can be characterized broadly as alternate vs. mixed (cf. separating vs. concurrent; Jacobson 1987); and functions can be characterized in terms of, for example, speech acts and interactional structures, as well as the curricular allocation of the languages for content area and literacy instruction (see subject allocation and oral/literate development under 'Languages in Curriculum'; cf. Fillmore and Valadez 1986: 655-667).

4. Enrichment Bilingual Education

Revisiting bilingual education typologies has served to extend the concept of enrichment bilingual education by, on the one hand, separating enrichment from maintenance, and, on the other, separating it from immersion. The former extension allows the enrichment model of bilingual education to be defined by its own unique goals of language development, cultural pluralism, and social autonomy; the latter extension reveals that enrichment bilingual education can be implemented via a range of program types, of which immersion is only one. The primary identifying characteristic for enrichment bilingual education is that the program structure incorporate a recognition that the minority language is not only a right of its speakers but a potential resource for majority language speakers (cf. Ruiz 1984).

It remains now to explore the extension of the practice of enrichment bilingual education. The enrichment bilingual education programs most often cited in the literature are the French immersion programs beginning in St. Lambert, Quebec in 1965. In these programs, native English speaking children learn the national minority language, French, in addition to their own language, English, and both languages are used as media of instruction (e.g. Conklin and Lourie 1983: 244; Fishman 1982: 26-28; Genesee 1987; Tucker 1986). These programs, whose students are from "the most fortunate socioeconomic backgrounds", are consistent with "elitist" bilingual education, of which enrichment bilingual education is a "direct descendant" (Fishman 1982: 25).

Nevertheless, extending enrichment bilingual education includes extending it beyond its elitist origins (cf. Fishman 1976a: 28-29; Trueba 1979: 57-58). Recently, there has been increasing attention in this country to another type of bilingual education program which belongs to the enrichment model and extends it beyond the majority to the minority group: the two-way, or interlocking, bilingual education program (cf. Collier 1989; Crawford 1989: 163-173; Lindholm 1987; Ovando and Collier 1985: 40-41; Tucker 1987). Programs mentioned in the press and in the nascent but growing literature include the two-way immersion program at The Oyster School in Washington D.C. (Collier 1989; Crawford 1989: 168-169; Days 1988; Marquand 1987); and a two-way maintenance program in Port Chester, New York ("Two-way bilingual programs"; Crawford 1989: 171, who terms this a two-way limited immersion program). In both structures, children of minority language groups learn English and native English speaking children learn the minority language; furthermore, both languages are used in instruction of content areas. The news articles note that the success of these programs goes beyond successful learning of English to a more general positive impact on understanding, communication, and integration across linguistic communities.

Lindholm provides a definition of bilingual (two-way) immersion and an informative directory of all such programs in operation in the U.S. in 1987.

Thirty programs are identified, of which the oldest are those in Dade County (since 1963), Washington D.C. (1971), and Chicago (1975); nineteen of the thirty date from only 1983 or later. As with other bilingual education types, Lindholm notes a proliferation of terms for these two-way immersion programs, including: bilingual immersion, two-way bilingual immersion, two-way bilingual education, two-way immersion education, language immersion, Spanish immersion, interlocking, and dual language education (1987: 12). Yet another increasingly popular name for it is dual language instruction (Lessow-Hurley 1990. See Morison 1990 for description of a dual language program in New York City). The criterial features Lindholm identifies for a two-way immersion program are: "1) the program essentially involves some form of dual language immersion, where the non-English language is used for at least 50% of the students' instructional day; 2) the program involves periods of instruction during which only one language is used; 3) both English speakers and non-English speakers (preferably in balanced numbers) are participants; and 4) the students are integrated for all content instruction" (1987: 5).

5. A Two-Way Maintenance Program

Here I would like to draw attention to another two-way enrichment bilingual education program type, which I call two-way maintenance. Using the typological framework introduced above, I will explore the characteristics of a program that has been functioning for two decades at the Potter Thomas School in Philadelphia (cf. Mezzacappa 1987). Data on the program come from my ongoing comparative ethnographic study on biliteracy in two Philadelphia public schools and their communities (cf. Hornberger 1989, 1990).

5.1 *Student Population*

Potter Thomas serves just over 1000 children in grades prekindergarten through five. It is primarily a neighborhood school, drawing its students from approximately twenty square blocks of North Philadelphia's Puerto Rican community. The population has changed over the two decades of the bilingual program's existence; furthermore, the population in the neighborhood at any one time is constantly changing. These two facts have consequences for the composition of the school's population.

First, over the past twenty years North Philadelphia's Puerto Rican population has grown in proportion to other groups (Philadelphia City Planning Commission 1986: 15); and there are larger numbers of second and third generation Puerto Ricans in the population (Ericksen et al. 1985: iv). Thus, whereas in the past Potter Thomas' English speaking students were primarily monolingual English speaking African-American children,now more than half of them are continent-born Puerto Rican students whose first or dominant language is English, but who have had some exposure to Spanish (18B 30^2; School District of Philadelphia 1987-1988: 376).

Second, the population in the school neighborhood at any one time is constantly changing due to continuing migration from Puerto Rico and to economic pressures within Philadelphia and on the Puerto Rican community in particular (both associated with Puerto Ricans' status as involuntary rather than immigrant minorities, cf. Ogbu 1987b). School District figures show that 67.7% of the children at Potter Thomas School come from families of low income (School District of Philadelphia 1987-1988: 377). The decline of factory jobs, the closing of factories, and poor housing in the neighborhood all contribute to high mobility in the population. Potter Thomas' assistant principal notes that the school registers 100 to 200 new students at the beginning of each school year (14A 40); many more arrive and leave during the school year. School District of Philadelphia records show 198 admits and 235 dismissals for Potter Thomas for the 1986-1987 school year (School District of Philadelphia 1987-1988: 377). An informal study of about 10 years ago found that only about 15% of the fifth grade had been at Potter Thomas throughout the six grades (15B 182). High mobility in the population means not only that the school continually receives new monolingual Spanish speakers of all ages who have just arrived from Puerto Rico; but also that it regularly loses students before they can complete the full bilingual language and literacy development the program envisions.

Assessment and placement of children into their reading and second language levels are regarded as crucial to the success of the program (14A 210). Assessment is individualized and systematic, carried out by the assistant principal (for Spanish reading and Spanish as a Second Language), the ESOL specialist, and the English reading specialist. Children are assessed upon arrival (18A 180-265; 15A 11); and are constantly re-evaluated and reassigned where necessary (e.g. at the end of levels and units; 14A 113; 18A 247; 18A 15, 73).

Assessment and placement play what appears at first to be a legitimizing role, but is in fact an advocacy one (Cummins 1986: 24). While the assessment instruments are primarily psychoeducational (e.g. tests accompanying the basal reading series, a check list of vocabulary items developed by the School District, an 'informal reading inventory', or a short dictation of ten words with instructions to make sentences with the words and use them in context), they are used not to locate a problem within the student, but to seek the best possible match between each individual and the range of learning environments available in the program.

5.2 *Teachers*

Philadelphia, like other parts of the country, suffers from a lack of trained bilingual teachers; the situation is exacerbated by the fact that Pennsylvania has as yet no certification in either bilingual education or ESOL. The result is, as the principal points out, that if a certified teacher happens to pass the Spanish test offered by the School District (also 13A 345; 13B 75), he or she becomes a bilingual teacher. That is, not necessarily all the teachers assigned to Potter Thomas School are trained as bilingual teachers. They are, instead, teachers who are bilingual.

On the other hand, the program also has some teachers who are monolingual: monolingual English teachers who were teaching at Potter Thomas before it became a bilingual school and have stayed on; and nearly monolingual Spanish teachers who were brought in during the first years of the program under emergency provisions. Other teachers, though bilingual, are clearly dominant in one language or the other. Finally, there is a core of teachers who are not only fully bilingual but also trained as bilingual teachers (14B 89). Most of the Spanish monolingual or bilingual teachers are of Cuban or Puerto Rican ethnic backgrounds.

Teaching roles at Potter Thomas take advantage of the range of language backgrounds and proficiencies of the teaching staff, and include homeroom teachers, reading aides, ESOL teachers, and Spanish support teachers. We will return to these under discussion of classroom language use.

5.3 *Program in School*

The bilingual program at Potter Thomas is a school-wide program; all children and all classes in the school participate. It is a two-way program. There are two streams in the school: the Latino stream, which consists of the children moving from Spanish dominance toward Spanish-English bilingualism; and the Anglo stream, which consists of the children moving from English dominance toward English-Spanish bilingualism. In the 1987-1988 school year, there were 451 and 567 students, grouped into 16 and 17 homeroom classrooms, respectively, in the Latino and Anglo streams.

When students first arrive at Potter Thomas, they are assigned to the Anglo or Latino stream according to their home language, that is, the dominant language in the home, as reported by the parents (2-19-87; 3-26-87; 14A 59; Kindergarten Child Intake Form). Parental preference also plays a role in children's placement: parents may choose, for linguistic or cultural reasons, to place their child in the Anglo stream, even if the child is Spanish-dominant; or vice versa. Thus Anglo and Latino are neither clear cultural nor monolingual language categories, but reflect two clusters along a continuum of language use, as well as a range of attitudes toward Spanish language maintenance and assimilation to U.S. culture.

5.4 *Languages in Curriculum*

The Potter Thomas bilingual program has been from its inception a two-way maintenance bilingual program in Spanish and English: Spanish speaking children learn English while maintaining their Spanish, and English speaking children learn Spanish while maintaining their English (14A 17). Both languages are developed beginning in prekindergarten and through fifth grade at the school, and both languages and literacies are used for subject matter instruction. When asked what were her goals for her students in terms of reading and writing in the two languages, the principal responded, "Well, to make them proficient in both languages, in reading and in writing, that's the ultimate goal ... With some children you can see that happening already by the fifth grade" (14A 130).

In the Anglo stream, children receive instruction in Spanish as a Second Language (SSL) each day for fifteen to thirty minutes in prekindergarten and kindergarten, and for forty-five minutes starting in first grade, until the point when they are ready for Spanish reading, which they have for 1 1/4 hours a day. All the rest of their instruction is in English.

In the Latino stream, children in prekindergarten and kindergarten receive fifteen to thirty minutes of English as a Second Language (ESL or ESOL –

English for Speakers of Other Languages) per day; in first and second grades, 1 1/4 hours per day; and in third through fifth grades, those children who for example have recently arrived from Puerto Rico and need ESOL instruction have it for 1 1/2 hours per day while their classmates have English reading. Just as in Spanish, so in English, students move from second language instruction to reading instruction as soon as they are ready (usually when they reach the intermediate ESOL level; 15A 35; 3-17-88). All the rest of their content area instruction is in Spanish until they reach the third grade, where the "transition" to English begins (18A 52).

Beginning at third grade, in theory, all instruction for all children in the school is in English, except for the 1 1/4 hours a day of Spanish reading instruction (2-19-87). Yet as we will see below in classroom language use, some content instruction in Spanish continues through the fifth grade.

For the first through fifth grades at Potter Thomas School, all of the morning hours are devoted to language development and reading. In general, the upper grades (3-5) have Spanish reading during first period (9-10:15) and English reading during second period (10:30-12); while the primary grades (1-2) have the reverse.

The structure for achieving this is the cycle structure, which circulates children out of their heterogeneously grouped homeroom classes (15A 210; 4-11-88) and into their Spanish and English reading cycles, homogeneously grouped by reading level. Reading groups from three or four homerooms are redistributed among the same three or four teachers, with the goal of each teacher's having no more than two reading groups (15A 130).[3]

The streams and cycles are merging structures. For example, in the English reading cycles at the fourth grade level, there may be a group made up of both Anglo and Latino stream children, reading at the fourth grade level (15A 85); or there may be a group, again with both Anglo and Latino stream children, reading at the primer level. Thus children from the two streams are integrated for part of their instructional day.

5.5 *Classroom Language Use*

The stream and cycle structure, combined with the range of language backgrounds and proficiencies of the teaching staff, provide for a highly varied spectrum of classroom language use. Highly proficient bilingual teachers function in self-contained bilingual homeroom classrooms and teach in both

English and Spanish reading cycles. Monolingual or one language-dominant teachers function in homerooms of the stream that matches their language and are paired with a counterpart of the other stream; they teach each other's reading cycles in the language of their respective proficiency. Paired classrooms lend themselves to alternate language use for all instruction, while in self-contained classrooms there is some mixed language use, especially outside of the reading periods. The overall goal is for "the children to have the best model for the language", that is, for each language (14B 205).

Some prekindergarten and kindergarten classes, though receiving only thirty minutes or less a day of instruction in their second language, share a classroom with their Anglo/Latino counterparts and thus share some team-taught lessons in science and social studies as well as daily activities such as singing and snack time. Most of the prekindergarten and kindergarten teachers are bilingual and use both languages with the children (e.g. 3-26-87).

In the upper grades (3-5), all the homeroom teachers but one are bilingual and language use in the classrooms is somewhat more flexible than the curricular sequencing outlined above implies, especially, for example, during social studies, science, and mathematics lessons, and in classroom management. Indeed, with the highly mobile student population, it could not be otherwise. Teachers in the upper grades regularly receive new students who have just arrived to Potter Thomas, to Philadelphia, or indeed, to the mainland United States, and who are monolingual Spanish speakers (e.g. 3-7-88). A bilingual program that expected such a student to immediately function for all but 1 1/4 hours of the day in English would be ignoring, rather than building on, important factors contributing to bilingualism.

This varied spectrum of classroom language use extends out to the support teaching staff as well: the reading aides, the ESOL teachers, and the Spanish support teachers. The English reading aides, who spend the morning at Potter Thomas, working first with the primary cycles and then with the upper grade cycles (15A 100), are, where possible, bilingual (4-11-88); nevertheless, it is also possible for a monolingual English speaking reading aide to function well in this structure (e.g. 3-17-88).

The situation is similar for second language support. ESOL teachers are not themselves necessarily fully bilingual. The four Spanish support teachers, who work in the morning with children from the Latino stream who are either very advanced or very low in their Spanish reading skills (18A 414) and in the afternoon with children from the Anglo stream who need additional support with Spanish reading, may not necessarily speak much English, but are able to contribute to the enrichment of both Anglo and Latino children's Spanish development.

The Potter Thomas program meets two (#2, #3) of Lindholm's four criteria for two-way immersion. That is, the program involves periods of instruction during which only one language is used, and both English speakers and non-English speakers are participants in the program. However, this program is not two-way immersion, but two-way maintenance bilingual education: rather than immerse its students in their second language, it provides for gradual introduction of their L2 with simultaneous maintenance of their L1 and it does so in two directions simultaneously.

6. Redirecting Bilingual Education Policy

Potter Thomas' two-way maintenance program functions as an oasis of optimism in the midst of a neighborhood plagued by poverty, drug-trafficking, and crime. I share this description of its program in the interests not only of recognizing its accomplishments as a rare example of enrichment bilingual education struggling against great odds, however, but also of challenging the bilingual education enterprise in the United States to foster and promote such initiatives.

Potter Thomas became a "Model Bilingual School" in the Philadelphia School District under funding from Title VII (the Bilingual Education Act) in 1969, but today continues under the school district budget. It has survived in part because it has been incorporated into the district's own operations. On the other hand, the model of bilingual education it represents has not been extended in the school district. While the originator of the Potter Thomas bilingual program envisioned similar schools operating in a variety of languages around the city (Chinese, Vietnamese, etc.), those schools have never been initiated (personal communication, Eleanor Sandstrom, 12-10-87). After many years of pressure from Hispanic educators and community leaders to provide a continuation of the Potter Thomas experience beyond the 5th grade, a Bilingual Middle Magnet School was finally opened in the fall of 1988; to date, however,due to a number of administrative and logistical constraints which have not been forcefully addressed by the school district, it has not moved beyond a transitional/maintenance model of bilingual education.

The inconsistencies and conflations across bilingual education typologies reviewed above have had significant consequences for bilingual education research and policy in the United States over the past 20 years (see Casanova and Cummins, this volume, and Hakuta 1986: 193-230, for an overview of that research and policy). The typological confusion has both contributed to the inconsistent results of bilingual education evaluation research and to some extent disguised the fact that U.S. bilingual education funds have gradually been redirected away from enrichment and maintenance of bilingual education and toward transitional and even non-bilingual programs.

Revisiting bilingual education typologies has allowed us to identify enrichment bilingual education in terms of its unique goals and structures. The defining characteristics of enrichment bilingual education, as we have seen, are that majority language speakers, as well as minority language speakers, learn a second language; and the minority language is recognized as a potential resource for the nation. It is perhaps not only to local sources, but also to policy makers and administrators who recognize the necessary complementarity between foreign language education and the education of language minority students that advocates must turn to redirect policy toward extending enrichment bilingual education.

Notes

1. This paper is based on discussions with students in my course on Bilingual Education over the past several years, and on research carried out beginning in 1987 with the permission and support of the School District of Philadelphia and the Potter Thomas School. I am grateful for a National Academy of Education Spencer Fellowship which enabled me to devote full-time to this research in 1989, and to the Dean's Fellowship, the Literacy Research Center, and the Research Fund at the Graduate School of Education, University of Pennsylvania, for providing support for graduate student research assistance. Thanks to Cheri Micheau for her research in the prekindergarten and kindergarten classes. I am especially grateful to the students, teachers and administrative staff at Potter Thomas who made possible the study reported on here.

2. This notation refers to a tape-recorded interview. Taped interviews cited in this paper are: #13-Rudolph Masciantonio, 1-22-88; #14-Myriam Wilches, Felicita Melendez, 1-25-88; #15-William Zinn, 1-25-88; and #18-Myriam Wilches, 4-25-88. A date in parentheses refers to a field note on that date.

3. While I am aware that the use of basal readers and reading groups is a debated and controversial practice, it is also a tenacious one (see Slavin 1987 for a synthesis of research on ability grouping). It is not my intention here to discuss the relative merits of this practice as against other possible ways of organizing reading instruction, but only to document what exists in this program.

SECTION V:

"THE BEAST AS A MULTISPLENDORED THING"

Languages in Education: Practices

Bilingual education ... the entire beast is indeed a multidsplendored thing.

Joshua A. Fishman, 1976a: x

Language Education in Bilingual Acadia:
An Experiment in Redressing the Balance

William Francis Mackey

Laval University

1. Acadia

Although it is not a state and no longer a colony, Acadia remains a unique, dynamic territorial and cultural entity. As an important colony of France, it included all of what is today the three Canadian Maritime provinces of Nova Scotia, Prince Edward Island and New Brunswick, east of a line between Campbellton and Calais, embracing all the lands between the Bay of Fundy and the Bay des Chaleurs.

By mid-18th century it had become a pawn in the great colonial wars between the French and British empires. In 1755, the English, in an effort to consolidate their gains in America took the drastic step of deporting the entire Acadian population of 13,000 to far-away lands in Europe, but mostly to other American colonies as far distant as the Gulf of Mexico. The cultural history of the Acadians has always been one of contact and accommodation, even before the tragedy of the great diaspora immortalized in American literature by Longfellow's epic "Evangeline".

Spearheaded by some 3,000 escapees, the Acadians gradually returned to their idyllic homeland, only to find that the fertile lands were now occupied by English settlers whose population had already grown from a nucleus of some 14,000 refugees fleeing the excesses of the American Revolution (the so-called United Empire Loyalists) strengthened by mostly Protestant newcomers from England, Scotland and Ireland who held title under grants from the British Crown. The returning Acadians had to settle for the less fertile coastal and forested regions to the North and East. But they were not joined by other settlers from France, since that country had by then ceded the entire area to Britain, according to the terms of the Treaty of 1763.

It was only generations later that they were joined in that sparsely populated tongue of land between Maine and Quebec, where the St. John River forms the international boundary between the USA and Canada, by an influx of Quebecers, to form the very French-speaking independent-minded self-styled Republic of Madawaska whose inhabitants (the Brayons) are famous for their buckwheat flapjacks. Nearby Grand Falls, with its yearly international potato festival, calls itself "the potato capital of the world" rivaling P.E.I. (Prince Edward Island) a.k.a. Spud Island.

Today, Acadia as a territorial and extra-territorial ethnic reality embraces dynamic communities in all the Canadian Maritime provinces, with the bulk of the population centered in New Brunswick where its quarter million French speakers makes up a third of the population concentrated in a crescent-shaped area following the coastline from the Nova Scotia border to the northernmost tip of Maine (see map). Within this area the degree of bilingualism of the population ranges from nil to practically equilingual, depending largely on the percentage of mother-tongue English speakers in the immediate area. If, for easy identification, we rename these areas by the names of their leading cities, we get a distribution arranged in ascending degree of contact which looks something like this: Edmundston (4% English mother-tongue), Bathurst (15%), Buctouche (20%), Campbellton (35%), Grand Falls (55%), Moncton (60%), Chatham-Newcastle (70%), Fredericton (93%), St. John (99%).

2. Language in Education in Acadia

In all these areas, until the middle of this century, the French speaking population was schooled largely in English, while tirelessly trying to negotiate the right to their own schools in their own language. By mid-century the Acadians had won this right, but only in New Brunswick; the others were under the jurisdiction of other provinces. For more than a generation the New Brunswick Acadians have even had their own educational system with schools at all levels including a university and several community colleges. The schools are governed within the Ministry of Education by a quasi-autonomous parallel division operating exclusively in French.

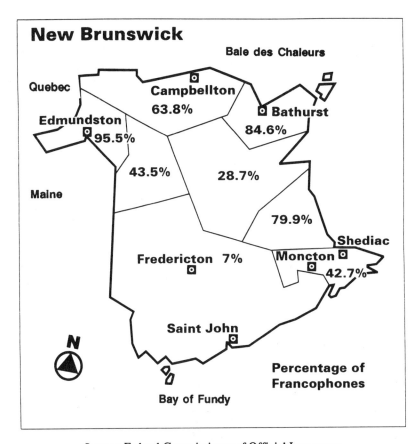

New Brunswick

Source: Federal Commissioner of Official Languages

Consequently French has become the dominant language of education to such an extent that, in some areas, parents and especially grandparents remark that the children are much less bilingual than they were. The question of bilinguality became crucial after 1969 when the New Brunswick Official Languages Act led to the requirement that applicants for many of the government post be fluent in both languages.

This requirement coupled with its counterpart at the federal level and bilingual policies in other areas created a strong demand for some sort of bilingual education. In this context, throughout the other part of the province with its population of some 700,000 English-speakers, parents also became disatisfied with the level of bilingualism which schools had provided their children, who had been allowed to study French simply as a school subject. Following the example of their Montreal cousins, they too in desperation began organizing classes in which all subjects were taught in the second language, the so-called immersion programs which by then were becoming increasingly popular from coast to coast. By 1990 more than 15% of the entire English-speaking school population of New Brunswick, about triple the national average, was doing its schooling in French. Much of this was financed with the help of a federal program for the promotion of bilingualism.

The apparent success of these programs attracted the attention of parents in the most unilingual French-speaking Acadian areas and they had their school boards emulate their Anglophone counterparts by requesting immersion programs entirely in English. The Ministry pointed out however that such programs were precisely what their parents and grandparents had fought against so long – before obtaining their own entirely French schools. Surely there must be other ways of improving the bilingual skills of their children without sacrificing their French schools of which they were so justly proud, by reverting to the old ways of an all-English education.

3. Restoring the Balance of Bilingualism through Schooling

It was at this point, in the autumn of 1984, that I was called in to meet with the parents and their school board, in one of the most isolated and most unilingual French-speaking districts in the Madawaska-Restigouche area, to see what options could be considered. Having been long involved in linguistic research in all parts of Acadia since the mid-forties, I well understood the dilemma with which the parents were faced. It was one of trying to restore the balance of bilingualism without taking away from the level of mother-tongue competence achieved in school.

Since the parents had been looking at the advantages of second language immersion in Anglophone Canada, this had to be the starting point of the discussion. A review of the extensive literature on immersion (some 400 titles) showed that one of its most remarkable achievements was in the high levels of comprehension of the second language. This to me was not surprising since the Anglophone children in immersion programs spend most of their class time hearing or reading French.

A second consideration was the great difference between the Anglophone population in Montreal and the Acadian population in the nature and degree of language contact outside the school. While uniformly low in the Anglophone areas, Acadian contact with the second language ranged from low to all-pervasive, not only between regions as had been pointed out, but also between individuals and families who had become more and more mobile. Any program which failed to take this difference into account could hardly reach the bilingual potential of the population!

In the areas of intense contact, mostly towns which were more than 50% English-speaking, it had been found that Acadian children could easily follow the same English mother-tongue language arts program as their Anglophone compatriots. Contrariwise, some of the other areas were as French unilingual as the most Francophone areas of neighboring Quebec.

Thirdly, in the most Francophone areas of New Brunswick the elementary school teachers themselves were no longer bilingual, although they were still required, from the early years on, to teach English as a subject. For some time past, but especially after the Communities Equality Act of 1981, teachers from the Anglophone districts could not be legally transferred to teach in the Francophone school districts, or vice versa.

Within the framework of these considerable constraints we had to come up with a feasible program which supplied the best models of the second language simultaneously to learners of differing levels of bilingual competence and different degrees of motivation for learning the second language. If English were maintained simply as a school subject it could occupy only a fraction of the time devoted to it in an immersion program. And we had to point out that in 100 minutes a week in less than 40 weeks, the parents could not reasonably expect a miracle. But they could expect that during this limited period, their children might obtain as much direct contact with the new language as one would during a comparable period in either an immersion program or in a conventional second language course – and perhaps more.

We could, ourselves, confirm this, thanks to some 20 years (1965-1985) of direct classroom observation, analysis, measurement and experimentation, including a review of many other studies in this area of research (Mackey 1965-1990). In our studies, we had tried to measure the extent to which each of some 30 types of learning and teaching in the classroom correlated with the students' ability to speak the second language. The results had been published as part of our center's research collection and were readily available. What concerned us here were the cost-benefit time-on-task aspects (Mackey, Loveless et al. 1987). Those who learn something, so it seems, do so not on account of the method but in spite of it (Huot 1988).

In the last analysis, it had become quite evident that no matter what method was used, the benefit obtained from the average speaking lesson was hardly proportional to the investment in learning time and teaching energy. And this was neither the fault of the teacher nor that of the learner. It was the inherent inefficiency of the system. Whether the lesson tended toward one extreme or the other in language behavior the results were certainly not impressive.

If the teacher did all the talking, the students had no speaking practice; if the learners did all or most of the talking, most of the utterances that impressed themselves on the learner's mind were in some way not correct. The most efficient lessons generated few correct utterances per hour of contact. You could have six correct utterances produced by a single student, and the rest of the class having said little or nothing at all. This is not surprising if you have 30 or more learners to share the talking time.

One of the reasons for the silences and mistakes was that the young learners were required to perform before their peers under pressure of time by speaking a language they did not know or had imperfectly absorbed. Some, because of individual learning styles and personality traits, performed better than others. This might have been because no single method can accommodate the infinite variations of the human brain – no two of which seem to learn in exactly the same way, since processing of the same stimulus is differently distributed between cerebral hemispheres as to both type and degree (Trocmé 1982, 1985). But it could not be said that in this context each learner acquired the language to the best of his or her capacity within the time allotted. If we were to offer an option to this type of teaching, it had to be something other than a new textbook or method. It had to be based on the rectification of observed deficiencies in the system, and consequently on a different rationale. The rationale was to include the following: (1) Give individual learners time to absorb the language you expect them to use; (2) let each advance according to individual capacities and interest; (3) make maximal individual use of the time available.

It would also have to be different from traditional teaching in respects other than an immediate comprehension objective. It would need to have the following features:

- Graded content and staged skills
- Interest individualized through variety of choice
- Self-paced and not class-placed
- Self-motivation and not teacher-motivation
- Self-reliance and not teacher-reliance
- High quality input and not simply peer-input
- Maximum exposure per classroom hour

It had to be realistic, operational, effective, affordable and compatible with school schedules. These were the features we set out to develop.

After a year of planning, materials acquisition, development and dry-runs, we came up with a program of staged multimedia self-directed second language acquisition.

4. Multimedia Self-Directed Second Language Acquisition

Although the staging of the skills became quite elaborate, it followed the general order of listening, reading, listening-speaking and reading-writing. For materials, we literally considered everything on the world market, including a lot of excellent out-of-print or out-of-stock material – books, tapes, videos and software. This material was computer-analysed for language level and difficulty, graded and re-graded into levels, and within each level into menus each containing a selection of material of roughly the same degree of difficulty. For each menu the aim was to supply the most abundant selection possible, so as to give to each learner the maximum freedom of choice according to interest and ability. From the beginning all texts were accompanied with a corresponding audio cassette. After picking an interesting text, each young learner (aged eight and up) through individual headphone and independently of others, was free to listen and look, listen and read, listen only or read only, for as long or as little, as fast or as slow, as each found it necessary or still interesting. There was no language teaching (Mackey 1987).

Instead there was a self-directed program with the following characteristics:

*   The first was emphasis on language learning and direct contact with the new language. This contrasted with teacher-based methods in which language lessons, indeed languages, are processed by the teacher before learners obtain direct access to the language.

* The second characteristic was based on the idea that the learners, even small children, should take responsibility for their own learning. Individualization was therefore unavoidable. It consequently became necessary to make sure that the classroom environment was conducive to learning. Needed was a climate of free, relaxed, indeed effortless learning, and elimination of such negative elements as: (1) competition, (2) intimidation and authoritarianism, (3) conditioning of pupils to be dependent.

* Thirdly, each skill and skill combination was progressively introduced, i.e. staged. Once introduced it was both maintained as an independent skill, transformed and linked with other skills. Work on each skill proceeded according to steps related to other sub-skills.

* Fourthly, use of now widespread and generally available technology. The technology, not teachers, handled the repetitive and physically exhaustive work. The technology took the wear and tear, while permitting (1) individualization and (2) the transmission of the most interesting recorded productions.

Most of the hundreds of illustrated books at the learner's disposal were appended to accompanying audio-cassettes that the children could listen to as they read. The sources included ESL materials, language arts and social studies materials, library books and magazines. Types of books covered:

– story-line illustrated readers;
– illustrated non-fiction;
– textbooks in which only parts were selected;
– illustrated dictionaries;
– "giant-size" readers;
– in-house photocopied materials.

Video was introduced after the initial reading/listening stage. The learners were in front of the television between two and three times a week. Currently there are some 300 episodes and/or individual video titles in the program. The video programs include TV-Ontario and the Canadian National Film Board productions as well as such series as "The Secret Garden", "The DeGrassi Kids" and "Anne of Green Gables". Most video is narrative in nature. The focus is on the subject matter, not on the new language itself.

From the very start, learners, including small school children, were expected to organize their own work. They chose their materials, and kept track of the work they had done. For this purpose, learners used individualized control sheets.

After four years of experimentation, field observations lead to expected and some unexpected findings, notably that children can learn a second language in the absence of trained specialized second language teaching staff or native speakers; that the approach lends itself to heterogeneous groupings of learners. It is possible to speculate from this that it is certainly conceivable to have pupils of different chronological ages; from different school grade levels; and having vastly different language proficiency – ranging from beginners to bilinguals – in the same program; – that is, studying together at the same time in the same room.

Other observations: Large classes were no problem. In 1990, we combined Grades 7, 8 and 9 – three classes of 30 learners each. Schools report a marked reduction in discipline problems in the experimental classes. Anyone, including parents and outsiders, can visit classes at any time without disturbing the work of the learners. Teachers report increasing requests for more books to read.

Once they got used to the approach, teachers were almost unanimously supportive and relaxed. Their main concern was not being able to assess regularly the children's learning – that is, to give tests and to correct work. In general, the teachers seemed to take pride in their project classes. ESL specialists were especially supportive.

Main problems encountered: (1) periodic internal evaluation is the biggest concern at the local level; (2) ongoing equipment repair, especially headsets; (3) as the approach is quite different from traditional classroom experience and orthodox teaching, there are people who are skeptical about its effectiveness; it is a controversial project; (4) a silent period worries people; (5) development is a time consuming activity. It takes time on the part of the Department to put together the components and the materials; (6) it requires keeping a lot of material in order within the classroom, as well as on order within the Department.

Since this was such a revolutionary concept of classroom learning, the Education Ministry did not decide to adopt it without some thorough-going and rigorous experimentation supplying hard evidence on its comparative effectiveness.

The Evaluation and Measurement Department of the Education Ministry who were given this task saw to it that the experimental design, the measurement and the evaluation be done independently of the designers and implementers of the new program. To this end, they commissioned an ongoing, long-term external evaluation from outside the province, from a research center that had not previously heard of the project and had had nothing to do with its development. It was the TESL Center at Concordia University in Montreal that was given this task, with an initial three-year mandate. The researchers succeeded in developing a powerful and rigorous experimental design comprising not only the school but also the community, including measurements of previous and ongoing out-of-class exposure to the two languages coupled with pretests to establish comparable control groups in varying contexts. Over a three year period, volumes of test results were accumulated in addition to term tests and final post-tests. The results after the first three years were reported by the director of the research team, Patsy Lightbown (1988 and forthcoming). They proved good enough to convince the Ministry to continue the experiment, to expand it and to extend it to the higher grades.

By 1990, in more than a hundred classrooms and control groups, there were some three thousand learners from Grade 3 to Grade 12 in most Acadian areas of the province involved in this new self-learning program. At the same time, some exploratory experimentation had been under way to extend the program through Grade 12 and the end of secondary school. Requests for information were so numerous that in 1989 the Ministry decided to put out a brochure in English and in French describing the structure and development of the new program (Ministère de l'Education 1990).[1]

5. Implications for Bilingualism and Education

Should this multimedia self-directed language acquisition program prove to be a viable option, it might have implications for those areas where bilingual education has as yet remained unfeasible, or for plurilingual classrooms, or for classes with learners at different levels, or for schools without qualified native teachers, or for individuals who learn better when free from regimentation. In school rooms where learners have been put into groups not of their own making, the overriding motif has often become one of conformity and compliance at the expense of learning and the individual pursuit of knowledge. There may be some wider implications. For our model is not one of transmission and control. It is rather an individual growth model as opposed to a production one. It is analogous to letting trees grow as opposed to manufacturing them, to gardening as opposed to food production, to culture as opposed to technique. It is a holistic approach rather than an analytic one. In a growth model, if the soil (context) is rich enough, many things happen at the same time at different levels within the same individual. Like the work of the artisan with the apprentice, the outcome is what counts. Problems are solved in context as they arise. You learn as you go. It is essentially product-oriented. Contrariwise, a production model has to be process-oriented. It requires conformity and specialization, uniformity and compliance. One learns to do one thing in one way at one time. That is why it is better suited to technology than it is to culture, more appropriate for techniques requiring the control of behavior then it is for the multivariate activities related to language and free expression. Often the need for compliance is achieved at the expense of learning. Operating within the hierarchical structure of public education our program has so far succeeded in reducing the use of learning as a tool for the control of behavior.

Note

1. This brochure, "An Experiment in Staged Self-Directed Language Acquisition" (English), "Projet expérimental d'auto-acquisition par étapes de la langue seconde: programme multimédia d'anglais" (French), is available from: Ministère de l'Education du Nouveau Brunswick, Box 6000, Fredericton, N-B. E3B 5H1, Canada.

Multilingualism is valuable to society ...
In this day and age, English speakers need
it most.

Joshua A. Fishman, 1978b: 47

Bilingual Education for All:
An Australian Pilot Study and Its Policy Implications

Michael Clyne

Monash University

1. Introduction

Joshua Fishman, whom we honour in this publication, has expressed enthusiasm for Australia's National Policy on Languages which calls for exposure to two languages – English and another language – as part of normal schooling (Fishman 1988a: 137). In another work (Fishman fc, b), he comments that the variety of languages offered in state schools in the south-eastern states of Australia and the proportion of students taking them is probably greater than anywhere else in the western world. We in Australia have greatly benefited over the years from Fishman's ideas, his theoretical frameworks, and his ideals, and we were especially delighted when he accepted a visiting distinguished professorship at Monash University for part of 1985. He became a rallying point not only for discussion on where we were going in our research, but he was able to give us advice, inspiration and encouragement in the language policy initiatives that were under consideration at the time. Fishman had frequently expressed his visions of a U.S.A. supportive of multilingualism (e.g. Fishman 1981b). Over the past decade, comprehensive policies of the kind envisaged have been formulated at the federal level and language in education policies have been developed in a number of Australian states. This has been due to a great deal of political lobbying by academics, teachers, ethnic groups, trades unions, and others, a change of government direction from assimilation to multiculturalism, and a broad consultative process (Clyne 1982, fc, Martin 1978, Ozolins 1988). Policies for language teaching have been facilitated by experimentation and evaluation. In this paper, I will describe the setting up and evaluation of some primary school German programs in Melbourne, their model-building function, and their significance in national and state language policies.

2. Language Teaching in Australia

According to the 1986 Census, 13.63% of the Australian population and 22.6% of the inhabitants of Melbourne then used a language other than English at home. The most widely used home languages other than English in Melbourne are (in order): Italian, Greek, Serbo-Croatian, Chinese, German, and Maltese. Most of the speakers are the product of postwar immigration. In addition, there are those who regularly use a language other than English but not at home, for instance in the homes of parents or other elderly relatives or within community organizations. And yet, there is a substantial shift away from bilingualism often associated with entry to school. Many pupils never study a second language at school. Fifteen percent of all secondary schools in Australia do not teach a language other than English. Only 12% of all students in the final two years of secondary school study one or more languages other than English. This is largely due to the politics of school organization and unflexible time-tables in which 'trendy' new options such as computer studies and consumer education are scheduled against languages.

It is then not surprising that, over the past one and a half decades, there has been substantial interest in starting second language study at primary school, for both monolingual English speakers and for those with a home background in a community (ethnic) language. There are diverse arguments supporting this early introduction:

1. Those who begin natural exposure to a language as children generally acquire it better than those who do not start until later (Krashen, Scarcella and Long 1982).

2. Young beginners still show much psychological flexibility. Children in the concrete operations stage of their development (Piaget 1971) are prepared to 'accept language as it is' rather than wanting to abstract from it or require individual translations ot grammatical explanations. They are still prepared to role play rather than to conform (cf. junior secondary pupils, especially boys). Thus:

2a. Early introduction facilitates a more natural mode of acquisition.

2b. The pronunciation of early beginners tends to be more native-like than that of later beginners (Haugen 1953, Penfield and Roberts 1959, Stock 1977) (but cf. Seliger 1980).

3. The early introduction of a community language can provide a link between home and school of bilingual children, giving the community language acceptance and status and enabling children to develop it beyond the essentials of the home domain. This could prevent the situation where the community language is unable to keep pace with the child's language development in English or their cognitive development. Thus, the school would support home language maintenance, not frustrate it as was the case in the 1950s and 1960s.

4. The linguistic and cultural relativity to which children are exposed in the second language program would represent an integral part of their total primary education.

5. Community languages are part of the shared heritage of all Australians. The earlier that children are exposed to them and respect and appreciate them, the better it is.

In the early 1970s, a number of state and non-government primary schools in Melbourne had introduced ad hoc programs in languages other than English. Some were taught by mothers as part of a once a week electives program in which children could take a term of photography, cookery or a language. Others were taught by the class teacher who happened to have some background in a particular language, still others (in non-government schools) by the secondary teacher of the language. Several schools received German programs from senior university students who were collecting data for theses or term papers. Thus, there was no guaranteed continuity, all the 'teachers' had deficiencies in their training for the job, and few of the programs were being evaluated (none independently). It was impossible to ascertain objectively whether some of the programs were more or less successful than others and why. South Australia had introduced languages into primary schools in the 1960s. By 1976, 10,364 pupils in that state were taking a second language (Murray and Lundberg 1977: 63, 79). Most of the classes started in Grade 3 or 4, were allocated brief time allotment each week, and many emphasized the cultural rather than the linguistic. Most of the teachers were itinerant.

3. German in Melbourne Schools

During discussions in Melbourne about 1980, there was a great deal of enthusiasm for putting primary school language teaching on a more permanent
footing and introducing at least some aspects of immersion education into
them. The Federal Government had recently started dispersing multicultural
education to the states. Committees were formed to take decisions on the
funding of programs. The Victorian committee was chaired by Terry Quinn,
an applied linguist from the University of Melbourne who was devoted to the
cause of a national languages policy. The Association of German Speaking
Communities, representing the various German-language ethnic interest
groups in Victoria, together with two state primary schools in Melbourne,
secured a major grant from the then Victorian Advisory Committee on Multicultural and Migrant Education to introduce German in the following year.
The two schools would share the one teacher. Both schools had at one time
offered German but had had to abandon programs because of the lack of a
teacher. The grant transferred responsibility for the second language program
from outside volunteers to the school. A small item in the budget was for
research assistance and, since several members of the Steering Committee had
connections with Monash University, a progressive evaluation was guaranteed. The results of this would be made available periodically to assure
others of what was feasible and to facilitate rectification of any problems. The
schools opted for different models, A for a bilingual (immersion) approach
and B for a more modest second language program. The effects of model and
differences in entry ages on proficiency would be assessed in the testing.

3.1 *Teaching German: Model A*

This model was based on principles of the Canadian early or delayed partial
immersion program (Swain and Lapkin 1982) where children acquire a
second language by being taught part of the curriculum in that language. The
model also took on features from the Australian pre-1916 German-English bilingual schools where different content in some subjects was taught in
English and German (Clyne 1988). Thus, German is acquired and/or
developed through use in some subjects. The German-medium teacher talks
to the children exclusively in German, from the beginning of the first lesson,
both inside and outside the classroom. Each of the subjects taught (partly or

wholly) in German contributes to second language development. As a classificatory and discovery subject, *Science* furthers a close link between linguistic and cognitive development in addition to facilitating frequent teacher-pupil interaction. *Art* introduces some basic notions (e.g. colour, size), emotional expressions (e.g. liking, disliking), and requests (e.g. asking for art and craft utensils). It also offers opportunities for interaction between individual pupils and the teacher. *Physical Education*, apart from teaching functions relating to human activity, may sharpen listening skills. These subjects are taught entirely in German in the first two years of the program. *Social Studies* and *Music* are both split into a German- and an English-medium segment of the curriculum each taught by the respective teacher. This facilitates integration of language and culture. The strong non-verbal component of Science and Physical Education assists the second language acquisition process, especially in the early stages. Beyond the first two years, various subjects (e.g. Science, Social Studies, Music) were integrated thematically and the integrated subject taught in German. By this time, the value of Art to the second language acquisition process had declined because of the long periods of passive activity and that of Physical Education had waned due to the repetitiveness of the language used. Model A provides 5 hours a week of German input in non-language subjects. (This was later decreased to three hours in the fifth and sixth year of the children's German program.) As the school is in the local government area of Melbourne with the largest number of German speakers, there are opportunities for children from non-German backgrounds to be exposed to German through neighbours, shops, and community organizations. (There are, in the district, three German-medium churches and three German-medium old people's homes. Older children at the school now not only join in on local German activities but also visit one of the old people's homes and conduct conversations with the residents as part of their social studies.)

Model A is a much less ambitious program than the Canadian Immersion type. No language other than English in Australia has the status or history of French in Canada. Model A is available to children from both German-speaking and non-German-speaking families. The latter group predominate by far in the school and the program (as in the others described in this paper. On children from German backgrounds, see below). German is not, on the whole, maintained very well in Australia. The program is of the kind "counteracting the conditions of linguistic and cultural segregation, being directed ... to any population seeking additional cognitive and emotional exposure to that available via 'monolingual deprivation'" (Fishman 1977b: 12).

The main features of this model are:

(i)   Functional specialization between the languages on 'one person, one language' principles (cf. Saunders 1988) with different subjects or different course content being taught in English and German. The German-medium teacher speaks nothing but German to the children from the beginning of the first lesson, both inside and outside the classroom.

(ii)   The stimulation of communicative need by making German the sole language of particular 'mainstream' subjects.

(iii)   Comprehensible input (Krashen 1981) provided in class and through school and community based extra-curricular activities.

3.2 Teaching German: Model B

While the school using Model A introduced German initially in only Grades 1 and 3, the other school started it in all grades. However, for comparative purposes, only Grade 1 and 3 beginners were tested in the first two years. As the school wished to have one class at each level exposed to German simultaneously, Model B received only two half hour periods of German per week. Thus, it is impossible to separate model from time of exposure. However, as we shall see later, these two factors are politically inseparable and language and other skills cannot really be differentiated. The teacher spoke German virtually throughout all lessons, which were based on functional syllabuses. However, there were also structured language classes and very much more emphasis on grammar (in an informal way) than in Model A. The school is in a neighbourhood with some German speakers and some German-speaking shops but not nearly as much presence of the language as in the district described above. However, there are German children's books in the local library and plenty of opportunities of hearing German, for instance, on radio and TV, where there are German children's programs. In this model and the others described, teachers do not formally correct ungrammatical forms but repeat utterances in grammatical form.

3.3 Teaching German: Model C

In the third year of the program, funding became available for additional teachers. Testing in the Model A school continued and two new cohorts were introduced into the testing schedule, starting in Grades 2 and 4. A third model – a compromise between A and B – was adopted in a third school. The main features of Model A also apply. The children received instruction in the German language (through German medium) for an hour per week and two hours per week of other subjects taught in German. These included segments of the curriculum in Social Studies, Science, and Music/Movement/Drama. All children at this school, which is in the same area as school A, are required to take either German or Italian, the latter also being taught according to Model C.

4. Evaluation of the Three Models: The Tests

Forty-nine tests were administered – 25 in the first two years and 24 in the next two. These were supplemented by observation and tapes of lessons made with a radio microphone as well as the perusal of diaries and letters to pen friends written in German by the children. The tests included listening-comprehension, sound discrimination, elicited sentence repetition (Adams 1978), conversation (including role-play, trialling and retelling of narratives, giving directions and other functional exercises), grammar (transformations), Cloze tests, dictation, written expression, and reading-comprehension.

In all the test measures in the first two years of a program, school A performed better than school C which, in turn, outperformed school B. (The one exception was Grade 2 starters in school C who did very marginally better than their counterparts in school A.) (See Table 1.) The difference between school B and the others is greater in Grade 1 than in Grade 3. The best results were obtained in sound discrimination and in listening comprehension and the weakest performances were recorded in grammar and in writing (Cloze). (See Table 2.)

The differences between schools A and B are greater in the grammar tests than in any other of the test measures, school B children obtaining less than half the marks of those at school A, which generally also outscored school C. In grammar more than in any other test measure, the classes seem to have performed in inverse proportion to their stress on language as an object rather than a medium. (ANOVA shows that the model is the only significant factor in these test results.)

The coefficient of variability (indicating dispersion of mean scores in a given class) shows the overall tendency for the spread to be lowest at school

Table 1
Mean scores for all skills over the first two years:
Comparison of models according to entry age.

Model	START YEAR			
	Grade 1	*Grade 2*	*Grade 3*	*Grade 4*
A	66.47	63.95	69.95	69.44
C	56.41	63.96	63.23	65.44
B	50.50	–	59.91	–

Table 2
Mean scores for test measures over the first two years:
Comparison between models

MDL	*ListCmp*	*OrlPrdc*	*OrlCmp*	*SndDisc*	*Grammar*	*Cloze*
A	87.16	80.23	75.83	92.90	27.16	50.44
C	81.36	72.58	71.97	88.09	23.76	44.39
B	67.68	70.47	65.25	86.09	12.45	31.73

A, except for Grade 4 beginners whose overall spread is equal at schools A and C. That is, children from a range of backgrounds and abilities can best cope with Model A because in bilingual education you do not need to pitch your instruction at the level of either the 'top' or the 'bottom' pupils. The difference between Grade 3 starters at B and C is quite slight (Table 3). (For details of the test results and the model as a factor, see Clyne 1986.)

On the whole, the older pupils in each school obtained better results than younger ones. However, the younger pupils would have more extra years in which to increase their proficiency. The only significant result relating to age was that Model B pupils who had started German in Grade 3 performed better than those who had begun in Grade 1. This does not apply to Models A and C. Grade 3 appears to be a 'threshold' year in which the maximum benefits of

Table 3
Average coefficient of variability (over six measures)
by model for different start years, first two years of program

Model	Grade 1	Grade 2	Grade 3	Grade 4
A	0.22	0.20	0.23	0.23
C	0.25	0.23	0.26	0.23
B	0.40	–	0.27	–

language learning are experienced. Grade 3 pupils obtained the highest or almost the highest overall scores in virtually all skills and all models (Reich 1986).

5. The Children's German

An actual analysis of the children's German speech shows four main phases in the development of their interlanguage:

(i)   English responses to German utterances, one and two word German utterances or unanalyzed formulaic utterances e.g.:

Zu Hause. Ich heiße Kate.

(ii)   The matrix language (usually determined by the language of the verb) is English, but individual German nouns, noun phrases or uninflected adjectives are transferred, with occasional code-switching, e.g.:

Mein Großvater und mein Großmutter have come to stay at our place because *meine Mutter* is in the *Krankenhaus* and she's had a baby.

(iii)   An attempt to speak German, with code-switching to English, as well as some creative integration of English items into the German phonological and grammatical systems, e.g.:

Heidi helfen die Vater get *dressen. Heidi machen die Hauscoat* on.

(iv)   German utterances with the integration patterns common in German-English bilinguals (Clyne 1967), e.g.:

> *Patrick, willst du kommen zu den Show an Samstag? Es ist ein Dollar fünfzig Cent. Mußt du ein Schnoball* [ʃnoːbal] (= snowball) *haben? Mein Mutter und Vater gehen.*

Examples of integrated lexical transfers from the children:

> *ich runne, er pullt, sie climbt, Heidi yawnt, readen, gewalkt* [ʃtɔkɪŋks];

Semantic transfers:

> *Trink* (= drink), *Mädchenfreund* (= girl friend), *Ist das right?*

Neologisms:

> *Händewascher* (face-washer, German Waschlappen), *Hampelfrau* (female Hampelmann, i.e. jumping jack), *Hauscoat* (dressing gown, German Schlafrock.)

The progression from one phase to another was determined by much individual variation (Clyne 1986) but those in Model A progressed much faster and were more creative in their use of German (e.g. integration, neologisms).

There was also a phased development of verb morphology:

(i)   formulaic unanalyzed verbs,

(ii)   generalization of *-st*, the ending of the *du* form (2nd person singular 'informal') which was used by the teacher to the pupils,

(iii)   unsystematic variation (e.g. *Ich habe, hast or hat, er hat or hast*), but *-st* generalization in inversion (e.g. *hast er?*) probably due to the teacher's questions,

(iv)   systematic variation but *-st* in inversion,

(v)   consistently grammatical forms.

Alongside this development we find the overgeneralization of *-en* forms with or without the auxiliary *ist* to form the equivalent of the English progressive (e.g. Heidi (ist) lesen = Heidi is reading). The development of the definite article takes place on fairly similar lines, from deletion (except in formulaic expressions) via generalization of *dein* (the second person informal singular possessive), then unsystematic variation, and finally (at a much later stage), grammatical variation.

These developmental phases are different to those usually described in either natural second language acquisition or classroom second language learning, and may be attributed to the sociolinguistic features of the acquisition situation. Other features, such as a tendency towards a generalization of SVO and proximity of discontinuous constituents, are not unusual in second language acquirers of German (Clahsen, Meisel and Pienemann 1983) or in German-English bilinguals (Clyne 1985).

Most of the children in Model A are good communicators and develop excellent comprehension skills from a very early stage although they take a long time to develop a high level of grammatical correctness. The pupils in all the schools have an almost faultless pronunciation, no doubt a product of the time of introduction. They also encounter few problems with reading (in some cases with *ö* and *ü*.) Proficiency in German spelling varies, partly due to the lexical context of the grapheme, but largely with age, with older children doing considerably better than younger ones (Clyne 1986: 73-81). This can be attributed to maturational factors and to the fact that they already have a stronger literacy basis in English. It concurs with the frequently held view that literacy skills can best be acquired in the first or dominant language and can be readily transferred to the second or weaker language (see e.g. Romaine 1989: chapter 6).

6. Comparing the Success of the Three Models

This is not the place to speculate why our experience differs from that of the Canadian immersion programs where literacy is acquired so successfully through the medium of L2 (Swain and Lapkin 1982). Writing is taught in all the Australian models under consideration through holistic and language experience methods.

As in the Canadian immersion programs, there is no evidence that the children are disadvantaged in their English or the subjects imparted through L2. Eckstein (1986) found that children in school A scored better or significantly better in scientific concepts, knowledge, and skills than comparable monolingually educated children in the same and a neighbouring school. On the whole, the control group could use specialized vocabulary as well as their monolingually taught peers. There were, however, some items of specialized vocabulary the experimental group did not know in English and which would need to be presented in language classes. The children were able to transfer skills from one language to another and did show great creativity in explaining in non-technical English anything for which they lacked a technical term.

In German, they were very proficient in expressing concepts but had some difficulties with processes. Far from the German program having an adverse effect on the children's English, it appeared to enhance their listening comprehension and their linguistic creativity.

So far we have dealt only with children from non-German-speaking backgrounds. Imberger (1986) compared the German language development, use and attitudes of children in schools A and C from German-speaking backgrounds. It appears that Model A, with its more extensive natural use of German in a wider range of subjects, is most appropriate for such children. Attitudinally, some families have greatly benefited from the German programs which have renewed their cultural self-esteem. Some children from homes where German is actively maintained, having transferred from another school in which they had been perceived as 'problems', have received a great boost from Model A. The value of the program to 'ethnic' children has depended largely on their level of their German and the attitudes of their family. Those with stronger German and more impetus for language maintenance have benefited most. On occasions (in the absence of a German-English bilingual school in Melbourne), school A has taken in recently arrived immigrant children from German-speaking countries and some temporary residents. The program has given these pupils a better chance of integrating into the Australian school and of maintaining their German. Summarizing, Model A appears to offer the following advantages:

(i)   A higher level of proficiency, and the ability to function effectively in German (albeit for some time with 'mixed language' responses).

(ii)   More uninhibited speech and a greater degree of linguistic creativity.

(iii)   A wider spread of subjects for acquisition of different functions and notions.

(iv)   The integration of language and culture.

(v)   Catering for a range of backgrounds and ability groups.

(vi)   Because well established primary school subjects are taught in L2, that language is, in effect, 'mainstreamed'.

(vii)   It is not necessary to argue for a sizeable allotment for the second language (as a new subject), since the L2-medium subjects need to be taught anyway and the language is an 'extra bonus'.

The only *possible* disadvantages of Model A compared to the other two models are:

(i)   The practice of replying in English may become habitual.

(ii)   Teacher-pupil interaction in the bilingual mode seems to induce unusual non-standard forms (see above).

(iii)   Having to keep the children in bilingual program in a separate stream each year can cause social problems.

However, (i) and (ii) seem to be a problem in Models B and C as well and there the overall language development is slower. (iii) becomes an issue only where the bilingual program is optional.

7. The Role of the Three Models in Building Programs

By the time the initial evaluation had been conducted for two years, a number of progress reports were available. The programs, particularly that of Model A, had been frequently visited by educational authorities whose plans were encouraged by what they saw. In 1983, the Victorian Ministry of Education decided to embark on an ambitious system to introduce languages other than English into state primary schools on a large scale. Supernumerary teachers would be appointed to schools preparing a successful submission to run approved second language or bilingual programs. This put the programs in schools A and B on a firm footing with separate teachers and facilitated the Model C compromise program. The mainstreaming of languages at the primary school was ensured by a Ministerial Policy Statement (No. 6) requiring school councils to ensure that their programs enable "students progressively to gain proficiency in a second language used in the Australian community" (Victoria 1984: 17). By 1985, 130 such teachers were assigned, eleven of them for German, in nine schools. German ranks third among the languages taught in state primary schools after Italian and Greek. Among other languages taught are Chinese, French, Japanese, Macedonian, and Turkish. Of these, Macedonian and Turkish are solely for mother tongue speakers, French, German, Italian, and Japanese are taken predominantly but not solely by second language learners, and Chinese and Greek programs often are planned for both groups. Although it had been intended that the number of supernumerary language teachers would rise by about 50 per year, a decrease in federal funding for multicultural education slowed down the development. In 1989, there were 17 languages other than English taught as part of regular school programs in Victorian state schools. There were full-scale second language programs in 117 schools (in addition to many more limited ones). Many of these programs were attempting to incorporate immersion principles at least to some degree. (A survey to be conducted during 1990 will hopefully throw more light on this.) This can be attributed directly to the German experiments with Models A and C.

In 1982, the Australian Government charged a group of six senators, three from each major party, with the task of inquiring into the need for a co-ordinated National Language Policy with broad terms of reference including the use, maintenance and teaching of languages other than English. The report of the inquiry (Australia 1984) established the four guiding principles for the National Language Policy, two of which were the maintenance and development of languages other than English and opportunities for learning second languages. The model A program was discussed in some of the hearings and in submissions from ethnic and professional associations. The Model A program receives four mentions in the report, which is rather cautious. It does not support immersion in spite of "evidence (being) persuasive" on the grounds that it was unlikely "programs of this kind will become a widespread model for second language learning in Australia, at least for some time to come" (p. 138).

As schools are a state responsibility in Australia, the actual strategies for applying language policies in primary and secondary education are in the hands of the states. The Senate Report's guiding principles and the Ministerial Policy Statement form the basis of the Victorian policy statement, *The Place of Languages other than English in Victorian Schools* (1985). Here, "Bilingual Education for all Children" regardless of home background is one of three possible models outlined for schools (the others being "Mother Tongue Maintenance and Development" and "Second Language Programs", Victoria 1985: 10-11). The need for ongoing research and evaluation is emphasized as is the necessity to develop strategies for continuity from primary to secondary school.

By the time the final National Policy on Languages (lo Bianco 1987a) was released, programs of Models A and C had been tried for several languages in a considerable number of schools in Victoria. The author of the policy, Joseph lo Bianco, was intimately familiar with the Victorian programs having been chairman of the Ministerial Advisory Committee on Multicultural and Migrant Education in Victoria, which funded the Community Language Program in primary schools, and of the working party which drafted the Victorian languages in education policy. He had also conducted research into Victorian Italian programs (lo Bianco 1987b). The lo Bianco Report presented the 'immersion' model as a normal one for the teaching of second languages. It refers to "increasing instances of immersion in a second language as a means of instruction". As a means of teaching a second language to monolingual English speakers it names "... where possible immersion bilingual teaching" (lo Bianco 1987a: 143). Model C is described as one of the case studies in the lo Bianco Report. It distinguishes between language awareness, limited exposure, and bilingual education (including Models A and C) programs. The lo Bianco Report stresses the importance of all programs being "accompanied by continuing and detailed evaluation to ensure that success is monitored and appropriate modifications made" (1987a: 155).

In 1983 and 1984, South Australia developed two complementary reports on second language teaching, *Voices for the Future* (1983) and *Education for a Cultural Democracy* (1984). The latter recommends that language maintenance be declared as right and that English and at least one other language be part of the education of all students from pre-school to the final year of secondary school. *Voices for the Future* argues that all languages taught in South Australia be accessible to both first and second language learners. It stresses that languages should be offered at different entry points and for school clusters to be established to facilitate transition from primary to secondary language programs. In late 1989, an implementation plan was drafted in South Australia, which outlines aims and procedures for mother tongue development and for second language development. Primary school programs are set to commence in Grade 4 due to limited resources but also to facilitate positive transfer, although it is stated that some community languages may be started in the preparatory year (age 5) in schools that have the same language for "mother tongue" programs. Immersion programs are mentioned indirectly when primary courses other than immersion are guaranteed a minimum allotment of 2 hours per week.

The Victorian counterpart *Languages Action Plan* (also authored by lo Bianco) appeared in 1989. The report includes a case study of the Model A program. The recommendations relevant to this discussion are the doubling of bilingual and immersion programs in the state every three years for the next decade, specific encouragement of such programs, and the training of bilingual teachers who can teach other subjects through the medium of a community language.

Languages for Western Australians, the report of the Western Australian languages in education working party (1988), recommends the setting up and trialling of a Primary Specialist Language Teacher Program over three years. A limited number of partial immersion programs would be established based on Model A. Other programs would have a minimum class contact time of an hour per week. The New South Wales equivalent originated in the same year. It recommended gradually extending primary school language programs to more languages. Bilingual programs are also to be established but for children from appropriate ethnolinguistic backgrounds (New South Wales 1988).

It can thus be seen that the original experiment with German in Victoria is having impact beyond the state boundaries and on programs in a range of languages. In Victoria, experimentation continues, with Model A and C programs and variations on them (e.g. different subjects, 4 hours per week) being introduced in more schools and more languages (especially Italian, Japanese, French, and Hebrew, as well as German). On the other hand, former Model B programs are receiving components of immersion (e.g. Science plus German taught in German). More structured grammar instruction is finding its way into Model A courses due to the results of the evaluation.

However, the general tendency has been to set up Victorian second language programs starting in the preparatory year (age 5). This is an affirmation of the policy that a second language should be a normal part of the education of all primary school children. In some other states, Grade 4 (or 5) is the proposed starting year, due to limited resources. School A has now made German compulsory in the first three years. The attrition rate is very small.

8. The Role of the Secondary School

It has been observed that, where continuity to secondary school is guaranteed, primary school language programs are far more successful than otherwise (cf. Sweden, Holmstrand 1982; Braunschweig, Doyé and Lüttge 1977; with England, Burstall et al. 1974, Buckby 1976; Austria, Petri and Zrzavy 1976). It is particularly undesirable for children who have had extensive primary school language programs to have to start the same language from scratch at secondary school. It gives the impression that everything they have learnt is useless and wasted. A difficult situation then often arises where the secondary school teacher has different (e.g. more grammatical and less communicative) expectations and is frustrated by the children with a high level of communicative skills. Their confidence and consequently their motivation, in turn, are undermined by the teacher.

After the Model A program had been in operation for four years, a follow-on program was started at the local high school. This catered also for children from school C and from another primary school which had adopted Model B (but for two hours per week). The high school taught the second language, Geography and History through the medium of German and Italian. Studies of the development of German skills from primary school (Csipek 1986, Doblin 1986) showed a continuing improvement at high school. There was a gradual levelling of Model A and C children despite continuing individual variation. Model B children, for whom the high school program was a type of late partial immersion, performed either best of all or worse than the other pupils (Csipek 1986). The high school is not able to give the same centrality to the immersion program as the better primary school programs. The constant pressure on the children to opt for 'attractive electives' is great and leads to attrition of numbers.

In most districts, it is not possible to offer a bilingual follow-up, but at least the children receive an advanced language program which continues from the level they attained at primary school. This, however, is not always feasible since many children are withdrawn from the state system after Grade 6 and then attend non-government schools; others are sent to high schools other than the nearest one, and many families wait until their child (or one of their children) has left primary school before they move house. All this renders planning very difficult.

9. Some Closing Remarks

This paper has demonstrated, through one Australian example, the interaction between research and policy. The original programs were subject to careful scrutiny and continuous evaluation. This was useful for rectifying problems as well as for model building. It showed what was feasible and liable to be successful in the given context and what resources were required. It was significant that there were so few programs initially that progress could be assessed (cf. also Cahill (1984) for Greek in Melbourne, Rubichi (1983) for Italian in Adelaide, lo Bianco (1987b) for Italian in Melbourne). Adjustment to programs resulted from the evaluation through a consultation process involving regular meetings with parents and meetings of the entire teaching staff of the school. Experimentation and innovation are now continuing without much evaluation. This is likely to change with the recent establishment of the Languages Institute of Australia which will inform the National Policy on Languages through research, the dissemination of research results, and curriculum development. It is hoped that one of the projects of the Institute's Language and Society Centre at Monash University will be on models and sociolinguistic variables in second language and bilingual education at primary school.

Teacher education is much more than simply another professional endeavor. It is first and foremost an intellectual endeavor striving to increase knowledge about man and the process whereby he learns, grows, changes, and influences others.

Joshua A. Fishman, Congressional Record A, 3594, July 11, 1966

Active Teaching and Learning in the Bilingual Classroom: The Child as an Active Subject in Learning to Write

Gerardo Torres

The City College of New York

1. Introduction

Bilingual education programs throughout the world many times serve as an educational alternative to language minority populations. But this alternative is often purely *linguistic*, that is, only the language used in the classroom is different from that used in educating language majority children.

Although it has been widely recognized that language minority children use language differently at home than mainstream children (Heath 1983), schools fail to take this difference into account. And even bilingual education programs are guilty of doing very little to take into account the different ways of using language by language minority children. The bilingual classroom often becomes a reflection of practices in the monolingual traditional classroom that serves language majority children. And, both bilingual and monolingual classrooms many times fail to take into account the children's individual learning differences and the constructive character of all learning and knowledge.

The academic discourse surrounding bilingual education has looked at the question of which language is used when, where and for what purposes. And there are countries such as the United States where that question is still argued on a daily basis. But even in schools and classrooms where that language planning question has been solved, the question of *how* language is used in the bilingual education classroom is most often ignored.

If bilingual education is going to serve as a vehicle of language minority children's socio-cognitive development, then it is clear that it must not only deal with the question of language allocation within the curriculum, but also with the conceptualization of the child as a learner.

This paper describes my involvement as an educator of bilingual teachers who can look beyond language and into learning. In particular, it focuses on the young Latino child as an active learner of writing in Spanish within a bilingual classroom. It also looks at how teachers interact with children in situations where children are actively participating in the process of learning. After reviewing research on the role of the student as an active subject in the teaching-learning of writing, this paper describes my research with two bilingual kindergarten teachers as they learn to observe their children and change their traditional modes of teaching to those that see the child as an active learner. It is my belief that only these pedagogical changes can bring about the academic success of language minority children that the language question only begins to address.

2. The Research Base

Among the early defenders of the student as an active subject in learning to write in Spanish, one finds the theoretical work of Iglesias (1979) in Argentina and Saez (1978) in Puerto Rico. But this purely ideological discourse has lately been supported by research which demonstrates that pre-school age children have notions about specific aspects of the writing system, and that they use these notions to construct their understanding and further mastery of the written system (Ferreiro 1982). As we will see below, recent research has also shown that the understanding and development of the mastery of writing occurs in manners that the traditional school ignores or is not able to build upon, and that the acquisition and mastery of literacy is embedded within a cultural context which can either blend within the traditional school practices or be in opposition to them, thus increasing the possibilities of academic failure.

As a result of this research, there has been a recent shift of the pedagogical discourse on how to start children writing. Instead of discussing the effectiveness of methods of teaching initial writing, there has been much discussion about the role of the student as an active subject in the teaching-learning process (Sole i Gallart 1985: 8-10; Teale 1986: 1-2). The teaching of writing is now seen as a dynamic experience where there are multiple and complex activities taking place and not simply as a unidimensional experience where the teacher follows specific methodological guidelines.

The earlier discussion of the effectiveness of methods of teaching writing, ignored three important aspects of teaching and learning:

1. The capacities and knowledge the student brings and how s/he acquires and formulates them (Barr 1985; Ferreiro 1982; Ferreiro and Teberosky 1977: 21).

2. The student's historical and environmental experiences (Bennett and Pedraza 1984; Heath 1982).

3. The role of the teacher when confronted with the student's capacities, knowledge, formulation and experiences (Bentley 1987; Hankey and Brightmore 1987: 84-90; Clark and Florio 1987; Norman 1985; Rowland 1987; Wells and Wells 1984).

An actual change in the practices of the teaching of writing has come about in some informed classrooms. In these classrooms, chidren entering school for the first time are no longer asked to copy letters and their names. They are no longer expected to write simple sentences using the known letters and words. The practices have shifted from implementing specific objectives and prescribed activities and using quantitative tools to measure learning, namely exams that are standardized or that measure how well children spell or write complete sentences. Instead, teaching and learning of writing is beginning to take into consideration the capacities and knowledge that students bring and their historical and environmental experiences. In these enquiring classrooms, the role of the teacher is no longer determined by lesson plans.

Research on writing has also shifted. Instead of focusing on the effects of given methods, research now looks at the dynamics of learning to write and the teaching conditions that foster it. Pre-schoolers have been the focus of this research. It has been shown that before entering school, children have formulated their own notions of what the written symbol is and what its formal characteristics are. As children develop, their notions change until they meet the conventions set up by the adult community without these having been taught to them (Ferreiro 1982; Ferreiro and Teberosky 1977; Teale 1986).

Ferreiro (1982: 136) presents an example of the progress in a Mexican child's conceptualization of the function of written texts. At 3 years and 5 months, when a child is shown cards with a drawing and letters and asked what they say, the child replies, *Letras* ("Letters"). Even when the question was changed to *¿Qué dicen las letras?* ("What do the letters say?"), the child once more replies, *Letras* ("Letters"). Seven months later, however, at 4, when the child is asked what the letters say, the child replies, *No sabo* ("I don't know").

Children not only develop concepts about the written symbols, but also of their formal characteristics. Ferreiro (1982: 131) gives us another example of this. Jorge, 4 years and 9 months, prepares labels for a toy store. For the toy soldier, he makes a circle. The researcher asks him what he put on the card. Jorge answers, *Soldados* ("Soldiers"). She then asks whether it is a soldier or a letter. Jorge replies that it is a soldier. Finally, the researcher asks what it says, and he replies, *Una letra* ("A letter").

Hankey and Brightmore (1987) provide a profile of the development of one of their students, from his pre-literacy stage to his refining and mastery of writing in a classroom where there was no direct traditional teaching of writing. They describe the stages this child went through and the assistance he gets from the teacher and other students in discovering the spelling of words and in editing and structuring his writing. Their research shows that teaching-learning to write occurs without direct teacher involvement or specific methods.

In her account of groups of children working together in writing projects, Teberosky (1982) describes how children assist each other by providing information on spelling, structuring of texts and formulation of ideas. Clover and Hutchings (1986) also describe how a group of children assisted each other's writing without necessarily providing rules nor copying.

Theories, practices and research in teaching-learning of writing have been transformed in the last decade. But how much of this shift in theory, practices and research has found its way into bilingual classrooms?

In the United States, the remedial nature of many bilingual classrooms has succeeded in supressing the liberating aspects of these theories, practices and research. Much of the writing instruction in bilingual classrooms follows a reductionist curriculum that is skills-oriented and mechanical. Rather than liberate the child's expression (even in her/his native language), this reductionist curriculum limits it and silences it.

My work with the two bilingual teachers described below is but a small attempt to engage bilingual educators in liberating pedagogical practices, especially when it comes to written expression.

3. Teachers and Students as Researchers of the Writing Process

I teach a course in the Teaching of Reading and Writing in Spanish in the Spanish-English bilingual classroom for students pursuing a Masters Degree in Bilingual Education at The City College of New York. As part of this course, I introduce teachers to research carried out by Latin American and Spanish researchers in monolingual Spanish speaking countries. This serves the double purpose of familiarizing students with non-Anglo-American research, at the same time that it develops the students' own Spanish.

Although extensive research on the teaching of writing has been conducted with monolingual children (both Spanish speakers and English speakers), there is virtually no research of the development of Spanish writing among bilingual children in the United States. And there are few classrooms where the young Latino child with emerging biliteracy is engaged in active learning. Therefore, in September 1989 two kindergarten teachers (who had been my former students) and I set out to study their work as teachers and the Latino children's active involvement in the process of learning to write Spanish. As part of our study, we wanted to transform traditional practices of teaching writing in the bilingual classroom. Our goal was to carefully study and document the implementation of an active approach to writing development and to evaluate its effectiveness.

We agreed that in order to understand the implementation of an approach where the students were going to be active participants in the process, it was necessary to focus on two aspects. First, it was necessary to study how the children conceptualized and learned to master the written system. Second, it was important to study the interactions between the teacher and the children. The two teachers were asked to focus only on one child and to tape their conversations with that child. We met weekly to discuss the transcriptions of their work.

Two aspects of the study very quickly emerged. Firstly, a series of classroom events where the child actively participated in writing were identified and documented. Secondly, the taped conversations between the teacher and the child showed the very important dynamic role that the teacher plays in fostering, documenting and evaluating the development of the learner.

When teaching follows a specific method, the student responds to external plans. Students then participate in the same activities, planned ahead by the teacher, the State or the Publishing Houses. The teacher is also controlled by the planned curriculum. However, when teaching and learning follow an active approach, the objectives and activities are subject to continuous change. This was the situation of the two classrooms we studied. In these two kindergarten classrooms the teachers' writing activities changed according to what the teacher wanted to know and what the students responded. It is then questions by the teachers and responses by the students that are central to our study and that define the roles that teachers of active writing assume as planners, recorders and researchers of children's writing development.

The teachers first investigated the knowledge the child brought to the classroom in the area of literacy. Knowledge of literacy was divided into that dealing with formal aspects of the system and that dealing with what the writing system represented.

Initially the two children who were the object of study were given crayons, pencils and paper and told to get to work. The children's production of a drawing, label or text was carefully observed by each teacher who questioned the child about the work. Through this procedure, a profile began to emerge not only of the development of the child's writing, but also of the approach that the teacher used to understand and foster the development of the emerging writer.

Almost immediately at the start of our study the teachers were faced with the inadequacy of their traditional questions. After close analysis of the teachers' questions and lengthy discussion, we decided that the teachers' questions needed to change. But the evolution of the teachers' questions emerged from an analysis of the students' responses. It was the students' responses that informed the teacher as to the next set of questions or activities.

At the beginning of the academic year, we wanted to know if the two kindergarteners in the study were familiar with the distance that separates the function of drawing from the writing system. Ferreiro (1982: 130) has suggested that this is one of the first problems that children face and resolve when starting to write. One of the teachers focused on a five year old girl named Julia. When Julia finished her first drawing in kindergarten, the teacher asked: *¿Qué dibujaste?* ("What did you paint?") Julia replied: *El papel* ("The paper"). It became clear to the teacher that her question was inappropriate to find out if Julia knew the difference between writing and drawing. So, the teacher changed the question, *¿Qué has hecho?* ("What have you done?"). Julia replied, *Pinté la cara de mi hermano* ("I drew my brother's face"). This last question then led to another one that finally determined that

Julia did know the difference between drawing and writing. Next to the drawing, Julia had drawn some signs. When asked what they were, Julia replied: *El nombre de mi hermanito* ("My little brother's name").

Once we determined that Julia knew the difference between drawings and written texts, we started studying her conceptualization of the function of the written system. It has been demonstrated that children go through a stage in learning to write when they do not conceptualize written symbols as objects whose function is to represent something else. Ferreiro and Teberosky (1979) have established that at this stage children may distinguish written symbols from drawings, although they may call them names, letters or numbers without distinction. The teacher pursued her questioning of Julia to find out what she meant by the word "name".

> T: *¿Quiere decir algo el nombre?*
> "Does the name say something?"
> C: *Sí.* "Yes."
> T: *¿Que?* "What?"
> C: *Julia, Bebé, John.*

It was clear to the teacher that Julia called the text "names", but that these represented external meaning.

There were also numbers on this child's drawing. The teacher pointed to the numbers and asked Julia the difference between those signs and the previous ones:

> T: *¿Son éstos los mismos que ésos?*
> "Are these the same as those?"
> C: *No, porque los hice differente.*
> "No, because I did them differently."
> T: *Entonces, ¿qué son?*
> "Then, what are they?"
> C: *Números.*
> "Numbers."
> T: *¿Dicen algo?*
> "Do they say something?"
> C: *Sí.*
> "Yes."
> T: *¿Qué dicen?*
> "What do they say?"
> C: *Uno, dos, tres, cinco, diez.*
> "One, two, three, five, ten."

Our study into the teacher's role in developing the young Latino child as an active learner of writing in Spanish leads us to three important observations:

1. The writing development of language minority children is the same as that of all other children. We found no differences between our two children's development as writers in Spanish and those who were subjects in the study by Ferreiro (1982).

2. As soon as teachers are liberated from planned curriculum guides, they start to hear their own voices in interacting with children. Questions then become not just part of the formal classroom script, but questions become the instruments with which teachers probe children's thinking and engage them in inquiry.

3. The interaction between the teacher and the child as active learners and inquirers creates the successful teaching and learning environment in which both teacher and child are immersed.

3. Conclusion

The transitional and remedial nature of many bilingual classrooms in the United States leads to the silencing of the child's expression in his/her native language and a timid and reduced expression in English. While Spanish is neglected, English is controlled and structured. Language failure is sure to follow.

But in a few classrooms in the United States (and even a few schools), bilingual teachers are making the difference in liberating children's expression, and thus their own. My work with these two kindergarten teachers is indicative of the success that bilingual teachers and children can experience given a teaching-learning approach in which they are in control of their activity and in tune with each other's interaction.

Enrichment bilingual education ... gives an additional window on the world.... Enrichment bilingual education has in mind the expansion of intellect and personality.

Joshua A. Fishman, 1977b: 45

Becoming Bilingual
in English in a non-English Environment
(A Retrospective Essay in Honor of Joshua A. Fishman)[1]

Bonifacio P. Sibayan

Philippine Normal College, Emeritus

1. Introduction

This essay in honor of Joshua A. Fishman is an attempt at a retrospective 'documentation' of how my classmates and I learned to speak, read and write English in an absolutely non-English environment under American colonial rule in the twenties when the vast majority of the people, especially those outside Manila, had no choice of school nor of language of instruction. The only place where we pupils heard or read any English was in a government school where we spent about seven hours or more a day, five days a week, forty weeks a year, for seven years.

At the time, there were a few schools, mostly operated by the Roman Catholic Church in Manila where the language of instruction was Spanish[2] where the rich sent their children. In practically all parts of the Philippines, however, the English-only public school was the only place where a child could get a school education. There was no alternative.

Since then, times have changed. In late 1939 grades one and two teachers were allowed to use the native language as 'auxiliary language' of instruction when pupils had difficulty in understanding what was being taught in English. In June 1940 the national language based on Tagalog (called Pilipino in 1959 and Filipino in 1987) was taught as a subject in the senior year of high school and teacher education curricula. Not too long after the opening of schools after the end of the second world war, the national language was taught as a subject in all classes from first grade to the university. In June 1974 the entire school system adopted a bilingual education program where science and mathematics subjects are taught in English and the social sciences and other subjects in Filipino. I am happy to say that I helped write that official policy.

In spite of the rapid ascendancy of Filipino, however, English is still the preferred language of instruction because it is the main language used in what I have called the controlling domains of language, namely, those of government, legislation, the judiciary, higher education and the professions, science and technology, business, commerce and industry and print media (Gonzalez and Sibayan 1988; Otanes and Sibayan 1969; Sibayan 1985).

I am one of the staunchest advocates of bilingual education in the Philippines. I do not advocate a return to the English-only (immersion) rule that I retrospectively 'document' in this essay for many reasons, reasons which are the concerns of another essay (Sibayan 1970). However, we have much to learn from many of the pedagogical practices of the period that I describe here.

2. Bakun: a non-English Environment

The Philippine public school system established by the United States in 1900 was in its twenty-third year when as a seven-year old I was sent to the thatch-roofed one-room schoolhouse in Bakun, a town in the minority region of the Cordilleras in Northern Luzon, Philippines. As an index of how remote this place is, up to now (year 1990) the automobile has not yet reached the place. At that time perhaps less than one hundred families comprised the community served by the school. The people were farmers who planted rice in paddies and sweet potatoes and vegetables in clearings on hillsides. They raised pigs and chickens in their yards.

There were just three persons who spoke, read and wrote English in Bakun then: the male school teacher, the sanitary inspector, and my father. The sanitary inspector's duty was to see to it that sanitation and health rules were observed and to dispense quinine to those sick with malaria, aspirin, the universal cure-all medicine, for most ailments, and denatured alcohol and tincture of iodine for wounds. My father who was in the civil service was municipal treasurer, town secretary, postmaster and local civil registrar all rolled into one. The three men were pioneers; they tried to bring government services to that remote community. The place was completely a non-English environment.

All the official reports of the three men to their superiors were rendered in English. The teacher reported to the supervising teacher whose office could be reached after approximately three days of hiking over mountains and across rivers and streams; the sanitary inspector made his reports to the provincial health officer (a physician) in the capital of the province which could be reached after approximately ten days of hiking, less if on horseback. My father rendered his reports to the provincial treasurer, the provincial governor and sometimes to the district (provincial) engineer in the provincial capital.

3. My First Schoolroom

There are certain things that stand out in our memories. For me, one of them was my first schoolroom. I can still see that room very clearly. It was full of pictures – of animals, birds, fruits, etc. on manila paper charts all labeled with their names. Everything in that room had a label – windows, the blackboard, desks, the teacher's table, the sand table, even the broom had a tag on it. Above the blackboard, the upper and lower case of the letters of the alphabet in script were conspicuously displayed. There were black and white reproductions of the "The Sower" and the "The Gleaners" by Millet.

The seats of the front desks of the rows of seats were full of cardboard cut-outs of animals, fruits, vegetables, objects such as chairs, tables, hoes, etc. in various colors.[3] There were several pocket charts made of manila paper hanging on the walls and strips of black flash cards which the teacher used for writing words and phrases for us to read. Sometimes we wrote words to form sentences on these flash cards. There were many sets of letters of the alphabet, both capital letters and small (lower case) in print (not script) which we used for forming (spelling) words.

There was one equipment that we used a lot for learning: the sand table. It was used in Language to arrange cardboard cutout figures to tell the story of the three pigs, three bears, big bad wolf, etc. In Arithmetic almost anything could be arranged for counting, adding, subtracting, multiplying, dividing, etc.

4. Monolingual Education: Immersion in English

When I started going to school I was bilingual in two Philippine languages, Ilocano, my ethnic language, one of the eight major languages of the Philippines, which I spoke at home with my parents and my brothers and sisters; and Kankanaey, one of the many minor languages of the country, the language of the Bakun community, which I spoke with my Kankanaey playmates. All my classmates in the first grade were monolingual speakers of Kankanaey.

Education in school was completely given in English. We were required to speak only English in the classroom and in the school premises. Anyone who spoke the local language was punished. The favorite form of punishment for the boys was carrying stones from the river bank for building the fence around the vegetable garden and around the school ground. The punishment for girls usually consisted of cleaning the school grounds or the schoolroom. Sometimes, especially when it was raining, the boys were simply whipped with a stick on the buttocks by the teacher.

We were 'immersed' in English long before Wallace Lambert and his associates at McGill used the term immersion. The Philippine immersion I describe here was practically forced on us; there was no alternate choice unlike the Canadian type which is voluntary and has options to offer. Some of us, though, never surfaced from the immersion. The dual task of learning English and using it to learn the content of the various subjects was a task that overwhelmed many children. Failure to learn English for understanding the subject matter content of the various subjects meant failure in school. Most pupils failed. Among the few who completed grade seven, many did not go to high school because of poverty. Worse, the nearest high school was too far away. I recall now that among my classmates in the first grade I know of only one who graduated from high school with me. He went on to become municipal treasurer of Bakun.[4]

Immersion consisted of many activities not generally done, if ever, today. For example, we did four things with a song: we sang it, we recited the words (lyrics) like we did with poems, we read the words in print and in script so we knew how they looked when written down and how they were spelled. More often than not, when the teacher was especially fond of the song or we ourselves liked it, we wrote the song in our notebooks.

By the time we completed the seventh grade we knew dozens of poems and literary pieces which included *The Charge of the Light Brigade, O Captain My Captain, The Wreck of the Hesperus,* and Lincoln's *Gettysburg Address* which were rendered as declamations. We could sing more than a hundred songs which included Philippine songs rendered in English. Songs like *O Worship the King, Come Thou Almighty King, Nearer my God to Thee, Lead Kindly Light, Onward Christian Soldiers, Rock of Ages, My Country 'Tis of Thee, Oh, Beautiful for Spacious Skies* became a part of our repertory of songs, many permanently stored in our memories for retrieval during appropriate occasions.

It seems to me now that we were always singing – during opening exercises, during rest breaks, before we went out of the classroom for recess, and before we were dismissed from our morning and afternoon classes; we bid our teacher goodbye in the afternoon with a song. Immersion in English meant committing to memory many poems, maxims and proverbs and retelling stories that we read. It meant reading a lot, orally and silently, and being asked questions afterwards about what we read. It meant writing on the blackboard and on paper, words, sentences and short paragraphs.

We were made to understand quite early that to get an education, we had to learn how to read and write and speak English. School life was dominated by reading, both silently and orally. Oral reading was done before one's classmates. We had a subject called phonics which was spent in reading and pronouncing words and sentences. Reading was the chief key to learning.

5. Oh, Jose, Can You See? and Guabas Aray

Every morning before we could read, we lustily sang "Oh, Jose, can you see ..." It was only later when we could read that we knew the version "Oh, say, can you see by the dawn's early light" etc. Every morning we sang the "Star Spangled Banner" and the Philippine National Anthem, in that order, in English during the flag raising ceremony in front of the schoolhouse. This ritual started the schoolday.

Reading corrected many mishearings like the song we heard as "Guabas aray, de mayas sang wan de" which read "Guavas are ripe, the mayas sang one day", etc.

6. Recitations from Memory, Dramatizations, Retelling Stories

My classmates and I were the first pupils to be enrolled in Bakun school. During the first two years, there was only one teacher, Guillermo Perez. I give his name out of respect for the memory of this wonderful man and extraordinary teacher. In the third year, another male teacher, Pedro Abuan, also an excellent teacher, joined Mr. Perez. In the fifth year, a lady teacher, Miss Doctolero, joined the teaching staff. She sang very well. In the sixth year, two teachers joined the teaching staff; there were now five teachers. Mr. Perez had married and his wife became the home economics teacher.

Not one of these Filipino teachers ever finished high school or secondary normal school. Some of them were pupils of teachers from the United States. Every summer vacation they attended summer school classes to learn subject matter content and methods of teaching. Most important of all, they observed demonstration classes on methods of teaching, preparation and use of teaching materials by selected model teachers.[5]

English was taught not as a language but as a means of giving us an education. It was the only language used for teaching us arithmetic, geography, history, civics, good manners and right conduct, reading and writing, gardening and industrial arts for the boys and home economics for the girls. We had to learn to speak, read, and write English so that we could get an education. The first objective was for us to learn subject-matter content; English was just a tool.

How well did the teachers succeed? In retrospect, I think they succeeded very well. Teaching was very difficult work. Because only English was allowed, in the beginning when the teacher wanted a child to learn action words such as "jump", "run", "sit down", "walk to the window", etc., he himself had to demonstrate by acting out the words himself.[6]

We memorized and recited the Latin alphabet so that we could locate words in the dictionary. We learned the eight parts of speech so that we could use the dictionary effectively not only to learn the pronunciation and spelling of a word, but also the use of the words including their various forms. We had to learn how to give the plural form of nouns, how to conjugate verbs, compare adjectives, make nouns out of verbs, etc.[7] When we wrote compositions there was no excuse for misspelling a word because there was the dictionary to refer to. We chose "big" words for our compositions. Our sentences were a combination of 'book' English and translations or renditions of Filipino words and expressions into English. This contributed to the formation of our 'Filipino' English.

Using the dictionary as a tool for learning English started in the fourth grade. A special abridged edition of Webster's dictionary was printed in the United States for use in Philippine schools. Every classroom from the fourth grade was furnished these dictionaries, at least one for every two pupils. The dictionary became one of the most important aids to learning English. The skills needed for using the dictionary were taught as early as the first grade through mastery of the alphabet by means of songs and plain memory. How a word was pronounced through the use of diacritical marks as found in the dictionary was taught to us with the aid of key words. These key words were generally nouns that were easy to illustrate with pictures. The chart containing the key words, diacritical marks and illustrations was prominently displayed on the classroom wall for everyone to see.

We learned the rudiments of grammar such as subject and predicate, transitive and intransitive verbs, adverbial and adjective modifiers, position of single word and phrase modifiers, simple, compound, complex sentences. In the seventh grade we were taught how to diagram sentences. Emphasis was laid on the eight parts of speech in connection with the use of the dictionary as a help to learning. The dictionary became one of the most important books in our lives.

We committed to memory rules of English grammar. In retrospect, memorizing grammar rules made sense. Because we did not have the so-called 'native feel for English' we had to know the grammatical 'rules' in order to have a guide especially in writing.[8]

One of our favorite subjects was geography. By the time we were in grade five we could draw from memory on paper or on the blackboard the map of the Philippines complete with provinces and capitals, the map of the United States complete with the forty-eight states and their capitals, the various countries of Asia, Africa, Europe, North and South America and Australia. We could locate from memory almost any city or place, mountains, seas, rivers, deserts, etc. We could name the most important products of a province of the Philippines, a country or region.

Relief maps out of paper pulp showing mountains, rivers, divides, plains and other geographical features were best learned through the sand table. The most important products of each region were indicated on the sand table relief map.

Our books were either direct imports of books used in schools in the United States or Philippine adaptations of those books. The first books to be written by Filipino authors to be used in Philippine schools were *A Brief History of the Philippines* by Leandro Fernandez which we used in the seventh grade – while it is true that we were immersed ('steeped' seem to be a more appropriate term) in English, the subject matter of history that we learned had much to do with our own history, not with United States history – and *The Philippine Readers* (series) by Camilo Osias in the fifth, sixth and seventh grades. *The Philippine Readers* became a classic and were known by generations of Filipinos as Osias Readers. I have since been convinced that one reason the Osias Readers became a classic was the fact that the stories were so interesting that we read them over and over again. This cannot be said of the contents (based on so-called 'word counts') of most readers that replaced them.

7. Surreptitious Bilingual Education under the Schoolhouse

When we were in the third grade, a new schoolhouse was built by the people of the community. The schoolhouse was built on stilts called "posts" to keep the floor from being flooded when it rained. The floor was about four feet above the ground. It was high enough for us to seek shelter under when it rained or when the sun shone very hot. That schoolhouse was typical of the schoolhouses of the period.

That space under the schoolhouse turned out to be one of the most useful spaces for education in the school compound. It was under the schoolhouse where we practiced and checked on each other's knowledge of the poems and stories we were to recite or tell in class before our classmates or before the teacher. We practiced our dramatizations of such delightful stories as "The Three Pigs", "Goldilocks", "The Three Bears", and other classics for presentation in class. It was under the schoolhouse where we tried to check on each other's knowledge of spelling, and of the names of the towns, cities, rivers, mountain ranges, etc. on the maps of the Philippines and of the continents.

The most important use of that space under the schoolhouse was for doing our homework. It seems strange to me now, but it was not then, why we were assigned homework when the teacher knew that with the exception of the homes of the teacher, the sanitary inspector and my father's, the homes in the community had no light at night except that from the fireplace. Not only that, the parents of my classmates were illiterate. But we were assigned homework anyway.

We did our homework under that schoolhouse. The most important homework was that of arithmetic problems. By the time we were in grade six we were solving problems on percentage and on compound denominate numbers. The arithmetic problems in the seventh grade involved measurements of surface, volumes of solids, the sphere, square and cube root, the Pythagorean theorem, isosceles and equilateral triangles, the three types of percentage, and believe it or not, business terms and forms, banking, and methods of investing money including real estate investments and stocks and bonds. The greatest wonder to me, in retrospect, is how the teacher tried very hard to make us understand these things.

We had to do two things with problems: solve the problems (the answers to the problems were at the back of the book so we could check our work) and, task of tasks, practice how to explain the solution to the problem in order to be ready to be called by the teacher to explain in English the solution on the blackboard before the entire class. That was the most difficult part of the homework.

The understanding of and arriving at the solutions to the problems, however, were done, in fact had to be done, in a mixture of English and Kankanaey. We could not help that mixture. It made things 'clear' to us. We found out that what we could not explain with the help of Kankanaey was practically beyond our understanding. As I look back now that experience confirms the importance of the native tongue.

We had to be careful, though, not to be heard speaking in Kankanaey by the teacher. We spoke the English explanations very loudly but toned down our voices in Kankanaey. In retrospect those sessions were some of the most effective experience of bilingual education in my own life.

I am sure now that there was more pupil interaction and perhaps as much understanding of difficult concepts under that schoolhouse because we were free to talk with the use of our native language, whereas inside the classroom there was our apprehension of the teacher calling on us and the constant fear that we were inadequate in English.

Fortunately, the classic architecture of a Philippine schoolhouse, the 'Gabaldon' named after the legislator-author of the law that appropriated money for this type of school building all over the Philippines, had this space under the schoolhouse. The Gabaldon schoolhouses built of poured concrete can still be found in many places all over the Philippines. It was a sad day when schoolhouses were built with no space under for such educational activities.

8. How a Teacher Managed to Listen to Fifty Stories, Each Twenty Times, in One Year

I recall that when we were in the fifth grade we were told that we would be promoted to the sixth grade if we could retell all the fifty famous stories in the book *Fifty Famous Stories, Retold* by Baldwin before the class and before the teacher. Mostly before the teacher. How?

Those old-time Filipino teachers of the twenties who never completed high school had industry and imagination in teaching to make up for their inadequacies. They reported to school early in the morning, before classes started to write their 'boardwork' or stayed after physical education which was always the last activity in the afternoon to write their lesson plans, correct papers, or do their boardwork. These before-and-after-class periods provided good opportunities for the teacher to listen to a pupil or two tell a story or recite a poem or sing a song.

The teacher did not wait for the regular class period to listen to pupils. A pupil could approach the teacher whenever he/she was ready to recite a poem or tell a story or sing a song. While the teacher wrote his/her lesson plans or boardwork the pupil recited a poem or told a story or sang a song. If the teacher was satisfied with the performance, the pupil was directed to go and draw a star with a colored crayola opposite his/her name under the appropriate title of the poem, story or song which were listed in a manila paper chart hanging on the wall. Every fifth star had to be a different color to make it easy to count how many stories, poems, or songs a pupil had satisfactorily rendered.

Another occasion when these poems, stories, or songs could be rendered by the pupil and get credit for them was the ten-minute opening exercise period which was the first classroom activity every morning. These opening exercises were planned by the pupils themselves. Before the end of the year, practically all of us had recited all the poems, told all the stories, and sung all the songs listed by the teacher.

Stories from *Tales from the Arabian Nights* such as "Aladdin and his Magic Lamp", "Ali Baba and the Forty Thieves", "Sinbad the Sailor", many of the stories of Hans Andersen, Grimm's Fairy Tales, Aesop's Fables, had become parts of our lives. These imaginative stories were as vivid to us in that remote part of the world as our own lives through the printed word and the beautiful illustrations.[9]

When we were in grade four, our teacher told us the story of "Tarzan and the Apes" by Edgar Rice Burroughs. The story was serialized in the *Philippines Free Press*, a weekly. Our teacher told the story of Tarzan to us without using a single word in our native language. He showed us the illustrations which fired our imagination and heightened our interest. Sometimes it took him the whole morning to tell one installment and we missed our regular subjects but we enjoyed the story more than our subjects. Later when I was a school teacher I knew that he had violated a strict rule in teaching – not to deviate from the program – but he must have noted how relaxed and interested we were when he told the story.

We had to participate in dramatizations or playlets. We dramatized "Goldilocks and the Three Bears", "Little Red Riding Hood", "The Three Little Pigs", "Billy Goat Gruff and the Troll", etc. The dramatizations would be repeated with each pupil acting out a different character for the voice and mood variations. We memorized the multiplication table, the various tables of measures of weight, length (English and metric), volume, capacity, time, etc.[10] Often, we did our memorization as we hiked to school and back home.

9. Garden Days, District Meets, and Other Celebrations

There were various officially-planned activities to 'show off' and check on our knowledge of English and our knowledge of the various subjects outside our schoolrooms. One of these was the graduation or closing exercises at the end of the school year preceding the long summer vacation. The two other occasions were the 'Garden Day' and the 'District Meet' as they were popularly known then.

During the closing exercises which parents attended dutifully (in their best finery), pupils recited poems and told stories, participated in dramatizations, sang duets, trios, and choruses – everyone had a part. The strangest thing was that with the exception of the teacher(s), the sanitary inspector and my father as well as the pupils, all the parents did not understand a word of the English language. But they were pleased and proud that their children could now speak what must have been to them a status or prestige, if exotic, language.

The garden days were occasions when the school pupils and the people of the community were given an opportunity to exhibit the the best of their products: the pupils exhibited their drawings of characters of stories, maps of various parts of the world, samples of their written work of poems and songs accompanied with illustrations. The pupils proudly showed their work to their parents and relatives. The people of the community exhibited their produce, usually the choicest samples, of their vegetable gardens – string beans, pechay, cabbage, radish, carrots, sweet potatoes, squash, etc. These were labeled, by the pupils and the teachers, with their proper names and, if intended for sale, with their prices as well. Only the pupils and teachers, however, could read the names and price tags. During the garden day, there were held what were then called group games in which the pupils participated: crab relay, hop and skip, running relays and others. All instructions were given in English.

The schools in the Philippines then were, as they are even up to the present, administratively organized into divisions and districts. School divisions coincided with the political unit called province or city (such as the City of Manila). Each division was under a division superintendent of schools. A division was divided into districts under supervising teachers. A district consisted of several towns, usually three or four towns, or two if the towns were big and had many schools. A large town would have a central school in the town proper and several barrio schools in the countryside. Bakun was a one-school town and it belonged to a three-town district.

The district meet was something all of us, young and old, looked forward to. During the district meet, which was generally held in a central school of one of the towns of the district before the end of the school year, the brightest pupils in the various subjects such as arithmetic computation and problem solving, spelling, geography, composition, dramatizations, declamations, singing (solo, duet, trio and chorus) were selected as contestants.

The contests were held outdoors so the people could watch and applaud the winners. Problems and directions were either dictated or written on pieces of paper. Winners were decided by boards of judges composed of teachers and sometimes the sanitary inspector and the municipal treasurer.

District meets would last two or three days. Winners in the various contests were awarded prizes. First prize winners would get three pencils, second prize winners, two pencils, and third price winners, one pencil, etc. Valued prizes because of their usefulness in school were pencils, notebooks, colored crayolas and ruled pad papers. Winners were also awarded certificates indicating what they won. Various points were assigned to first, second and third prize. The points were added up for each school and town and champions, second place winners, etc. were declared. The certificates became permanent and valued exhibits on the walls of the schoolrooms of the winning schools.

10. Compensation Enough

I have often wondered how we learned to speak, read and write English in that non-English environment. It seems that the key to our learning English consisted of the following: reading and more reading of English, both silently and orally; committing to memory poems and stories and reciting and retelling these pieces before the class and the teacher. We were required to explain what we read. Most important of all, we were taught to love books. As a symbol for this love, we were taught how to cover our books with manila paper and how to take care of them.

In retrospect, I think one of the secrets of our success was our isolation. There was practically nothing to distract us from concentrating on learning the English language. Also perhaps because we were allowed to speak and use only English in school, we separated the languages – in the case of my classmates, Kankanaey for their home and the community, and English for their school world. In my case I had the three languages well separated, Ilocano at home with my parents, brothers and sisters, Kankanaey with my Kankanaey playmates outside the school, and English in school and sometimes with my father and younger brother when we did our homework especially in arithmetic.

I learned enough English in that remote and completely non-English world to enable me to compete in the secondary normal school where we had several American teachers. I am happy that we learned enough English to learn subject matter content and thus to have made it possible for us to compete through a language not our own.

The apprehensions and fears, the struggle and the frustrations sometimes mixed with anger and resentment for being forbidden to speak one's language are forgotten now or have simply vanished with the years. In my particular case, the many advantages derived by me through my education and my love for books and learning are more than enough compensation for the difficulties I went through in learning the English language.

Notes

1. I want to thank Bro. Andrew Gonzalez, FSC, President of De La Salle University, Dr. Edilberto P. Dagot, President, Philippine Normal College and Professor Benjamin M. Pascual for critically reading an earlier draft of this paper resulting in its improvement. All mistakes, however, are mine.

2. The schools that used Spanish as the language of instruction shifted to English when English became an instrument for socio-economic mobility.

3. Those cut-outs were some of the most useful materials for teaching free and spontaneous speaking and conversations. We acquired communicative competence (an avowed goal of second language learning in the seventies) through those cut-outs and with real objects in the schoolroom.

4. The reader not familiar with the Philippine experience may ask why I experienced 'success' although schooled in a language not my mother tongue and why others failed. In my particular case, I had the advantage of having a father who spoke, read and wrote English. My father was typical of the first generation of Filipinos who obtained some education in the public schools taught exclusively in the English language. I also had the advantage of leaving Bakun because of the reassignment of my father to other places. My Kankanaey classmates in that remote community never left the place. They never had any opportunity to use the English they learned.

5. The teaching of English in the Philippines was mainly the work of Filipinos, many of whom learned their English from other Filipinos who were partly taught their English by North Americans.

6. In the 1970s language teachers 'discovered' this technique and labeled it 'physical response' in language teaching.

7. My father believed in words. He required us to come home from school everyday knowing at least five new words which we kept in a notebook that he examined regularly. He was also a lover of books.

8. Years later when I lived in a dormitory suite with three American college boys, they were surprised to find out that I knew more 'grammar rules' to explain the 'correctness' of English constructions than they did.

9. We used to have many distinguished visitors in our house. They would reward us with silver coins for reciting poems and telling stories we had learned in school.

10. Later, just before and after World War II, memorizing was abandoned as a way of learning; emphasis was on understanding. This change of teaching methods resulted in pupils having nothing to 'retrieve' from their brains.

If there is anything that bilingual education has to contribute to language teaching more generally it is its maximization of language learning for the communication of messages that are highly significant for senders and receivers alike, both in their individual, as well as in their actual and potential societal capacities.

Joshua A. Fishman, 1976a: 36

ESL in Bilingual Education

Christina Bratt Paulston
University of Pittsburgh

1. Introduction

The objective of this paper is to identify some significant questions, features, and issues which relate to second language acquisition in a school setting, to children's language learning in the classroom. It will readily be seen that our state of knowledge is very unsatisfactory. We know surprisingly little about how children learn a second language. Barry McLaughlin concludes his *Language Learning in Bilingual Instruction: Literature Review* (1982: 89) with this caution: "The point is that we are not at the conclusion stage but at the hypothesis stage. The quality and quantity of the research is simply not sufficient to support definitive statements". This is probably the most important point that arises from examining the research in general, and it is one that I cannot sufficiently emphasize. We are beginning to be able to ask significant questions, to see trends and directions. This paper should be read as an explorative discussion, not as any expounding of finite knowledge. It is my strong conviction that in the long run we only harm the children we want to help by pretending to a state of affairs which is inaccurate, however appealing.

I will write in generalities because we urgently need to be able to generalize about the practices and effects of bilingual instruction, but we should not forget that it is individual children of flesh and blood we are discussing. The joy and delight of the third grade Mexican-American boy, brutally raped some months earlier, who had finally learned to read in Señora Olga's class, is also a valid evaluation of bilingual education. My visit to her Texas classroom reminded me again that the most significant feature of bilingual education in the United States may well be that it helps ease the schooling of young children some of whom have a very rough life. Although this paper deals with second language acquisition, we need to remember that there are other matters in these children's life that are of higher importance, and that it is only as English language acquisition becomes an indicator of school achievement, social success and integration, and the possibility for upward social mobility that second language learning becomes truly important.

Bilingual education in the United States takes place in a setting of language shift. However, the various groups shift at different rates. The Koreans (Kim et al. 1981) and Vietnamese (Rupp 1980) manifest a very rapid shift, whereas the Navajos show the slowest rate of shift (Lieberson and Curry 1971; Spolsky 1977a). There really are no accurate figures for the Southwest because of continued illegal migration, but certainly shift among Hispanics is taking place (Teitelbaum 1976). In situations of language shift, language maintenance tends to become an emotional matter as a marker of the old ethnicity. Some of this tension manifested itself in the early seventies as a conflict between English as a Second Language (ESL) and bilingual education (BE), as well as between the perceived goals of bilingual education programs as promoting shift to English (transitional) or developing the mother tongue along with English (maintenance).

The general and unanimous first goal of most bilingual education programs in the United States as perceived by the teachers is for the children to learn English and learn it well. In general, I think it is much more common today to find BE administrators who are willing to settle for transitional BE than it would have been twenty years ago. As a result, there is less conflict and controversy within bilingual education as the goal orientation of the program participants comes to coincide more with the legal objectives as Congress saw them.

Another consequence of what I see as an implicit shift to a transitional goal orientation is the attempt at alternatives to bilingual education, primarily ESL programs and immersion programs, which will be discussed below. Since the goal orientation of these programs are the same as those of transitional BE, they have become more acceptable than they were earlier.

The other major goal of BE program is an affirmation of the children's cultural values and beliefs. This is in accordance with BE legislation and typically meets with little or no controversy in the school setting. I suspect this may also represent a slight shift from earlier positions. *Bilingual/bicultural* was the slogan of the maintenance proponents but now it has become generally acceptable across the board, by Anglos as well as by bilingual teachers.

2. Instruction and Teaching

My impression from reading the Significant Bilingual Instructional Features Study (SBIFS), conducted by Tikunoff and his associates (1982) is that _the_ most important teacher characteristic is efficient classroom management, and my own classroom experience supports that conclusion. Everyone interested in second language teaching would probably agree that one of the teacher's major roles is to structure the school environment so that the students can learn. This is what all good classroom management does. Good teaching allows for both learning and acquisition in Krashen's (1981) terms, where learning is the result of teaching while acquisition results from the student's processing of meaningful language input. Learning would include such activities as study of sound-symbol relationship, work with vocabulary cards, and fill-in-the-blank exercises. Activities for second language acquisition focus on the content or function of language, and they include writing free compositions, making shopping lists for the make-believe store where the learning objectives include addition and getting correct change, as well as all those other activities which take place in English without focusing on form, such as the teaching of Science and Mathematics.

The integrative approach, that is, methods of teaching in bilingual education classes which have been identified in the SBIF study as academically excellent,[1] makes certain of this acquisition phase of language development, and all the evidence is quite clear that without such a stage, i.e. language used for communication, language teaching is not very efficient (Savignon 1971). The Canadian immersion programs were founded on the belief that unless the second language is used for teaching content matter rather than just taught as a subject, language learning will not take place (Swain and Barik 1978; Swain and Lapkin 1981). This is not to say that the learning stage can be ignored. Children also need the formal aspect of language learning, and presumably the failure of many ethnic children in submersion classes (regular mainstream classes in English which ignore some children's lack of knowledge of English) results from ignoring this need.

Competent student participation consists of accurate decoding and understanding, active participation, and obtaining feedback. A student cannot perform a task if s/he cannot understand the task expectations, but it is not clear which are the parts of language that second language learners must understand. Hatch (1978) documents what children learn in her *Second Language Acquisition* but not really how they do it. We do know, however, that the second language learning "process is a very long, very demanding, and frequently frustrating one for the child" (Hatch 1978: 12). I think children probably focus on vocabulary and then work out the semantic relationship between lexical items from their pragmatic knowledge of the real world. In any case, it is clear that good teachers spend a lot of effort, their own and that of students, on vocabulary development.

I would like to make a few comments here on learning vocabulary and the use of mother tongue translation. It is perfectly possible to learn vocabulary in English without access to the native language, and children with non-standardized mother tongues do just that. They use vocabulary cards with pictures and sometimes speech, and the teachers make games with points and prizes out of such learning. The children guess meaning from context, which is also how one learns words in the mother tongue. This is fairly easy with concrete items, except of course that one might guess wrong. When it comes to abstract items like *think*, teachers complain that it becomes much more difficult to get the meaning across, and when possible they resort to the easiest way, translation. For vocabulary acquisition, if the children know the corresponding item in their mother tongue, translation makes it an easier and probably much less frustrating task. Even in the Canadian immersion programs, there are instances of translation. I have many times heard a child ask things like: "Comment dit-on *because* en français?" asking for some word they needed.

But children don't know in either L1 or L2 much of the vocabulary learned in school, and then they have to work out the meaning in English with synonyms or dictionary definitions and practice in context. Translation is of no help. Probably the major advantage of subject matter taught in the L1 is that it develops the children's vocabulary knowledge of their mother tongue into that of a full-fledged functional language.

Much of what is perceived as vocabulary teaching is not that at all but teaching concepts like zero and its placement and capital letters for which the children then are taught labels. It seems self-evident that it is easier to explain the zero-concept in a language the children understand, but it is less clear that learning the label *mayúscula* is really any easier than the label *capital letter*. The Canadian immersion programs also make clear that it is perfectly possible to go directly from concept to labels in the L2 rather than the concept to L1 to L2 route, which is often done in US bilingual classrooms. This is especially true in classes like Geography and Science which use many concrete props and so turn themselves into veritable language learning classes (Cazden 1979; Rodriguez 1981).

We see then that the use of L1 and L2 in the classroom is problematic for the task of second language acquisition and that a claim like "Obviously, using L1 for instruction better ensures ... understanding task expectations" (Tikunoff 1982: 19) is probably premature. McLaughlin comes to the same conclusion in his literature review: "It would be premature to regard the issue (use of the first language) as settled. Most likely, decisions as to when and to what extent each of the bilingual child's two languages should be used in the classrooms depends on social, psychological, *and* linguistic factors. Some children, in some circumstances, need more support in their first language than others do" (McLaughlin 1982: 34). And that is exactly what the teachers, as reported in the SBIFS (1982) case studies, actually do. The majority of their first language use during instruction in English is in translation to *individual* students who seem lost during instruction. And until we have more definite answers, that seems a practice they may as well continue.

Feedback is as important in language learning as it is in any learning in a school setting. But feedback in L2 learning may be even more important since it is often a way of clarifying and sorting input, meaningful input being at the very core of successful language learning. Let me illustrate the importance of feedback using Wagner-Gough's data on Homer, (5 years, 11 months), an Assyrian speaker learning English. He is playing with his friend Mark, building something with blocks.

> Mark   : Quit making it so tall!
> Homer : What is this sulta! (angry voice) What is this sulta!
> Mark   : Don't make it so tall!
> Homer : (whispering to himself) What is this sulta? (Then in Assyrian: I ask what sulta is. He says sulta is something. I say there's no such thing as sulta.) (Wagner-Gough, 1978: 156)

Homer is processing *so tall* as *sulta* with consequent confusion and he actually asks for feedback (note his frustration). Mark does what most of us do when we are not understood the first time; he merely repeats. This is one instance where an instant translation would have been helpful, but Homer needs more than the meaning, he also needs to learn the correct forms. In a classroom a good teacher would have done that for him.

In language learning, there is feedback on more than the formal aspects of language. There is also feedback on the functional use of language as communication, and many, including myself hold that this is the more salient aspect of language acquisition. Homer knows well enough that Mark is making a mand, a request of some kind. In the classroom children get feedback on their requests all day long, permission to go to the bathroom, to sharpen the pencil, to read in the library corner. Making mands that one very much wants to have approved is a highly motivating factor in language learning, and it is a legitimate question to wonder if such language learning occasions should automatically be ignored because requests are more readily accomplished in the L1. On the other hand, one certainly does not want to put some poor child through torture beacuse he does not know how and does not dare to ask permission in English to go to the bathroom. Tact and common sense will take a good teacher further than any linguistic knowledge about the role of feedback in language acquisition today because our knowledge is minimal.

3. Effective Instruction

Brophy's summary of effective teaching is hard to quarrel with:

> ... learning gains are most impressive in classrooms in which students receive a great deal of instruction from and have a great deal of interaction with the teacher, especially in public lessons and recitations that are briskly paced but conducted at a difficulty level that allows consistant success. (1979: 747)

These teaching behaviors are likely to be equally true of second language teaching as of teaching in the mother tongue, and I know of no evidence which contradicts Brophy. However, in second language acquisition there is an additional consideration. Language is mainly acquired through social interaction, and some of the best language "instructors" are in fact the other English-speaking students. Fry found that "language use played an important role in social interaction and inclusion in the daily activities of classroom life. It was found that the students learned the language by being in the environment, interacting, and developing associations with English-speaking peers.

As they learned more English, their interactions and associations with English-speaking students increased. They also became more active and involved in the classroom" (1981: abstract). The findings are supported by those of Johnson (1980) who found peer tutoring and Milk (1980) who found small group settings efficient for language learning.

Mack (1981) found that interaction between English speakers and Spanish speakers in first grade was more efficient for English language acquisition than a structured ESL program. This topic should be further pursued and studied. All indications are that in the long run these mixed language classes are more of an asset for the students than a complication for the teacher, which it no doubt also is. Mack concludes her study by saying "that segregation of second language learners in an ESL class where all children are beginners in the language is an unwise policy" (1981: abstract). It should be noted that Mack's comparison is between an ESL-only class and a regular monolingual class in English, not with a Bilingual Education program. Nevertheless, the study addresses the problem of segregating ESL students, and this issue needs to be considered for ESL in bilingual education as well (see the work of the Office of Educational Equity, Massachusetts Department of Education, 1990 and of its director, Charles Glenn 1990).

The literature on second language learning is unanimous in supporting the enormous importance of *motivation* in L2 acquisition. On the whole, language learning or its absence is motivated by social forces which tend to have much stronger influence than any teaching methods or program types *per se* (Paulston 1980b). One of the strongest arguments for BE lies exactly in its being able to counteract negative social forces. For example, there is little socio-economic motivation for Amerindian children on the Navajo reservation to learn English, and they do learn more English in a bilingual program than in an all English program (Rosier and Holm 1980). Bilingual education is not a quick fix. The Navajo children in the Rosier and Holm study took six years to come up to national norms.

There are many indicators for successful BE programs. Students in BE programs have fewer behavior problems (Albino-Cordero 1981), achieve at higher levels (Chavez 1980; Dimas 1981), have higher educational aspirations (Caples-Osorio 1979), and have higher attendance and lower drop-out rates (Dimas 1981) than students in mainstream programs. These factors are all motivational in nature, and they make a lot more sense for evaluating bilingual education than do reading scores and syntax measures. They make clear that language acquisition is not the most important aspect of bilingual education.

But effective instruction also focuses on language development, both L1 and L2. And this brings us to the issue of ESL instruction. The integrative approach to language development is supported both by experience and by theory. The Canadian immersion programs were founded in the belief that young students will never learn a second language well unless it becomes the medium of instruction (Lambert and Tucker 1972), and the experience so far has borne this out. There is, however, a distinction between immersion and submersion programs (Cohen and Swain 1976). The Canadian immersion programs are maintenance programs with the instruction split half and half in French and English. The US submersion programs ignore the fact that the children do not know English and allow them to sink or swim. Most US immersion programs are misnomers which operate only in English with a combination language arts/ESL approach. It is doubtful that a program for middle class mainstream Canadian children can successfully be adopted to the needs of children of subordinate ethnic groups in the United States.

We believe on the basis of other experience that an integrative approach is necessary for language learning at the elementary level. That belief does not necessarily invalidate ESL instruction. As a matter of fact, *any* Language Arts development in English in a bilingual program is plain and simple instruction in English as a second language. All the activities of vocabulary development in English which permeate many BE case studies are instances of successful ESL instruction. Why then are ESL and bilingual education sometimes considered mutually exclusive?

Rather than question whether an integrative approach is better than ESL instruction, one should ask whether children in a bilingual program, which of course means an integrative approach, stand to profit from a formal component in language learning. Some will answer that negatively. Terrell (1981) claims that sentences which are taught to children to illustrate rules or grammar will not help them use the rule in speech. Others reserve judgement. McLaughlin states:

> As children mature, however, they are more capable of dealing abstractly with language. Older children may profit from instruction that involve rule-isolation and attention to grammatical usage (Canale and Swain 1979; Gadalla 1981). There has been little research on this particular issue, but anecdotal evidence suggests that older children do make use of

grammatical information and profit from instruction that focuses on grammatical usage. (1982: 30-31)

I think Terrell's position is overstated. In fact, learning to read in the mother tongue contains a multitude of rule-oriented activities, and there is evidence that children switch from a semantic language orientation to formal analysis about the time they enter school (Galambos 1982). If children can process rule-oriented explanations in the L1, they probably can do it in the L2 as well, but as McLaughlin says, there is little research on this issue. Until such research is carried out, common sense would seem to dictate an integrative approach with a formal ESL-component, a practice which is prevalent among effective teachers.

There is also the question of whether a modified language arts program for ESL purposes in a monolingual English program can substitute for bilingual education. The answer to that question is the core argument for the BE movement in the United States. This paper is not the place for an exhaustive answer, and the issue is more complicated than we thought ten years ago. Baker and de Kanter (1981) in their much discussed report argue for an ESL approach on the basis of evaluative data from BE programs. I have argued repeatedly that one cannot just examine the programs but that one must also take into account the social conditions (Paulston 1975, 1980a). It seems, that in social circumstances which do not favor rapid language shift, children from subordinate ethnic groups at the lower rungs of the social structure in fact do better in bilingual programs. Swain and Cummins (1979) also support the same argument but on the basis of linguistic factors. Cummins claims that the support of the child's first language is needed for effective L2 acquisition and socio-cognitive growth (Cummins 1976, 1982).

4. Methods for Teaching ESL

I was surprised to find some twenty teachers at a workshop in Texas assure me unanimously that audio-lingual techniques, such as choral substitution, repetition, and transformation drills, work in the classroom and that the children learn from them. Although I find it very surprising that doing mechanical substitution drills with elementary school children would work, I am loathe to contradict the judgement of experienced classroom teachers. We know very little about language teaching methodology at the elementary level. (For practical considerations, see Pialorsi 1974; Saville-Troike 1976; von Maltitz 1975.)

At the adult level (or post-puberty or post-critical period) there is general agreement on a communicative approach to language teaching (Canale and Swain 1979) with the major argument that the focus of language teaching should be on language use rather than on language form. This is of course what happens in a bilingual education program, but it also can (and I would add should) happen in a good ESL program (Murphy 1978). In my opinion the ESL component of BE programs has been seriously neglected. When children come from multiple language backgrounds, it is not possible to implement bilingual programs of instruction. At such times, a good ESL program is a lot more helpful than a regular program (Scudder 1979).

The question of age also influences preferred methods of L2 teaching. Scholars do not agree on critical period issues, but adults (past puberty) seem in some regards to learn an L2 differently than children. In his study of the impact of BE programs, Huang (1980) found that the majority of High School teachers favored ESL program over BE programs in helping High School students with limited English proficiency improve English language skills. There has been an unfortunate tendency among BE proponents to categorically criticize an ESL approach, but such criticism may be premature as ESL may be more effective than it has been given credit for.

5. Conclusion

Most BE program evaluation research compares BE programs with regular, unmodified monolingual programs. I suspect that this dearth of research is founded on ideological grounds. Many BE proponents regard ESL with misgivings. I would expect that a good ESL program, with a bilingual teacher, who code-alternated in English and the children's L1 for purposes of explanation, would be quite efficient for English learning purposes. That is after all how children in Europe learn English as a foreign language. But we don't know, and until we know more about an ESL approach, we need to be judicious in our conclusions. We gain nothing with unsupportable claims.

Note

1. The SBIF study identifies three underlying principles of the effective integrative approach in order to meet the two major goals of bilingual education: attainment of English language proficiency and growth in academic skills. The three principles are: 1. The recognition of the interaction between acquisition of English-language proficiency and academic skills. 2. The use of some L1 to ensure understanding of the intent of instruction. 3. The critical role of the bilingual teacher in using both L1 and L2, focusing on language-development, and using cues from the child's culture.

References

Abdulaziz, M.H. 1971. "Tanzania's National Language Policy". *Language and Social Change* ed. by W.H. Whiteley, London: OUP.

Abdulaziz, M.H. 1980. "The Ecology of Tanzanian National Language Policy". *Language in Tanzania* ed. by E.C. Polomé and C.P. Hill, 139-175. London: OUP.

Abdulaziz, M.H. 1985. "Aspects of Lexical and Semantic Elaboration in the Process of Modernization of Swahili". *Swahili Language and Society* ed. by J. Maw. Wien: Beitrage Zur Afrikanistik.

Academic Excellence Project Awarded. 1989 *National Clearinghouse for Bilingual Education Forum* 12.4.

Academy for Educational Development and the Edward W. Hazen Foundation. 1982. "A New Direction for Bilingual Education in the 1980's". *Focus* 10.1-4. National Clearinghouse for Bilingual Education.

Adams, M.A. 1978. "Methodology for Examining Second Language Acquisition". In Hatch, ed., 1978.277-296.

Albino-Cordero, H.P. 1981. An Investigation of the Effects of Bilingual and Non-Bilingual School Programs on Pupil Adjustment. Ph.D. diss., University of Connecticut.

Allardt, E. & C. Starck. 1981. *Språkgränser och samhällsstruktur. Finlandssvenskarna i ett jämförande perspektiv.* Stockholm: Almqvist and Wiksell.

Andrezejewski, B.W. 1974. "The Introduction of a National Orthography for Somali". *ALS* 15.199-203.

Andrezejewski, B.W. 1980. "The Use of Somali in Mathematics and Science". *Baund* 63.

Andrezejewski, B.W. 1983. "Language Reform in Somalia and the Modernization of the Somali Vocabulary". *Language Reform* ed. by I. Fodor, 69-84. Buske Verlag: Hamburgh.

Annamalai, E., ed. 1980. *Bilingualism and Achievement in School.* Mysore: Central Institute of Indian Languages.

Appel, R. & P. Muysken. 1987. *Language Contact and Bilingualism.* London: Edward Arnold.

Arnaldi de Olmeda, C. 1976. *Claves de Reconocimiento en la Enseñanza de la Lectura.* Río Piedras, Puerto Rico: Ed. Cultural.

Au, K.H. 1981. "The Comprehension-Oriented Reading Lesson: Relationships to Proximal Indices of Achievement". *Educational Perspectives* 20.13-15.

Au, K.H., & C. Jordan. 1981. "Teaching Reading to Hawaiian Children: Finding a Culturally Appropriate Solution". *Culture and the Bilingual Classroom: Studies in Classroom Ethnography* ed. by H. Trueba, G. Guthrie and K. Au, 139-152. Rowley, Mass.: Newbury House.

Australia. 1984. *A National Language Policy*. Report of the Senate Committee on Education and the Arts. Canberra: Australian Government Publishing Service.

L'Avenir du Luxembourg. 1988. No. 94, 7. "150 ans d'indépendance du Grand-Duché de Luxembourg".

Baetens Beardsmore, H. 1986. *Bilingualism: Basic Principles*. Clevedon and Philadelphia: Multilingual Matters.

Baetens Beardsmore, H. & J. Kohls. 1988. "Immediate Pertinence in the Acquisition of Multilingual Proficiency: The European Schools". *The Canadian Modern Language Review* 44.680-701.

Baetens Beardsmore, H. & M. Swain. 1985. "Designing Bilingual Education: Aspects of Immersion and 'European School' Models". *Journal of Multilingual and Multicultural Development* 6.1-15.

Bain, B. 1974. "Toward a General Theory". *Bilingualism, Biculturalism, and Education: Proceedings from the Conference at College Universitaire Saint Jean, Edmonton* ed. by S.T. Carey. Alberta: The University of Alberta.

Baker, K. 1987. "Comment on Willig's 'A Meta-Analysis of Selected Studies in the Effectiveness of Bilingual Education'". *Review of Educational Research* 57.351-362.

Baker, K.A. & A.A. de Kanter. 1981. *Effectiveness of Bilingual Education: A Review of the Literature*. Washington, D.C.: Office of Planning, Budget and Evaluation, U.S. Department of Education.

Baker, K.A. & A.A. de Kanter. 1983. *Bilingual Education: A Reappraisal of Federal Policy*. Lexington, Mass.: Lexington Books.

Barr, J. 1985. *Understanding Children's Spelling*. Edinburgh: The Scottish Council for Research in Education.

Barth, F. 1969. "Introduction". In Barth, ed., 1969.9-38.

Barth, F., ed. 1969. *Ethnic Groups and Boundaries. The Social Organization of Culture Difference*. Oslo.

Barthes, R. 1953 [1972]. *Le Degré zéro de l'écriture*. Paris: Editions du Seuil.

Barthes, R. 1970. *S/Z*. Paris: Editions du Seuil.

Batibo, H.M. 1986. The English Language Teaching and Learning in Tanzanian Primary Schools. Unpublished manuscript.

Becker, W. & R. Gersten. 1982. "A Follow-up of Follow Through: The Later Effects of the Direct Instruction Model on Children in the Fifth and Sixth Grades". *American Educational Research Journal* 19.75-92.

Ben-Zeev, S. 1977. "The Influence of Bilingualism on Cognitive Strategy and Cognitive Development". *Child Development* 48, 1,009-1,018.

Bender, M.L., J.D. Bowen, R.L. Cooper & C.A. Ferguson, eds. 1976. *Language in Ethiopia*. London: OUP.

Bennett, A.T. & P. Pedraza. 1984. "Discourse, Consciousness, and Literacy in a Puerto Rican Neighborhood". *Language and Power* ed. by C. Kramarae, M. Schulz and W. O'Barr, 243-259. Beverly Hills, Ca.: Sage Publications.

Bennett, W.J. 1988. *The Condition of Bilingual Education in the Nation: 1988.* A Report to Congress and the President.

Bensman, D. 1987. "Quality Education in the Inner City: The Story of the Central Park East Schools". New York: Community School Board, District #4.

Bentley, P. 1987. "The Development of Writing Profiles". *Primary Teaching Studies* 3.91-97.

Benton, R.A. 1979. *Who Speaks Maori in New Zealand?* Wellington: New Zealand Council for Educational Research.

Benton, R.A. 1981. *The Flight of the Amokura: Oceanic Languages and Formal Education in the South Pacific.* Wellington: NZCER.

Benton, R.A. 1985. *Bilingual Education Programmes Evaluation 1984-5: Final Report.* Wellington: NZCER.

Benton, R.A. 1988. *The Matawaia Declaration: Some Educational and Administrative Implications.* Wellington: NZCER

Benton, R.A. 1990. "Biculturalism in Education: Policy and Practice under the Fourth Labour Government". In Boston and Holland, eds., 1990.192-212.

Berger, P. & T. Luckmann. 1966. *The Social Construction of Reality.* London: Allen Lane.

Betances, S., R.R. Fernández & L.A. Baez. November 1981. Hispanics, Educational Policies, and the Politics of Bilingual Education. Typescript.

Bethell, T. 1979. "Against Bilingual Education". *Harper's.* February.

Bilingual Education Act (April 28, 1988). Public Law 100-297.

Bilingual Educator Becomes Director of OBEMLA. 1989. *National Association for Bilingual Education News* 13.4,6.

Boggs, S.T. 1985. *Speaking, Relating, and Learning: A Study of Hawaiian Children at Home and at School.* Norwood, NJ: Ablex Publishing Corp.

Boos-Nunning, U. & M. Hohmann. 1989. "The Educational Situation of Migrant Workers' Children in the Federal Republic of Germany". In Eldering and Kloprogge, eds., 1989.39-59.

Boston, J. & M. Holland, eds. 1990. *The Fourth Labour Government* (second edition). Auckland: Oxford University Press.

Bourdieu, P. 1975. "Le Langage autorisé. Note sur les conditions sociales de l'efficacité du discours rituel". *Actes de la Recherche en Sciences Sociales,* 183-190.

Bourdieu, P. 1977. "L'Economie des échanges linguistiques". *Langue Française* 34. 17-34.

Bourdieu, P. 1979. *La Distinction.* Paris: Editions de Minuit.

Boyd, S. 1985. *Language Survival. A Study of Language Contact, Language Shift and Language Choice in Sweden* (*Gothenburg Monographs in Linguistics,* 6). Goteborg: University of Gothenburg, Department of Linguistics.

Brophy, J.E. 1979. "Teacher Behavior and its Effects". *Journal of Teacher Education* 71.733-750.

Buckby, M. 1976. "Is Primary French in the Balance?" *Audio-Visual Language Journal* 44.

Burstall, C., M. Jamieson, S. Cohen & M. Hargreaves. 1974. *Primary French in the Balance*. Slough, Bucks: National Educational Research Foundation.

Cahill, D. 1984. *A Greek-English Bilingual Program: Its Implementation in Four Schools*. Coburg: Philip Institute of Technology.

Canale, M. & M. Swain. 1979. *Communicative Approaches to Language Teaching and Testing*. Ontario: Ministry of Education.

Caples-Osorio, R.W. 1979. Educational Aspirations of Selected Mexican American School Children Enrolled in Bilingual Education. Ph.D. diss., Texas A & M University.

Caruso, N., ed. 1989. *Folk's Lore: A History of the Jewish Public Library 1914-1989*. Montreal: The Jewish Public Library. [Text in English & Yiddish.]

Cazden, C. 1979. "Curriculum/Language Contents for Bilingual Education". *Language Development in a Bilingual Setting*, 129-138. Pomona, Ca.: National Multilingual Multicultural Material Development Center.

Cazden, C. 1985. "The ESL Teacher as Advocate". Plenary presentation to the TESOL Conference. New York.

Cazden, C.B. & C. Snow, eds. 1990. *English Plus: Issues in Bilingual Education* (*The Annals of the American Academy of Political and Social Science*, 508). Newbury Park, Ca.: Sage.

Center for Applied Linguistics. 1977. *Bilingual Education: Current Perspectives*. Arlington, Virginia: Center for Applied Linguistics.

Chaturvedi, M.G. & B.V. Mohale. 1976. *Position of Languages in School Curriculum in India*. Delhi: National Council of Educational Research and Training.

Chaturvedi, M.G. & S. Singh, eds. 1981. *Position of Languages in School Curriculum in India*. New Delhi: National Council of Educational Research and Training.

Chavez, R.C. 1980. A Study of Students' Perception in Bilingual/Bicultural Classroom Climates and Non-Bilingual Classroom Climates. Ph.D. diss., New Mexico State University.

Cheng, L. 1987. "English Communicative Competence of Language Minority Children: Assessment and Treatment of Language 'Impaired' Preschoolers". In Trueba, ed., 1987b.49-68.

Chomsky, N. 1987. *On Power and Ideology: The Managua Lectures*. Boston: South End Press.

Churchill, S. 1986. *The Education of Linguistic and Cultural Minorities in the OECD Countries*. Clevedon: Multilingual Matters.

Clahsen, H., J. Meisel & M. Pienemann. 1983. *Deutsch als Zweitsprache: Der Spracherwerb ausländischer Arbeiter*. Tübingen: Naar.

Clark, C. & S. Florio. 1983. "Understanding Writing Instruction: Issues of Theory and Method". *Research on Writing* ed. by P. Mosenthal, 237-264. New York: Longman.

Clover, J. & H. Hutchings. 1986. "The Variety of the Urban Environment". *Primary Teaching Studies* 1.29-37.

Clyne, M. 1967. *Transference and Triggering*. The Hague: Nijhoff.

Clyne, M. 1982. *Multilingual Australia*. Melbourne: River Seine.

Clyne, M. 1985. "Typological and Sociolinguistic Factors in Grammatical Convergence: Differences between German and Dutch in Australia". *Australia Meeting Place of Languages* ed. by M. Clyne, 151-160. Canberra: Pacific Linguistics.

Clyne, M., ed. 1986. *An Early Start. Second Language at the Primary School*. Melbourne: River Seine.

Clyne, M. 1988. "Bilingual Education – What Can We Learn from the Past?" *Australian Journal of Education* 32.93-111.

Cohen, A.D. 1975. *A Sociolinguistic Approach to Bilingual Education: Experiments in the American Southwest*. Rowley, Mass.: Newbury House.

Cohen, A. & M. Swain. 1976. "Bilingual Education: The Immersion Model in the North American Context." *TESOL Quarterly* 10.45-53.

Cohen, A.D. 1983. "Researching Bilingualism in the Classroom". *Bilingualism: Social Issues and Policy Implications* ed. by Andrew W. Miracle Jr., 133-148. Athens, Georgia: University of Georgia Press.

Cohen, A.D. & Luis M. Laosa. 1976. "Second Language Instruction: Some Research Considerations". *Journal of Curriculum Studies* 8.149-165.

Cole, M. 1985. "The Zone of Proximal Development: Where Culture and Cognition Create Each Other". *Culture, Communication and Cognition: Vygotskian Perspectives* ed. by J.V. Wertsch, 146-161. New York: Cambridge University Press.

Cole, M., & S. Scribner. 1974. *Culture and Thought: A Psychological Introduction*. New York: Basic Books.

Collier, V.P. 1987. "Age and Rate of Acquisition of Second Language for Academic Purposes". *TESOL Quarterly* 21.617-641.

Collier, V.P. 1989. "Academic Achievement, Attitudes, and Occupations among Graduates of Two-Way Bilingual Classes". Paper presented at the American Educational Research Association. San Francisco, California.

Commission on International Education: American Council on Education. 1984. *What We Don't Know Can Hurt Us: The Shortfall in International Competence*. Washington, D.C.: American Council on Education.

Conklin, N. & M. Lourie. 1983. *A Host of Tongues*. Free Press.

Cook-Gumperz, J., ed. 1986. *The Social Construction of Literacy*. Cambridge: Cambridge University Press.

Crawford, J. 1989. *Bilingual Education: History, Politics, Theory and Practice*. Trenton, N.J.: Crane Publishing Co.

Csipek, C.M. 1986. A Study of Year 7 Students Learning German by Immersion. B.A. Honors Thesis, Monash University.

Cummins, J. 1976. "The Influence of Bilingualism on Cognitive Growth: A Synthesis of Research Findings and Explanatory Hypothesis". *Working Papers on Bilingualism* 9.1-43.

Cummins, J. 1978. "Metalinguistic Development of Children in Bilingual Education Programs: Data from Irish and Canadian Ukranian-English Programs". *The Fourth Locus Forum 1977* ed. by M. Paradis, 127-138. Columbia, S.C.: Hornbeam Press.

Cummins, J. 1981. "Age on Arrival and Immigrant Second Language Learning in Canada: A Reassessment". *Applied Linguistics* 2.132-149.

Cummins, J. 1982. "Linguistic Interdependence among Japanese and Vietnamese Immigrant Students". *The Measurement of Communicative Proficiency: Models and Applications* ed. by C. Rivera, Washington, D.C.: Center for Applied Linguistics.

Cummins, J. 1984. *Bilingualism and Special Education: Issues in Assessment and Pedagogy.* Clevedon and Philadelphia: Multilingual Matters.

Cummins, J. 1986. "Empowering Minority Students: A Framework for Intervention". *Harvard Educational Review* 56.18-35.

Cummins, J. 1988. "From Multicultural to Anti-Racist Education: An Analysis of Programmes and Policies in Ontario". In Skutnabb-Kangas and Cummins, eds., 1988.127-160.

Cummins, J. 1989. *Empowering Minority Students.* Sacramento, California: California Association for Bilingual Education.

Cummins, J. & M. Swain. 1986. *Bilingualism in Education: Aspects of Theory, Research and Practice.* London: Longman.

Danoff, M.V., G.J. Coles, D.H. McLaughlin & D.J. Reynolds. 1977, 1978. *Evaluation of the Impact of ESEA Title VII Spanish/English Bilingual Education Program.* Palo Alto, California: American Institutes for Research.

Daun, Å. 1984. "Swedishness as an Obstacle in Cross-Cultural Interaction". *Ethnologia Europea* 14.95-109.

Daun, Å. 1989. *Svensk mentalitet.* Stockholm: Raben and Sjögren.

Daun, Å. & B. Ehn, eds. 1988. *Blandsverige.* Stockholm: Carlssons Bokförlag.

Daun, Å., C.-E. Mattlar & E. Alanen. 1989. *Personality Traits Characteristic for Finns and Swedes.* Enthologia Scandinavica.

David, A. 1978. "Bilingual Education: an Alternative Strategy in India". M. Litt. Dis. Hyderabad, India: Central Institute of English and Foreign Languages.

Days, M. 1988. A Class Success in any Language. *Philadelphia Daily News,* March, pp. 4, 27.

Delgado-Gaitan, C. 1986. "Teacher Attitudes on Diversity Affecting Student Socio-Academic Responses: An Ethnographic View". *Journal of Adolescent Research* 1.103-114.

Delgado-Gaitan, C. 1987a. "Mexican Adult Literacy: New Directions for Immigrants". In Goldman and Trueba, eds., 1987.9-32.

Delgado-Gaitan, C. 1987b. "Traditions and Transitions in the Learning Process of Mexican Children: An Ethnographic View". In G. Spindler and L. Spindler, eds., 1987c.333-359.

Delgado-Gaitan, C. 1987c. "Parent Perceptions of School: Supportive Environments for Children". In Trueba, ed., 1987b.131-155.

Delgado-Gaitan, C. 1988a. "The Value of Conformity: Learning to Stay in School". *Anthropology and Education Quarterly* 19.354-381.

Delgado-Gaitan, C. 1988b. "Sociocultural Adjustment to School and Academic Achievement". *Journal of Early Adolescence* 8.63-82.

Delgado-Gaitan, C. 1990. *Literacy for Empowerment: The Role of Parents in Children's Education.* London: Falmer Press.

Delgado-Gaitan, C. & H.T. Trueba. 1991. *Crossing Cultural Borders: Education for Immigrant Families in America.* London: Falmer Press.

Department of Education: Bilingual Education Regulations. 1986 (June 19). *Federal Register,* 22422-22447.

De Vos, G. 1966. "Essential Elements of Caste: Psychological Determinants in Structural Theory". In De Vos and H. Wagatsuma, eds., 332-384.

De Vos, G. 1973. "Japan's Outcastes: The Problem of the Burakumin". *The Fourth World: Victims of Group Oppression* ed. by B. Whitaker, 307-327. NY: Schocken Books.

De Vos, G. 1980. "Ethnic Adaptation and Minority Status". *Journal of Cross-Cultural Psychology* 11.101-124.

De Vos, G. 1983. "Ethnic Identity and Minority Status: Some Psycho-Cultural Considerations". *Identity: Personal and Socio-Cultural* ed. by A. Jacobson-Widding, 90-113. Uppsala: Almquist Wiksell Tryckeri AB.

De Vos, G. 1988. "Differential Minority Achievement in Cross Cultural Perspective: The Case of Korean in Japan and the United States". Paper presented at the American Anthropological Association Meetings, Phoenix, Nov., 1988.

De Vos, G. & H. Wagatsuma. 1966. *Japan's Invisible Race: Caste in Culture and Personality.* Berkeley, CA: University of California Press.

Diaz, R.M. 1985. "The Intellectual Power of Bilingualism". *The Quarterly Newsletter of the Laboratory of Comparative Human Cognition* 7.16-22.

Diaz, S., L. Moll & H. Mehan. 1986. "Sociocultural Resources in Instruction: A Context-Specific Approach". *Beyond Language: Social and Cultural Factors in Schooling Language Minority Students* ed. by Bilingual Education Office, 187-230. Los Angeles, CA: Evaluation, Dissemination and Assessment Center.

Dimas, W.A. 1981. The Relative Effectiveness of the Title VII Bilingual Program and Regular Mainstream Program in Trenton as Revaled by the Students' Grade Point Averages (GPA), Attendance Records and Drop-Out Rates. Ph.D. diss., Rutgers University.

Doblin, J.C. 1986. The Second Language Development of Year 8 Students in a German Partial Immersion Program. B.A. Honors Thesis, Monash University.

Dodson, C. 1981. "A Reappraisal of Bilingual Development and Education: Some Theoretical and Practical Considerations". *Elements of Bilingual Theory* ed. by H. Baetens Beardsmore, 14-27. Brussel: Vrije Universiteit Brussel.

Doyé, P. & D. Lüttge. 1977. *Untersuchungen zum Englishunterricht in der Grundschule.* Braunschweig: Westermann.

Drobizheva, L. & M. Gouboglo. 1986. "Definitions". Appendix to papers given by the authors at the Symposium on Multilingualism: Aspects of Interpersonal and

Intergroup Communication in Plurilingual Societies. Brussels, 13-15 March 1986.

Dulay, H. & M. Burt. 1978. *Why Bilingual Education? A Summary of Research Findings*. San Francisco: Bloomsbury West.

Dumon, W. & L. Michiels. 1987. OCDE, *Système d'observation permanente des migrations, Belgique, Sopemi 1987/2*. Leuven: Sociologisch Onderzoeksinstituut, Departmenent Sociologie.

Dunn, L.M. 1987. *Bilingual Hispanic Children on the U.S. Mainland: A Review of Research on Their Cognitive, Linguistic, and Scholastic Development*. Circle Pines, Minnesota: American Guidance Service.

Dunsky, S., ed. 1961. *Shloime Wiseman Book*. Montreal: Jewish People's School. [Text in Yiddish, Hebrew & English.]

Durkheim, E. 1961. *Moral Education*. Glencoe, IL: Free Press.

Eckstein, A.L. 1986. "Effect of the Bilingual Program on English Language and Cognitive Development". In Clyne, ed., 1986.82-99.

Education Amendment Act 1989 No 156. 1989. Wellington: Government Printer.

Edwards, J. 1984a. *Linguistic Minorities. Policies and Pluralism*. London: Academic Press.

Edwards, J. 1984b. "Language, Diversity and Identity". Edwards 1984.77-310.

Ehn, B. & K-O. Arnstberg. 1980. *Det Osynliga Arvet. Sexton Invandrare Om Sin Bakgrund*. Stockholm: Författarförlaget.

Eldering, L. 1989. "Ethnic Minority Children in Dutch Schools: Underachievement and Its Explanations". In Eldering and Kloprogge, eds., 1989.107-136.

Eldering, L. & J. Kloprogge, eds. 1989. *Different Cultures Same School: Ethnic Minority Children in Europe*. Amsterdam: Swets & Zeitlinger.

Eldering, L. & J. Kloprogge. 1989. "Introduction". In Eldering and Kloprogge, eds., 1989.9-13.

Emeneau, M.B. 1974. "Bilingualism and Structural Borrowing". *Proceedings of the American Philosophical Society* 106.43-44.

Enquête sur les habitudes et besoins langagiers au Grand-Duché de Luxembourg. 1986. Luxembourg: Ministère de l'Education Nationale et de la Jeunesse.

Entin, Yoel. 1946. "Di naye yidishe dertsiung (der onheyb fun di yidishe folksshuln)." *Yidish natsyonaler arbeter farband 1910-1946 (geshikhte un dergreykhungen)*, 145-197. New York: Jewish National Workers Alliance.

Epstein, N. 1977. *Language, Ethnicity and the Schools: Policy Alternatives for Bilingual-Bicultural Education*. Washington, D.C.: The George Washington University Institute for Educational Leadership.

Ericksen, E.P. et al. 1985. *The State of Puerto Rican Philadelphia*. Philadelphia, Pennsylvania: Temple University.

Erickson, F. 1984. "School Literacy, Reasoning, and Civility: An Anthropologist's Perspective". *Review of Educational Research* 54.525-544.

Erickson, F. 1986. "Qualitative Methods in Research on Teaching". In Wittrock, ed., 1986.119-158.

Erickson, F. 1987. "Transformation and School Success: The Politics and Culture of Educational Achievement". *Anthropology and Education Quarterly* 18.335-356.

Even-Zohar, I. 1978. *Papers in Historical Poetics*. Tel Aviv: The Porter Institute for Poetics and Semiotics.

Ferguson, C.A. 1959. "Diglossia". *Word* 15.325-340.

Ferguson, C.A. & S.B. Heath, eds. 1981. *Language in the USA*. Cambridge: Cambridge University Press.

Fernández, R.M. & F. Nielsen. 1986. "Bilingualism and Hispanic Scholastic Achievement: Some Baseline Results". *Social Science Research* 15.43-70.

Ferreiro, E. 1982. "Los Procesos Constructivos de Apropiación de la Escritura". In Ferreiro and Palacios, eds., 1982.128-154.

Ferreiro E. & M. Palacios, eds. 1982. *Nuevas Perspectivas sobre los Procesos de Lectura y Escritura*. México: Siglo XXI.

Ferreiro, E. & A. Teberosky. 1977. *Los Sistemas de Escritura en el Desarrollo del Niño*. México:Siglo XXI.

Fillmore, L.W. & C. Valadez. 1986. "Teaching Bilingual Learners". In Wittrock, ed., 1986.648-685.

Fishman, G. Schweid. Forthcoming. "A Bibliography of Joshua A. Fishman's Work". *The Influence of Language on Culture and Thought: Essays in Honor of Joshua A. Fishman's Sixty-Fifth Birthday* ed. by R. Cooper and B. Spolsky. Berlin: Mouton de Gruyter.

Fishman, J.A. 1949. Bilingualism in a Yiddish School: Some Correlates and Non-Correlates. New York: Yiddish Scientific Institute. Unpublished manuscript.

Fishman, J.A. 1956. *Language Loyalty in the United States*. The Hague: Mouton Co.

Fishman, J.A. 1959. Attitudes of American Jewish Parents toward the Jewish Education of Their Children. Unpublished manuscript. August 1959.

Fishman, J.A., ed. 1968. *Readings in the Sociology of Language*. The Hague: Mouton.

Fishman, J.A. 1970. *Sociolinguistique*. Bruxelles: Labor et Nathan.

Fishman, J.A., ed. 1971a. *Advances in the Sociology of Language*, Vol. I. Mouton: The Hague.

Fishman, J.A. et al. 1971b. *Bilingualism in the Barrio*. Bloomington: Indiana University Publications.

Fishman, J.A., ed. 1972a. *Advances in the Sociology of Language*, Vol. II. The Hague: Mouton.

Fishman, J.A. 1972b. "Societal Bilingualism. Stable and Transitional". *Language in Sociocultural Change*, 135-152. Stanford: Stanford University Press.

Fishman, J.A. 1972c. "The Sociology of Language". *Language in Sociocultural Change*, 1-15. Stanford: Stanford University Press.

Fishman, J.A. 1972d. *The Sociology of Language: An Interdisciplinary Social Science Approach to Language in Society*. Rowley, Mass.: Newbury House.

Fishman, J.A. 1974. Language and Culture in the Globah Community. Lecture. Albuquerque, New Mexico.

Fishman, J.A. 1976a. *Bilingual Education: An International Sociological Perspective*. Rowley, Mass.: Newbury House.

Fishman, J.A. 1976b. "Bilingual Education: What and Why?" *English as a Second Language in Bilingual Education* ed. by K. Twaddell. Washington, D.C.: TESOL.

Fishman, J.A. 1977a. "Bilingual Education: The State of Social Science Inquiry". *Papers in Applied Linguistics, Bilingual Education Series.* Arlington, VA: Center for Applied Linguistics.

Fishman, J.A. 1977b. "The Social Science Perspective: Keynote". *Bilingual Education: Current Perspectives. Social Science*, 1-49. Washington, D.C.: Center for Applied Linguistics.

Fishman, J.A. 1977c. "The Sociology of Bilingual Education". In Spolsky and Cooper, eds., 1977.94-105.

Fishman, J.A. 1978a. "A Gathering of Vultures, the 'Legion of Decency' and Bilingual Education in the U.S.A". *NABE* 2.13-16.

Fishman, J.A. 1978b. "Positive Bilingualism: Some Overlooked Rationales and Forefathers". *Georgetown Roundtable on Languages and Linguistics* ed. by James E. Alatis, 42-52.

Fishman, J.A. 1978c. "Talking about Bilingual Education". *Newsletter* (BESC) 5.1-2.

Fishman, J.A., ed. 1978d. *Advances in the Study of Societal Multilingualism.* The Hague: Mouton.

Fishman, J.A. 1979. "Bilingual Education: What and Why?" In Trueba and Barnett-Mizrahi, eds., 1979.11-19.

Fishman, J.A. 1980a. "Ethnic Community Mother Tongue Schools in the USA: Dynamics and Distributions". *International Migration Review* 14.235-247.

Fishman, J.A. 1980b. "Minority Language Maintenance and the Ethnic Mother Tongue School". *Modern Language Journal* 64.167-173.

Fishman, J.A. 1981a. "Attracting a Following to High-Culture Functions for a Language of Everyday Life: The Role of the Tshernovits Language Conference in the 'Rise of Yiddish'". In Fishman, ed., 1981d.369-394.

Fishman, J.A. 1981b. "Language Policy: Past, Present and Future". *Language in the USA*. In Ferguson and Heath, eds., 1981.516-526.

Fishman, J.A., ed. 1981c. "The Need for Language Planning in the United States". *Profession 81* (Modern Languages Association), 34-36.

Fishman, J.A., ed. 1981d. *Never Say Die! A Thousand Years of Yiddish in Jewish Life and Letters.* Berlin: Walter de Gruyter.

Fishman, J.A. 1982. "Sociolinguistic Foundations of Bilingual Education". *Bilingual Review / La Revista Bilingüe* 9.1-35.

Fishman, J.A. 1985a. "Non-English Language Ethnic Community Schools in the USA: Instruments of more than Literacy and less than Literacy". *Working Papers on Migrant and Intercultural Studies*, No. 1, July.

Fishman, J.A., ed. 1985b. *Readings in the Sociology of Jewish Languages.* Leiden: E.J. Brill.

Fishman, J.A. 1987a. *Ideology, Society and Language: The Odyssey of Nathan Birnbaum*. Ann Arbor: Karoma.

Fishman, J.A. 1987b "Language Spread and Language Policy for Endangered Languages". *Language Spread and Language Policy: Issues, Implications and Case Studies* (Georgetown University Round Table on Languages and Linguistics 1987). Washington D.C: Georgetown University Press.

Fishman, J.A. 1988a. "'English Only' – Its Ghosts, Myths and Dangers". *International Journal of the Sociology of Language* 74.125-140.

Fishman, J.A. 1988b. *The Rise and Fall of the Ethnic Revival*. Berlin: Mouton de Gruyter.

Fishman, J.A. 1988c. "The Significance of the Ethnic-Community Mother-Tongue School". *The Rise and Fall of the Ethnic Revival*, 363-376.

Fishman, J.A. 1989a. "Societal Factors Predictive of Linguistic Homogeneity/Heterogeneity at the Inter-Polity Level". *Cultural Dynamics* 1.414-437.

Fishman, J.A. 1989b. *Language and Ethnicity in Minority Sociolinguistic Perspective*. Clevedon, Avon: Multilingual Matters Ltd.

Fishman, J.A. Forthcoming, a. "My Life from My Work; My Work from My Life". *First Person Singular*, Vol. II, ed. by Konrad Koerner. Amsterdam: John Benjamins.

Fishman, J.A. Forthcoming, b. "Prospects for Reversing Language Shift in Australia: Evidence from its Aboriginal and Immigrant Languages". *Reversing Language Shift; Theory and Practice of Assistance to Threatened Languages*. Clevedon: Multilingual Matters.

Fishman, J.A. Forthcoming, c. *Yiddish: Turning to Life: Sociolinguistic Studies and Interpretations*. Amsterdam: John Benjamins.

Fishman, J.A., R.L. Cooper & A.W. Conrad. 1977. *The Spread of English*. Rowley, Mass.: Newbury House.

Fishman, J.A. & J. Lovas. 1970. "Bilingual Education in a Sociolinguistic Perspective". *TESOL Quarterly* 4.215-222.

Fishman, J.A. & J. Lovas. 1972 [1970]. "Bilingual Education in a Sociolinguistic Perspective". In Spolsky, ed., 1972.83-93.

Fishman, J.A. & V. Nahirny. 1964. "The Ethnic Group School and Mother Tongue Maintenance in the United States". *Sociology of Education* 37.306-317.

Fishman, J.A. & R. Solano. 1989. "Societal Factors Predictive of Linguistic Homogeneity/Heterogeneity at the Inter-Polity Level". *Cultural Dynamics* 1.414-437.

Frankel, J. 1981. *Prophecy and Politics: Socialism, Nationalism & the Russian Jews, 1862-1917*. Cambridge: Cambridge University Press.

Freire, P. 1986 [1970]. *Pedagogy of the Oppressed*. New York: Continuum.

Fry, J.J.S. 1981. English Language Acquisition through Social Interaction in Classrooms in which Children Speak Various Languages. Ph.D. diss., Michigan State University.

Fuchs, C.L., ed. 1980. *Hundert yor yidishe un hebreishe literatur in Kanade*. Montreal: Chaim Leib Fuchs Book Fund Committee.

Gaarder, A.B. 1976. "Linkages between Foreign Language Teaching and Bilingual Education". *English as a Second Language in Bilingual Education* ed. by J.E. Alatis and K. Twaddell, 199-203. Washington D.C.: TESOL.

Galambos, S.J. 1982. "Development of Metalinguistics Awareness in Bilingual and Monolingual Children". Paper presented at the University of Pittsburgh.

García, H.D.C. 1981. *Bilingualism, Confidence and College Achievement*. Center for the Social Organization of Schools: John Hopkins University.

García, O. 1990. "Interview with Joshua Fishman: Schooling, Bilingual Education, Sociology of Language and Yiddish". Unpublished interview, 8/23/90.

García, O. & R. Otheguy. 1987. "The Bilingual Education of Cuban-American Children in Dade County's Ethnic Schools". *Language and Education* 1.83-95.

García, O. & R. Otheguy, eds. 1989. *English across Cultures: Cultures across English. A Reader in Cross-Cultural Communication.* Berlin: Mouton de Gruyter.

General Accounting Office (GAO). 1987. *Bilingual Education: A New Look at the Research Evidence.* U.S. General Accounting Office Briefing Report to the Chairman, Committee of Education and Labor, House of Representatives.

Genesee, F. 1987. *Learning through Two Languages: Studies of Immersion and Bilingual Education.* Cambridge, Mass.: Newbury.

Gersten, R. 1985. "Structured Immersion for Language Minority Students: Results of a Longitudinal Evaluation". *Educational Evaluation and Policy Analysis* 7.187-196.

Gersten, R. & J. Woodward. 1985a. "A Case for Structured Immersion". *Educational Leadership*, September, 75-79.

Gersten, R. & J. Woodward. 1985b. "Response to Santiago". *Educational Leadership*, September, 83-84.

Ghosh, R.N. 1980. "Indian Bilingualism". *Bilingual Education* ed. by L.K. Boey, 36-46. Singapore University Press: SEAMEO Regional Language Center.

Glazer, N. & J. Cummins. 1985. "Viewpoints on Bilingual Education". *Equity and Choice* 2.47-52.

Glenn, C. 1990. "How to Integrate Bilingual Education without Tracking". *The School Administrator*, May, 1990.28-31.

A Glossary of Bilingual-Education Terms. 1987. *Education Week*, p. 29, April 1.

Goldman, S. & H. Trueba, eds. 1987. *Becoming Literate in English as a Second Language: Advances in Research and Theory.* Norwood, NJ: Ablex Corporation.

Goldsmith, E.S. 1976. *Architects of Yiddishism at the Beginning of the Twentieth Century: A Study in Jewish Cultural History.* Rutherford: Fairleigh Dickinson University Press & Associated University Press.

Gonzalez, A. & B.P. Sibayan, eds. 1988. *Evaluating Bilingual Education in the Philippines (1974-1985).* Manila: Linguistic Society of the Philippines.

González, J. 1978. "The Status of Bilingual Education Today: Un vistazo y un repaso". *NABE* 2.13-20.

Goodman, K. 1982. "El Proceso de Lectura: Consideraciones a través de las lenguas y del desarrollo". In Ferreiro and Palacios, eds., 1982.13-28.

Gorman, T.P., ed. 1970. *Language in Education in Eastern*. Chicago: University of Chicago Press.

Gouboglo, M.N., A. Tabouret-Keller & R. Kinnear, eds. Forthcoming. *Language and Ethnicity: East-West Experiences and Perspectives*. Wien: European Coordination Centre for Research and Documentation in the Social Sciences.

Grace, G. 1990. "Labour and Education: The Crises and Settlements of Education Policy". In Boston and Holland, eds., 1990.

Greene, M. 1986. "In Search of a Critical Pedagogy". *Harvard Educational Review* 56.427-441.

Grift, W. van de & N.A.J. Lagerweij, eds. 1988. *Hoe verbeteren we onderwijs?* De Lier: Academisch Boeken Centrum.

Grosjean, F. 1982. *Life with Two Languages: An Introduction to Bilingualism*. Cambridge, Mass.: Harvard University Press.

Gumperz, J. 1961. "Speech Variation and the Study of Indian Civilization". *American Anthropologist* 63.976-988.

Gumperz, J. 1962. "Types of Linguistic Communities". *Anthropological Linguistics* 4.28-40.

Gumperz, J. 1964. "Linguistic and Social Interaction in Two Communities". *American Anthropologist* 66.37-53.

Gumperz, J., ed. 1982. *Language and Social Identity*. Cambridge, MA: Cambridge University Press.

Gumperz, J. 1986. "Interactional Sociolinguistics in the Study of Schooling". *The Social Construction of Literacy* ed. by J. Cook-Gumperz, 45-68. Cambridge, MA: Cambridge University Press.

Gumperz, J., & D. Hymes, eds. 1964. *The Ethnography of Communication*. (*American Anthropologists*, 66).

Gumperz, J. & D. Hymes, eds. 1972. *Directions in Socio-Linguistics: The Ethnography of Communication*. New York: Holt, Rinehart, and Winston.

Guthrie, G.P. 1985. *A School Divided: An Ethnography of Bilingual Education in a Chinese Community*. Hillsdale, New Jersey: Lawrence Erlbaum.

Hagman, T. & J. Lahdenperä. 1988. "Nine Years of Finnish-Medium Education in Sweden – What Happens Afterwards? The Education of Minority Children in Botkyrka". *Minority Education. From Shame to Struggle* ed. by T. Skutnabb-Kangas and J. Cummins, 328-335. Clevedon: Multilingual Matters.

Hakuta, K. 1986. *Mirror of Language: The Debate on Bilingualism*. New York: Basic Books.

Hakuta, K. 1987. "Introduction". At the Harvard Institute on Bilingual Education: Research to Policy to Practice. Cambridge, Mass.

Hakuta, K. Forthcoming. "Language and Cognition in Bilingual Children". *Advances in Bilingual Education*. Los Angeles: UCLA, CLEAR.

Hamayan, E.V. 1986. "Is it really Bilingual Education? An Examination of Program Models". Paper presented at the 15th Annual International Bilingual/Bicultural Education Conference. Chicago: National Association for Bilingual Education.

Hamers, J. & M. Blanc. 1989. *Bilinguality and Bilingualism*. Cambridge: Cambridge University Press.

Hankey, G. & R. Brightmore. 1987. "Najero: A Record of His Development as a Writer". *Primary Teaching Studies* 3.84-90.

Harley, B. & M. Swain. 1984. "The Interlanguage of Immersion Students and Its Implications for Second Language Teaching". *Interlanguage* ed. by A. Davies, C. Criper and A.P.R. Howatt, 291-311. Edinburgh: University of Edinburgh Press.

Harley, B., P. Allen, J. Cummins & M. Swain. 1990. *The Development of Second Language Proficiency*. Cambridge: Cambridge University Press.

Hatch, E.M., ed. 1978. *Second Language Acquisition*. Rowley, Mass.: Newbury House.

Haugen, E. 1953. *The Norwegian Language in America*. Philadelphia: University of Pennsylvania Press.

Heath, S.B. 1981. "English in Our Language Heritage". In Ferguson and Heath, eds., 1981.6-20.

Heath, S.B. 1982. "What no Bedtime Story Means: Narrative Skills at Home and School". *Language and Society* 11.49-76.

Heath, S.B. 1983. *Ways With Words*. Cambridge, MA: Cambridge University Press.

Hechinger, F.M. 1987. "Cultural isolation". *New York Times*, January 13.

Henderson, K.J. 1974. "Bilingual Schooling: Meeting a Basic Need". *The Christian Science Monitor*, November 11.

Henderson, K.J. 1978. "Bilingual Education: Good or Bad?" *Wisconsin State Journal*, June 15.

Het onderwijs in het Fries op de basisschool: Stand van zaken 1988-1989. 1989. Zoetermeer: Ministerie van Onderwijs en Wetenschappen.

"Hindrance?" *The Philadelphia Inquirer*, October 6.

Hoffman, F. & J. Berlinger. 1978. *Die Neue Deutsche Mundartdichtung*. Hildesheim, New York: Olms.

Holmstrand, L. 1982. *English in the Elementary School*. Uppsala: Education Department, Uppsala Technical College.

Hornberger, N.H. 1988a. *Bilingual Education and Language Maintenance: A Southern Peruvian Quechua Case*. Providence, Rhode Island: Foris Publications.

Hornberger, N.H. 1988b. "Iman Chay?: Quechua Children in Peru's Schools". In Trueba and Delgado-Gaitan, eds., 1988.99-117.

Hornberger, N.H. 1989. "Continua of Biliteracy". *Review of Educational Research* 59(3).271-296.

Hornberger, N.H. 1990. "Creating Successful Learning Contexts for Biliteracy". *Teachers College Record* (Winter).

"House Boosts Title VII Funding for Developmental Bilingual Education and Graduate Fellowships". 1989. *National Association for Bilingual Education News* 13.1,10.

Housen, A. & H. Baetens Beardsmore. 1987. "Curricular and Extra-Curricular Factors in Multilingual Education". *Studies in Second Language Acquisition* 9. 83-102.

Houtveen, Th. 1988. "Onderwijsbegeleiding en onderwijsverbetering". *Hoe verbeteren we onderwijs?* ed. by W. van de Grift and N.A.J. Lagerweij, o.c., 139-173.

Huang, B-D. 1980. The Impact of Bilingual-Bicultural Education Programs on an Urban High School: A Descriptive Case Study. Ph.D. diss., Columbia University Teachers College.

Huot, D. 1988. *Etude comparative de différents modes d'enseignement/apprentissage d'une language seconde; Aspects de l'intégration des pédagogies des langues maternelle et seconde pour un public adulte.* Berne: Peter Lang.

Ianco-Worrall, A.D. 1972. "Bilingualism and Cognitive Development". *Child Development* 43. 1,390-1,400.

Iglesias, L. 1979. *Didáctica de la Libre Expresión.* Buenos Aires, Argentina: Ediciones Pedágogicas.

Imberger, B. 1986. "Children from German-Speaking Families". In Clyne, ed., 1986. 112-27.

Jacobson, R. 1979. "Can Bilingual Teaching Techniques Reflect Bilingual Community Behaviors?" In Padilla, ed., 1979.483-497.

Jacobson, R. 1987. "Allocating Two Languages as a Key Feature of Bilingual Methodology". Paper presented at the 16th Annual International Bilingual/Bicultural Education Conference. Denver: National Association for Bilingual Education.

Jayasuriya, D.L. 1986. "Ethnic Minorities and Issues of Social Justice in Contemporary Australian Society". Keynote Address at Australian Adult Education Conference. "Learning for Social Justice". Australian National University, Canberra, 7-9 December.

Jensen, A.R. 1981. *Straight Talk about Mental Tests.* New York: The Free Press.

Jeppesen, K.J. 1989. *Unge Indvandrere. En undersogelse af andengeneration fra Jugoslavien, Tyrkiet of Pakistan. (Rapport,* 89.6). Copenhagen: Socialforskningsinstituttet.

Johnson, D.M. 1980. Peer Tutoring, Social Interaction, and the Acquisition of English as a Second Language by Spanish-Speaking Elementary School Children. Ph.D. diss., Stanford University.

Jordan, D. 1984. "The Social Construction of Identity. The Aboriginal Problem". *The Australian Journal of Education* 28.3.

Jordan, D. 1988. "Rights and Claims of Indigenous People: Education and the Reclaiming of Identity". In Skutnabb-Kangas and Cummins, eds., 1988.189-222.

Kachru, B.B. 1983. *The Indianization of English.* New Delhi: Oxford University Press.

Kachru, B.B. & S.N. Sridhar, eds. 1978. *Aspects of Sociolinguistics in South Asia (International Journal of the Sociology of Language,* 16). The Hague: Mouton.

Kage, J. 1961. "Tsvey hundert yor yidishe dertsiung in Montreal". Dunsky 1961. 160-180.

Kallen, H. 1956. *Cultural Pluralism and the American Idea: An Essay in Social Philosophy*. Philadelphia: University of Pennsylvania.

Kanungo, G.B. 1962. *The Language Controversy in Indian Education*. University of Chicago: The Comparative Education Center.

Keller, G.D. & K.S. van Hooft. 1982. "A Chronology of Bilingualism and Bilingual Education in the United States". *Bilingual Education for Hispanic Students in the United States*, ed. by J.A. Fishman and G.D. Keller. New York: Teachers College Press.

Kern, R., ed. 1989. *Deutsch als Umgangs -und Muttersprache in den europaeischen Gemeinschaften*, Eupen: Ined.

Kessler, C. & M.E. Quinn. 1987. "Language Minority Children's Linguistic and Cognitive Creativity". *Journal of Multilingual and Multicultural Development* 8.173-186.

Khubchandani, L.M. 1983. *Plural Languages, Plural Cultures*. Hawaii: East-West Center.

Kim, K. K-O, K. Lee & T-Y. Kim. 1981. *Korean Americans in Los Angeles: Their Concerns and Language Maintenance*. Los Alamitos, Ca.: National Center for Bilingual Research.

Kjolseth, R. 1972. "Bilingual Education Programs in the United States: For Assimilation or Pluralism?" In Spolsky, ed., 1972.94-121.

Kloss, H. 1976. "Abstand und Ausbausprachen". *Zur Theorie des Dialekts* ed. by J. Gösche et al., 301-322. Wiesbaden: Steiner.

Kloss, H. 1978, *Die Entwicklung neuer germanischer Kultursprachen*. Düsseldorf: Schwann.

Kloss, H. 1983. "Europas Sprachprobleme Heute und Morgen". *Regionalismus in Europa*, 125-133. Munich: Bayerische Landeszentrale.

Kloss, H. & G.D. McConnel. 1984. *Composition linguistique des nations du monde*. Volume 5: *L'Europe et L'URSS*. Québec: Presses de l'Université Laval.

Kloss, H. & A. Verdoodt. 1969. *Research Possibilities on Group Bilingualism, A Report*. B-18, Québec: CIRB, Université Laval.

Kothari, D.S. 1970. *Education, Science, and National Development*. Bombay: Asia Publishing House.

Krashen, S.D. 1981. *Second Language Acquisition and Second Language Learning*. Oxford: Pergamon.

Krashen, S.D., R.C. Scarcella & M. Long, eds. 1982. *Child/Adult Differences in Second Language Acquisition*. Rowley, Mass.: Newbury House.

Krashen, S. & D. Biber. 1987. *Bilingual Education in California*. Report prepared for the California Association for Bilingual Education.

Krishnamurti, Bh. 1979. "Language Planning and Development: The Case of Telugu". *Contributions to Asian Studies* 9.38-56.

Krishnamurti, Bh. 1989. "A Profile of Illiteracy in India: Problems and Prospects". Typescript.

Kristeva, Julia. 1969. *Séméotikè: Recherches pour une sémanalyse*. Paris: Editions du Seuil.

Lambert, W.E. 1975. "Culture and Language as Factors in Learning and Education". *Education of Immigrant Students* ed. by A. Wolfgang. Toronto: O.I.S.E.

Lambert, W.E. & D.M. Taylor. 1986. *Cultural and Racial Diversity in the Lives of Urban Americans: The Hamtramck/Pontiac Study*. Preliminary Report. Toronto, Canada: McGill University.

Lambert, W. & R. Tucker. 1972. *Bilingual Education of Children: The St. Lambert Experiment*. Rowley, Mass.: Newbury House.

Lamy, P. 1975. "The Impact of Bilingualism Upon Ethnolinguistic Identity". *Social Studies* 4.172-207.

Larter, S. & M. Cheng. 1984. *Bilingual Education and Bilingualism: A Review of Research Literature*. Toronto, Canada: Toronto Board of Education.

Lau vs. Nichols, 414 U.S. 563 (1974).

Legaretta, D. 1979. "The Effects of Program Models on Language Acquisition by Spanish Speaking Children". *TESOL Quarterly* 13.521-534.

Legarreta-Marcaida, D. 1981. "Effective Use of the Primary Language in the Classroom". *Schooling and Language Minority Students: A Theoretical Framework*, 83-116. Los Angeles: Evaluation, Dissemination, and Assessment Center, California State University.

Leitin, D.D. 1977. *Politics, Language and Thought. Africa*. Nairobi: OUP.

Lessow-Hurley, J. 1990. *The Foundations of Dual Language Instruction*. New York: Longman.

Lieberson, S. & T.J. Curry. 1971. "Language Shift in the United States: Some Demographic Clues". *International Migration Review* 5.125-137.

Liebkind, K. 1984. *Minority Identity and Identification Processes: A Social Psychological Study*. Commentationes Scientiarum Socialium 22, 1984. Helsinki: Societas Scientiarum Fennica.

Liedtke, W.W. & L.D. Nelson. 1968. "Concept Formation and Bilingualism". *Alberta Journal of Educational Research* 14.225-232.

Lightbown, P. & R.H. Halter. 1988. *Evaluation of ESL Learning in Regular and Experimental Programs in Four New Brunswick School Districts*. Montreal: Concordia University TESL Centre (Vol. I: 1985-1986/1986/1987; Vol. 2: 1987-1988).

Lightbown, P. Forthcoming. "Can They Do it Themselves? A Comprehension-Based ESL Course for Young Children." *Proceedings of a Conference on Comprehension-Based Language Teaching* (Ottawa, May 11-13, 1989).

Lindholm, K.J. 1987. "Directory of Bilingual Immersion Programs: Two-Way Bilingual Education for Language Minority and Majority Students". Los Angeles: Center for Language Education and Research. University of California, Los Angeles.

Linet, M. 1989. Analyse des visites d'étude organisées par la Commission des Communautés Européennes et le Bureau Européen pour les langues moins répandues. Diss. Louvain-la-Neuve, Faculté de Philosophie et Lettres.

lo Bianco, J. 1987a. *National Policy on Languages*. Canberra; Australian Government Publishing Service.

lo Bianco, J. 1987b. "Linguistic Interaction in Second Language Classrooms: Italian in Victoria". *Australian Review of Applied Linguistics* 4.172-96.

lo Bianco, J. 1989. *Victoria – Languages Action Plan.* Melbourne: Ministry of Education.

Lyons, J. 1988. "View from D.C.". *National Association for Bilingual Education News* 11.8,10.

Lyons, J. 1989. "The View from Washington". *National Association for Bilingual Education News* 12.2,5,9,10.

Lyons, J. 1990. "The Past and Future Directions of Federal Bilingual-Education Policy". In Cazden and Snow, eds., 1990.66-80.

Mack, M. 1981. The Effect of a Curriculum Designed to Improve the Self-Concept and English Oral Language Skills of Spanish Speaking Migrant Children in First Grade. Ph.D. diss., University of Florida.

Mackey, W.F. 1965. *Language Teaching Analysis.* London: Longman.

Mackey, W.F. 1972 [1970]. "A Typology of Bilingual Education". *Advances in the Sociology of Language* ed. by Joshua A. Fishman, 413-432. The Hague: Mouton.

Mackey, W.F. 1987. "Is Language Teaching a Waste of Time?" Epilogue to Mackey, Loveless et al. 1987.

Mackey, W.F., G. Loveless, P. Louisy & V. Heechung. 1987. *Polychronometric Techniques in Behavior Analysis: Language Teaching* (ICRB Publication B-163). Quebec: International Center for Research on Bilingualism.

Major Civil Rights Report Issued; Developmental Bilingual Education Urged. 1989 *National Association for Bilingual Education News* 13.4.

Maori Language Act 1987 No. 176. Wellington: Government Printer.

Marquand, R. 1987. "Model Bilingual Education". *The Christian Science Monitor*, September 25.

Martin, J. 1978. *The Migrant Presence.* Sydney: Allen and Unwin.

McConnell, G.D. & J.D. Gendron. 1988. *Dimension et mésure de la vitalité linguistique*, G-9, Vol. I. Quebec: CIRB.

McDermott, R. 1987a. "Achieving School Failure: An Anthropological Approach to Illiteracy and Social Stratification". In Spindler, ed., 1987.173-209.

McDermott, R. 1987b. "The Explanation of Minority School Failure, Again". *Anthropology and Education Quarterly* 18.361-364.

McKay, S.L. 1988. "Weighing Educational Alternatives". *Language Diversity: Problem or Resource?* ed. by Sandra McKay and Sau-ling C. Wong, 338-366. Cambridge, Mass.: Newbury House.

McLaughlin, D. 1982. Language Learning in Bilingual Instruction: Literature Review. University of California at Santa Cruz. Unpublished manuscript.

Meestringa, Theun. 1985. *Naar een Schoolwerkplan Fries.* Enschede: Stichting voor Leerplan Ontwikkeling.

Mezzacappa, D. 1987 "Learning in 2 Languages: Advantage or Hindrace?" *The Philadelphia Inquirer.* October 6, 1987.

Milk, R.D. 1980. Variation in Language Use Patterns across Different Group Settings in Two Bilingual Second Grade Classrooms. Ph.D. diss., Stanford University.

Ministère de l'Education du Nouveau-Brunswick. 1990. *An Experiment in Staged Self-Directed Language Acquisition.* New Brunswick.

Minorités (les) linguistiques dans les pays de la Communauté Européenne. 1986. Rapport de synthèse par l'Istituto del l'Encyclopedia italiana, Luxembourg: Office des publications officielles des Communautés Européennes.

Miron, D. 1987. "Sifruyot hayehudim: bein mamashut lemisha'lot lev". *Im lo tihye Yerushalaim: masot 'al hasifrut ha'ivrit beheksher tarbuti-politi,* 93-171. Tel Aviv: Hakibbutz Hameuchad.

Moll, L. & E. Diaz. 1987. "Change as the Goal of Educational Research". *Anthropology and Education Quarterly* 18.300-311.

Morison, S.H. 1990. "A Spanish-English Dual Language Program in New York City". In Cazden and Snow, eds., 1990.160-169.

Mullard, C. 1985. *Race, Power and Resistance.* London: Routledge and Kegan Paul.

Mullard, C. 1988. "Racism, Ethnicism and Etharcy or Not?" In Skutnabb-Kangas and Cummins, eds., 1988.350-378.

Muller, S. 1980. "America's International Illiteracy". *New York Times Higher Education Supplement,* November 11.

Municio, I. 1983. *Hemspråk i förskolan. En undersökning om genomförande.* EIFO-Report 21. Stockholm: EIFO.

Municio, I. 1987. *Från lag til bruk – hemspraksreformens genomförande.* Stockholm Studies in Politics 31. University of Stockholm: Department of Political Studies.

Municio, I. Forthcoming. "Medpart, motpart eller icke-part? Finska föräldrar som brukare i svensk skola". In Peura and Skutnabb-Kangas, eds. In press.

Murphy, B.J. 1978. The Identification of the Components Requisite for the Teaching of English to Primary School Navajo Students: Guidelines for English as a Second Language in Navajo/English Bilingual Education. Ph.D. diss., University of Massachusetts.

Nadkarni, M.V. 1977. "Educational Level and Educational Choice". *Seminar in Sociolinguistics* (no editor). Hyderabad: Telugu Academy.

National Governors' Association. 1989. *America in Transition: The International Frontier.* Report of the Task Force on International Education.

New Language Planning Newsletter. 4.1, September 1989. Mysore: Central Institute of Indian Languages.

New South Wales. 1988. *Report of the Ministerial Working Party on the State Language Policy.* Sydney: Ministerial Working Party on the State Language Policy.

Nielsen, F. & S.J. Lerner. 1982. Language, Skills and School Achievement of Bilingual Hispanics. Unpublished manuscript. Chapel Hill: University of North Carolina.

Norman, P. 1985. "A Sense of Authorship". *Primary Teaching Studies* 1.47-54.

Nurullah, S. & J.P. Nayak, eds. 1964. *A Student's History of Education in India, 1800-1965.* Bombay: Macmillan.

O'Malley, J.M. 1978. "Review of the Evaluation of the Impact of ESEA Title VII Spanish/English Bilingual Education Program". *Bilingual Resources* 1.6-10.

Office of Educational Equity, Massachusetts Board of Education. 1990. *Two-Way Integrated Bilingual Education.*

Office of the Minister of Education. 1988. *Tomorrow's Schools: The Reform of Education Administration in New Zealand.* Wellington: Government Printer.

Ogbu, J. 1974. *The Next Generation: An Ethnography of Education in an Urban Neighborhood.* New York: Academic Press.

Ogbu, J. 1978. *Minority Education and Caste: The American System in Cross-Cultural Perspective.* New York: Academic Press.

Ogbu, J. 1983. "Minority Status and Schooling in Plural Societies". *Comparative Education Review* 27.168-190.

Ogbu, J. 1987a. "Variability in Minority Responses to Schooling: Nonimmigrants vs. Immigrants". In G. Spindler and L. Spindler, eds., 1987c.255-278.

Ogbu, J. 1987b. "Variability in Minority School Performance: A Problem in Search of an Explanation". *Anthropology and Education Quarterly* 18.312-334.

Ogbu, J. 1989. "The Individual in Collective Adaptation: A Framework for Focusing on Academic Underperformance and Dropping out among Involuntary Minorities". *Dropouts from School: Issues, Dilemmas, and Solutions* ed. by L. Weis, E. Farrar and H. Petrie, 181-204. Albany, NY: State University of New York Press.

Otanes, F.T. & B.P. Sibayan. 1969. *Language Policy Survey of the Philippines.* Manila: Language Study Center, Philippine Normal College.

Ovando, C.J. & V.P. Collier. 1985. *Bilingual and ESL Classrooms: Teaching in Multicultural Contexts.* New York: McGraw Hill.

Ozolins, U. 1988. The Politics of Migrant Languages in Australia. Ph.D. Diss., Monash University.

Padilla, R.V., ed. 1979. *Bilingual Education and Public Policy in the United States.* Eastern Michigan University: Bilingual Bicultural Education Programs.

Pandit, P.B. 1977. *Language in a Plural Society.* New Delhi: Devraj Channa Memorial Committee.

Parreren, C.F. van. 1988. *Ontwikkelend onderwijs.* De Lier: Academisch Boeken Centrum.

Pattanayak, D.P. 1971. *Distribution of Languages in India, in States and Union Territories.* Mysore: Central Institute of Indian Languages.

Pattanayak, D.P. 1981. *Multilingualism and Mother-Tongue Education.* Delhi: Oxford University Press.

Pattanayak, D. 1986. "Educational Use of the Mother Tongue". *Language and Education in Multilingual Settings* ed. by B. Spolsky, 5-15. Clevedon and Philadelphia: Multilingual Matters.

Paulston, C.B. 1978 [1975]. "Education in a Bi/Multilingual Setting". *International Review of Education* 24.309-328.

Paulston, C.B. 1975. "Ethnic Relations and Bilingual Education: Accounting for Contradictory Data". *Proceedings of the First Inter-American Conference on Bi-*

lingual Education ed. by R. Troike and N. Modiano, 368-401. Arlington: Center for Applied Linguistics.

Paulston, C.B. 1980a. *Bilingual Education: Theories and Issues.* Rowley, Mass.: Newbury House.

Paulston, C.B. 1980b. *English as a Second Language.* Washington, D.C.: National Education Association.

Peal, E. & W.E. Lambert. 1962. "The Relationship of Bilingualism to Intelligence". *Psychological Monographs* 76, whole no. 546.

Penfield, W. & L. Roberts. 1959. *Speech and Brain Mechanisms.* Princeton: Princeton University Press.

Petrella, R. 1971. *Le Développement régional en Europe.* Paris: Mouton.

Petrella, R. 1978. *La Renaissance des cultures régionales en Europe.* Paris: Editions Entente.

Petri, G. & A. Zrzavy. 1976. *Untersuchungen zur Evaluation des Schulversuchs "Fremdsprachliche Vorschulung".* Graz.

Petrushka, S. 1945. *Mishnayes mit iberzetsung un peyresh in yidish. Seder Zera'im.* Montreal: Northern Printing & Stationery Co.

Peura, M. Forthcoming. "Mobilisering som motstånd". In Peura and Skutnabb-Kangas, eds.

Peura, M. & T. Skutnabb-Kangas, eds. Forthcoming. *"Man kan väl vara tvåländre också"* – *den sverigefinska minoritetens väg fran tystnad till kamp.* Stockholm: Carlssons Förlag.

Philadelphia City Planning Commission. 1986. North Philadelphia Plan (draft). Philadelphia, Pennsylvania. November. Typescript.

Phillipson, R. 1990. *English Language Teaching and Imperialism.* Tronninge, Denmark: Transcultura.

Phillipson, R. & T. Skutnabb-Kangas. 1986. *Linguicism Rules in Education,* 3 volumes. Roskilde: Roskilde University Centre.

Phillipson, R., E. Kellerman, L. Selinker, M. Sharwood Smith & M. Swain, eds. Forthcoming. *Foreign/Second Language Pedagogy Research: A Commemorative Volume for Claus Faerch.* Clevedon: Multilingual Matters.

Piaget, J. 1971. *Science of Education and the Psychology of the Child.* London: Longman.

Pialorsi, F. 1974. *Teaching the Bilingual.* Tucson: University of Arizona Press.

Pifer, A. 1979. *Bilingual Education and the Hispanic Challenge.* New York: Carnegie Corporation.

Pilovsky, A.L. 1986. *Tvishn yo un neyn: yidish un yidish-literatur in Erets-Yisroel 1907-1949.* Tel Aviv: Veltrat far yidish un yidisher kultur.

Pinker, S. 1979. "Formal Models of Language Learning". *Cognition* 1.217-283.

Piven, F.F. & R. Cloward. 1971. *Regulating the Poor: The Functions of Public Welfare.* New York: Vintage.

Pomerantz, I.C., Y. Mark, S. Bercovich & M. Brownstone, eds. 1948. *Shul-pinkes.* Chicago: Sholem Aleichem Folk Institute.

President's Commission on Foreign Language and International Studies. 1979. *Strength Through Wisdom: A Critique of U.S. Capability.* Washington D.C.: U.S. Government Printing Office.

Ramirez, J.D., R. Wolfson & F. Morales. 1985. *Description of Immersion Strategy Programs in the U.S.* Washington, D.C.: US Department of Education.

Ramos, M., J. Aguila & B. Sibayan. 1967. *The Determination and Implementation of Language Policy.* Quezon City: Phillipine Center for Language Study, Alemar-Phoneix.

Rapport van de projectgroep invoering Fries als verplicht vak op de scholen voor gewoon lager onderwijs in de provincie Friesland. 1985. 's-Gravenhage: Ministerie van Onderwijs en Wetenschappen.

Reagan, Ronald. 1981. Speech delivered to the National League of Cities in the International Ballroom of the Washington Hilton. *Weekly Compilation of Presidential Documents.* US Department of Archives: Washington, D.C., 213-220.

Reich, H. 1986. "The Effect of Age on Performance in Different Language Skills". In Clyne, ed., 1986.57-70.

Rodriguez, I.Z. 1981. An Inquiry Approach to Science/Language Teaching and the Development of Classification and Oral Communication Skills of Mexican American Bilignual Children in Third Grade. Ph.D. diss., University of Texas at Austin.

Rodriguez, R. 1982. *Hunger of Memory: The Education of Richard Rodriguez.* Boston: David. R. Godine.

Rodriguez, R. 1985. "Bilingualism, Con: Outdated and Unrealistic". *New York Times,* Education, Fall Survey, Sunday, November 10, Section 12, p. 83.

Rohter, L. 1986. "Two Systems of Bilingual Education, but which is Best?" *New York Times,* November 24, B1.

Rokkan, S. 1968. "The Structuring of Mass Politics in the Smaller European Democracies". *Comparative Studies in Society and History* 10.173-210.

Rokkan, S. 1971, *Nation Building: A Review of Recent Comparative Research.* Paris: Mouton.

Rokkan, S. 1975. "Dimensions of State Formation and Nation-Building". *The Formation of National States in Western Europe* ed. by C. Tilly. Princeton: Princeton University Press.

Rokkan, S. & D. Urwin. 1983. *Economy, Territory, Identity.* London: Sage.

Romaine, S. 1989. *Bilingualism.* Oxford: Basil Blackwell.

Rome, D. 1975. "On the Jewish School Question in Montreal 1903-1931". *Canadian Jewish Archives* ns 3.

Roosens, E. 1989. "Cultural Ecology and Achievement Motivation: Ethnic Minority Youngsters in the Belgian System". In Eldering and Kloprogge, eds., 1989.85-106.

Rosier, P. & W. Holm. 1980. *The Rock Point Experience: A Longitudinal Study of a Navajo School Program.* Bilingual Education Series: 8. Washington, D.C.: Center for Applied Linguistics.

Roskies, D.G. 1986. "The People of the Lost Book: A Cultural Manifesto". *Orim: A Jewish Journal at Yale* 2.1.7-34.

Rossell, C.H. 1989. "The Effectiveness of Educational Alternatives for Limited English Proficient Children". *The Social and Cultural Context of Instruction in Two Languages: From Conflict and Controversy to Cooperative Reorganization of Schools* ed. by G. Imhoff. New York: Transaction Books.

Rossell, C.H. 1990. "The Research on Bilingual Education". *Equity and Choice* 6.29-36.

Rowland, S. 1987. *The Enquiring Classroom*. London: Falmer Press.

Rubichi, R. 1983. "Planning and Implementation of a Bilingual Program". *Journal of Intercultural Studies* 4.37-54.

Rueda, R. 1983. "Metalinguistic Awareness in Monolingual and Bilingual Mildly Retarded Children". *National Association for Bilingual Education Journal* 8(1). 55-68.

Rueda, R. 1987. "Social and Communicative Aspects of Language Proficiency in Low-Achieving Language Minority Students". In Trueba, ed., 1987b.185-197.

Rueda, R. & H. Mehan. 1986. "Metacognition and Passing: Strategic Interaction in the Lives of Students with Learning Disabilities". *Anthropology and Education Quarterly* 17.139-165.

Ruiz, Richard. 1984. "Orientations in Language Planning". *NABE Journal* 8.15-34.

Rupp, J.H. 1980. Cerebral Language Dominance in Vietnamese-English Bilingual Children. Ph.D. diss., University of New Mexico.

Saez, Antonia. 1978. *La Lectura, Arte del Lenguaje*. Río Piedras: Universidad de Puerto Rico.

Santiago, R.L. 1985. "Understanding Bilingual Education – Or the Sheep in Wolf's Clothing". *Educational Leadership*, September, 79-83.

Saravia-Shore, M. 1979. "An Ethnographic Evaluation/Research Model for Bilingual Programs". In Padilla, ed., 1979.328-348.

Saunders, G.W. 1988. *Bilingual Children from Birth to Teens*. Clevedon: Multi-lingual Matters.

Saussure, F. de. [1916] 1966. *Course in General Linguistics*. Trans. W. Baskin. New York: Mc Graw Hill.

Savignon, S. 1971. Study of the Effect of Training in Communicative Skills as Part of a Beginning College French Course on Student Attitude and Achievement in Linguistic and Communicative Competence. Ph.D. diss., University of Illinois at Urbana, Campaign.

Saville-Troike, M. 1976. *Foundations for Teaching English as a Second Language: Theory and Method for Multicultural Education*. Englewood Cliffs, N.J.: Prentice-Hall.

Saville-Troike, M. & J.A. Kleifgen. 1989. "Culture and Language in Classroom Communication". In García and Otheguy, eds., 1989.83-102.

SBIFS. 1982. *Significant Bilingual Instructional Features Study. Case Studies*. San Francisco: Far West Laboratory for Educational Research and Development.

Schmied, J. 1989. *English in East and Central Africa*. Bayreuth: Bayreuth University Press.

Schneider, S.G. 1976. *Revolution, Reaction or Reform: The 1974 Bilingual Education Act*. New York: Las Americas Publishing Co.

School District of Philadelphia. 1987-1988. *Superintendent's Management Information Center*. Philadelphia, Pennsylvania: Philadelphia School District Office of Research and Evaluation. Report No. 8818.

Scribner, S. & M. Cole. 1978. "Literacy without Schooling: Testing for Intellectual Effects". *Harvard Educational Review* 48.448-461.

Scudder, B.E.T. 1979. A Comparative Study of the Effects of the Use of a Diagnostic/Prescriptive Approach versus a Tutorial Approach to the Teaching of English to Non-English Speaking Elementary School Children in a Large Urban School District in Colorado. Ph.D. diss., University of Colorado at Boulder.

Secada, W.G. 1990. "Research, Politics, and Bilingual Education." In Cazden and Snow, eds., 1990.81-106.

Seidner, S.S. & M.M. Seidner. 1982. "In the Wake of Conservative Reaction: An Analysis". *Bilingual Education Paper Series* (November). Los Angeles: California State University.

Seliger, H. 1980. "Thomas Scovel – The Effects of Neurological Age on Second Language Acquisition". Paper presented at the 13th American TESOL Convention, Boston.

Sibayan, B.P. 1970. "For a Bilingual Education in the Philippines". *Curriculum Journal* 1.154-156.

Sibayan, B.P. 1985. "The Filipino People and English". *Scientific and Humanistic Dimensions of Language* ed. by K.R. Jankowsky, 582-593. Amsterdam/Philadelphia: John Benjamins.

Sibayan, B.P. & A. Gonzalez, FSC. 1990. "English Language Teaching in the Philippines: A Succession of Movements". *Teaching and Learning English Worldwide* ed. by J. Britton, R.E. Shafer and K. Watson, 270-297. Avon, England: Multilingual Matters.

Siguán M. & W. Mackey. 1987. *Education and Bilingualism*. International Bureau of Education.

Skutnabb-Kangas, T. 1981. *Bilingualism or Not*. Clevedon & Phildelphia: Multilingual Matters.

Skutnabb-Kangas, T. 1987. *Are the Finns in Sweden an Ethnic Minority – Finish Parents Talk about Finland and Sweden*. Research Project The Education of the Finnish Minority in Sweden, Working Paper 1. Roskilde: Roskilde University Centre.

Skutnabb-Kangas, T. 1988. "Multilingualism and the Education of Minority Children". In Skutnabb-Kangas and Cummins, eds., 1988.10-44.

Skutnabb-Kangas, T. Forthcoming, a. "Sverigefinnar forhandlar om etnisk identitet". In Peura and Skutnabb-Kangas, eds. In press.

Skutnabb-Kangas, T. Forthcoming, b. "Bicultural Competence and Strategies for Negotiating Ethnic Identity". In Phillipson et al., eds. In press.

Skutnabb-Kangas, T. Forthcoming, c. "Language as a Cultural Core Value in the Ethnic Self-Categorization of the Finnish Labour Migrant Minority in Sweden". Gouboglo et al., eds. In press.

Skutnabb-Kangas, T. 1990. *Language, Literacy and Minorities*. London: The Minority Rights Group.

Skutnabb-Kangas, T. & J. Cummins, eds. 1988. *Minority Education. From Shame to Struggle*. Clevedon and Philadelphia: Multilingual Matters.

Skutnabb-Kangas, T. & P. Leporanta-Morley. 1988. "Migrant Women and Education". *Scandinavian Journal of Development Alternatives*, VII: 1, 1988.83-112.

Skutnabb-Kangas, T. & R. Phillipson. 1987. "Aspects of Multilingualism". *Proceedings from the Fourth Nordic Symposium on Bilingualism* ed. by Erling Wande et al. *(Studia Multiethnica Upsaliensia, 2)*. Uppsala: Acta Universitatis Upsaliensis, 167-170.

Slavin, R.E. 1987. "Ability Grouping and Student Achievement in Elementary Schools: A Best-Evidence Synthesis". *Review of Educational Research* 57(3). 293-336.

Smith, G.H. 1989. "Kura Kaupapa Maori: Innovation and Policy Development in Maori Education". *Access* [University of Auckland] 8.26-28.

Smolicz, J. 1979. *Culture and Education in a Plural Society*. Canberra: Curriculum Development Center.

Smolicz, J. 1983. "Cultural Alternatives in Plural Societies: Separation or Multiculturalism?" *Journal of Intercultural Studies* 4.47-68.

Solé i Gallart, I. 1985. "Una reflexión sobre Montessori y Decroly". *Cuadernos de Pedagogía* 126.8-10.

Soltes, M. 1925. *The Yiddish Press: An Americanizing Agency*. New York: Columbia University Press.

SOU. 1974. *Invandrarutredningen. Invandrarna och minoriteterna*. Stockholm: Statens offentliga utredningar. 1974.69.

SOU. 1983. *Olika urgsprung – gemenskap i Sverige*. Stockholm: Statens offentliga utredningar. 1983.57.

South Australia. 1983. *Voices for the Future*. Adelaide: South Australian Education Department Languages Policy Working Party.

South Australia. 1984. *Education for a Cultural Democracy*. Adelaide: Task Force to Investigate Multiculturalism and Education.

Spener, D. 1988. "Transitional Bilingual Education and the Socialization of Immigrants". *Harvard Educational Review* 58.133-153.

Spindler, G. 1955. *Anthropology and Education*. Stanford, CA: Stanford University Press.

Spindler, G. 1963. *Education and Culture: Anthropological Approaches*. New York: Holt, Rinehart & Winston.

Spindler, G. 1974. "The Transmission of American Culture". In G. Spindler, ed., 279-310.

Spindler, G. 1977. "Change and Continuity in American Core Cultural Values: An Anthropological Perspective". *We the People: American Character and Social Change* ed. by G.D. DeRenzo, 20-40. Westport: Greenwood.

Spindler, G., ed. 1987. *Education and Cultural Process: Anthropological Approaches* (second edition). Prospects Heights, Illinois: Waveland Press, Inc.

Spindler, G. 1987a. "Beth Ann – A Case Study of Culturally Defined Adjustment and Teacher Perceptions". In Spindler, ed., 1987.230-244.

Spindler, G. 1987b. "The Transmission of Culture". In Spindler, ed., 1987.303-334.

Spindler, G. 1987c. "Why Have Minority Groups in North America Been Disadvantaged by Their Schools?" In Spindler, ed., 1987.160-172.

Spindler, G. & L. Spindler. 1983. "Anthropologists View American Culture". *Annual Review of Anthropology* 12.49-78.

Spindler, G. & L. Spindler. 1987a. "Cultural Dialogue and Schooling in Schoenhausen and Roseville: A Comparative Analysis". *Anthropology and Education Quarterly* 18.3-16.

Spindler, G. & L. Spindler. 1987b. "Teaching and Learning How to Do the Ethnography of Education". In G. Spindler and L. Spindler, eds., 1987c.17-33.

Spindler, G. & L. Spindler, eds. 1987c. *The Interpretive Ethnography of Education: At Home and Abroad.* Hillsdale, NJ: Lawrence Erlbaum Associates.

Spindler, G. & L. Spindler. Forthcoming. *The American Cultural Dialogue and its Transmission.* England: Falmer Press.

Spolsky, B., ed. 1972. *The Language Education of Minority Children.* Rowley, Mass.: Newbury House.

Spolsky, B. 1974. "Speech Communities and Schools". *TESOL Quarterly* 8.17-26.

Spolsky, B. 1977a. "American Indian Bilingual Education". *International Journal of the Sociology of Language* 14.

Spolsky, B. 1977b. "The Establishment of Language Education Policy in Multilingual Societies". In Spolsky and Cooper, eds., 1977.1-22.

Spolsky, B. 1987. *Report on Maori-English Bilingual Education.* Wellington: Department of Education.

Spolsky, B. 1989. "Maori Bilingual Education and Language Revitalisation". *Journal of Multilingual and Multicultural Development* 10.89-106.

Spolsky B. & R. Cooper, eds. 1977. *Frontiers of Bilingual Education.* Rowley, Mass.: Newbury House.

Sridhar, K.K. 1977. The Development of English as an Elite Language in the Multilingual Context of India: Its Educational Implications. Ph.D. Diss. Urbana: University of Illinois.

Sridhar, K.K. 1982. "English in South Indian Urban Context". *The Other Tongue: English Across Cultures* ed. by B.B. Kachru, 141-153. Urbana: University of Illinois Press.

Sridhar, K.K. 1985. "Bilingualism in South Asia (India): National/Regional Profiles and Verbal Repertoires". *Annual Review of Applied Linguistics* 6.169-186.

Sridhar, K.K. 1989. *English in Indian Bilingualism.* New Delhi: Manohar Publications.

Srivastava, R.N. 1988. "Societal Bilingualism and Bilingual Education: A Study of the Indian Situation". *International Handbook of Bilingualism and Bilingual Education* ed. by C.B. Paulston, 247-274. Connecticut: Greenwood Press.

Statistiques: Année Scolaire 1985-1986. Luxembourg: Ministère de l'Education Nationale et de la Jeunesse.

Stock, H.L. 1977. The Age Factor in Second Language Acquisition: German Speaking Migrants in South Australia. M.A. Thesis, Monash University.

Straka, M., ed. 1970. *Handbuch der Europaeischen Volksgruppen.* Vienne Stuttgart: Braumüller.

Suárez-Orozco, M. 1987. "Towards a Psychosocial Understanding of Hispanic Adaptation to American Schooling". In Trueba, ed., 1987b.156-168.

Suárez-Orozco, M.M. 1989. *Central American Refugees and U.S. High Schools: A Psychosocial Study of Motivation and Achievement.* Stanford, CA: Stanford University Press.

Swain, M. & H. Barik. 1978. "Bilingual Education in Canada: French and English". *Case Studies in Bilingual Education* ed. by B. Spolsky and R. Cooper, 22-71. Rowley, Mass.: Newbury House.

Swain, M. & J. Cummins. 1979. "Bilingualism, Cognitive Functioning and Education". *Language Teaching and Linguistics: Abstracts* 12.4-18.

Swain, M. & S. Lapkin. 1981. *Bilingual Education in Ontario: A Decade of Research.* Ontario: Ministry of Education.

Swain, M. & S. Lapkin. 1982. *Evaluating Bilingual Education: A Canadian Case Study.* Clevedon, England: Multilingual Matters.

Tarrant, L. 1984. "Kohanga Reo". *Tu Tangata* 19.9-11.

Task Force to Review Education Administration. 1988. *Administering for Excellence: Effective Administration in Education.* Wellington: Government Printer.

Teale, William H. 1986. "The Beginnings of Reading and Writing: Written Language Development During the Pre-School and Kindergarten Years". *The Pursuit of Literacy-Early Reading and Writing* ed. by R. Michael, 1-29. Dubuque, Iowa: Kendal/Hunt.

Teberosky, A. 1982. "Construcciones de Escritura a través de la Interacción Grupal". In Ferreiro and Palacios, eds., 1982.155-178.

Teitelbaum, H. 1976. Assessing Bilingualism in Elementary School Children. Ph.D. diss., University of New Mexico.

Terrell, T.D. 1981. "The Natural Approach in Bilingual Education". *Schooling and Language Minority Students: A Theoretical Framework*, 117-146. Los Angeles: Evaluation, Dissemination and Assessment Center.

Tikunoff, W.J. 1982. An Emerging Description of Successful Bilingual Instruction: An Executive Summary of Part I of the SBIF Descriptive Study. Typescript.

Title VII, Public Law 100-297. 1988 (April 28). Sec. 7001-8001.

Tomorrow's Schools Implementation Unit. 1989a. *Reform of Education Administration: Integration Working Group.* Wellington: Government Printer.

Tomorrow's Schools Implementation Unit. 1989b. *Reform of Education Administration: Kura Kaupapa Maori Working Group.* Wellington: Government Printer.

Torrance, E.P., J.J. Wu, J.C. Gowan & N.C. Aliotti. 1970. "Creative Functioning of Monolingual and Bilingual Children in Singapore". *Journal of Educational Psychology* 61.72-75.

Touret, B. 1973. *L'Aménagement constitutionnel des états de peuplement composite.* Québec: Presses de l'Université Laval.

Trocmé, Helène. 1982. "La Conscientisation de l'apprenant dans l'apprentissage d'une langue étrangère". *Revue de Phonétique Appliquée* 161-163.253-267.

Trocmé, Helène. 1985. "Brain Research and Human Learning". *Revue de Phonétique Appliquée* 73-75.303-315.

Troike, R. 1978. "Research Evidence for the Effectiveness of Bilingual Education". *NABE Journal* 3.13-24.

Troike, R.C. & M. Saville-Troike. 1982. "Teacher Training for Bilingual Education: An International Perspective". *Issues in International Bilingual Education* ed. by B. Hartford, A. Valdman and C. Foster, 199-219. New York: Plenum Press.

Trueba, H.T. 1979. "Bilingual Education Models: Types and Designs". In Trueba and Barnett-Mizrahi, eds., 1979.54-73.

Trueba, H. 1983. "Adjustment Problems of Mexican American Children: An Anthropological Study." *Learning Disabilities Quarterly* 6.395-415.

Trueba, H. 1987a. "Organizing Classroom Instruction in Specific Sociocultural Contexts: Teaching Mexican Youth to Write in English". In Goldman and Trueba, eds., 1987.235-252.

Trueba, H., ed. 1987b. *Success or Failure?: Learning and the Language Minority Student.* New York: Newbury/Harper & Row.

Trueba, H. 1987c. "Ethnography of Schooling". In Trueba, ed., 1987b.1-13.

Trueba, H. 1988a. "Peer Socialization among Minority Students: A High School Dropout Prevention Program". In Trueba and Delgado-Gaitan, eds., 1988.201-217.

Trueba, H. 1988b. "Culturally-Based Explanations of Minority Students' Academic Achievement". *Anthropology and Education Quarterly* 19.270-287.

Trueba, H. 1988c. "English Literacy Acquisition: From Cultural Trauma to Learning Disabilities in Minority Students". *Linguistics and Education* 1.125-152.

Trueba, H. 1989. *Raising Silent Voices: Educating the Linguistic Minorities for the 21st Century.* New York: Harper & Row.

Trueba, H.T. & C. Barnett-Mizrahi, eds. 1979. *Bilingual Multicultural Education and the Professional from Theory to Practice.* Rowley, Mass.: Newbury House.

Trueba, H. & C. Delgado-Gaitan, eds. 1988. *School and Society: Learning Content through Culture.* New York: Praeger Publishers.

Trueba, H., L. Jacobs & E. Kirton. 1990. *Cultural Conflict and Adaptation: The Case of Hmong Children in American Society.* London: Falmer Press.

Trueba, H., G. Spindler & L. Spindler, eds. 1989. *What Do Anthropologists Have to Say about Dropouts?* London: Falmer Press.

Tucker, G.R. 1980. "Implications for U.S. Bilingual Education: Evidence from Canadian Research". *Focus* 2.1-4. National Clearinghouse of Bilingual Education.

Tucker, G.R. 1986. "Implications of Canadian Research for Promoting a Language-Competent American Society". *The Fergusonian Impact* ed. by Joshua A. Fishman, Volume 2.361-369. Berlin: Mouton de Gruyter.

Tucker, G.R. 1987. "Educational Programs for Language-Minority Children". Paper presented at the Harvard Institute on Bilingual Education: Research to Policy to Practice. Cambridge, Mass.

Two-way Bilingual Programs: Focus on Port Chester, New York. 1987 *National Clearinghouse on Bilingual Education Forum*, 10.1,3.

U.S. Bureau of the Census. 1984. *1980 U.S. Census*. Current Populations Report. Washington, D.C.: Government Printing Office.

U.S. Congress. 1984. *Bilingual Education Reauthorization Act*.

U.S. Department of Commerce. Bureau of the Census. 1987. *The Hispanic Population in the United States: March 1986 and 1987 (Advance Report)*. Washington, D.C.: U.S. Government Printing Office.

United States General Accounting Office (GAO). 1987. *Bilingual Education: A New Look at the Research Evidence*. Washington, D.C.: Program Evaluation and Methodology Division.

Velzen, W.G. van, M.B. Miles, M. Ekholm, et. al., eds. 1985. *Making School Improvement Work*. De Lier: Academisch Boeken Centrum.

Verdoodt, A. 1969. *L'Université Bilingue*. Québec: CIRB.

Verdoodt, A. 1989. *Les Langues écrites du monde: Relevé du degré et des modes d'utilisation. 3. L'Europe occidentale*. Québec: Presses de l'Université Laval.

Victoria. 1984. *Ministerial Policy Statement 6. Curriculum Development and Planning in Victoria*. Melbourne: Ministry of Education.

Victoria. 1985. *The Place of Languages other than English in Victorian Schools*. Melbourne: State Board of Education and Ministerial Advisory Committee on Multicultural and Migrant Education.

Von Maltitz, F.W. 1975. *Living and Learning in Two Languages: Bilingual-Bicultural Education in the United States*. New York: McGraw-Hill.

Vygotsky, L. 1962. *Thought and Language*. Cambridge: M.I.T. Press.

Vygotsky, L.S. 1978. *Mind in Society: The Development of Higher Psychological Processes* ed. by M. Cole, V. John-Teiner, S. Scribner and E. Souberman. Cambridge: Harvard University Press.

Wagatsuma, H. & G. De Vos 1984. *Heritage of Endurance: Family Patterns and Delinquency Formation in Urban Japan*. Berkeley, CA: University of California Press.

Wagner-Gough, J. 1978. "Excerpts from Comparative Studies in Second Language Learning". In Hatch, ed., 1978.155-171.

Waitangi Tribunal. 1986. *Finding of the Waitangi Tribunal Relating to Te Reo Maori*. Wellington: Government Printer.

Wells, G. & J. Wells. 1984. "Learning to Talk and Talking to Learn". *Journal of the College of Education* 23.190-197.

Wertsch, J. 1985. *Vygotsky and the Social Formation of the Mind*. Cambridge: Harvard University Press.

Western Australia. 1988. *Languages for Western Australia*. Perth: Ministerial Working Party on the Development of a Policy for the Teaching of Languages other than English (LOTE) in Western Australian Schools.

Westin, C. 1988. *Den Toleranta Oppinionen. Inställningen till invandrare 1987.* (DEIFO-rapport, 8). Stockholm: DEIFO.

Widgren, J. 1986. "Interview. Widgren ehdottaa itsetutkiskelua: 'Vähemmistöasema ei ole ajankohtainen'" (Widgren suggests self-reflection: "Minority Status is not Prevalent"). *Ruotsin Suomalainen* 1.1986.

Willig, A.C. 1985. "A Meta-Analysis of Selected Studies on the Effectiveness of Bilingual Education. *Review of Educational Research* 55.269-317.

Wiseman, S. 1943. "Amerike in undzer yidisher dertsiung". rpt. in Dunsky 1961.72-82.

Wiseman, S. 1948a. "Di yidishe yontoyvim un di yidishe dertsiung". In Pomerantz et al., 1948.216-252.

Wiseman, S. 1948b. "Yidishe tog-shuln in Montreal". In Pomerantz et al., 1948.45-52.

Wiseman, S. 1982. "A memuar fun mayn lebn". *Kanader yidisher zamlbukh* ed. Jacob Zipper and Chaim Spilberg, 380-414. Montreal: National Committee on Yiddish, Canadian Jewish Congress.

Wisse, R.R. 1977. "A Golus Education". *Moment* 2.4.28,62.

Wittrock, M.C., ed. 1986. *Handbook of Research on Teaching*. New York: Macmillan Publishing Co.

Zentella, A.C. 1981. "Tá Bién, You Could Answer Me en Cualquier Idioma: Puerto Rican Codeswitching in Bilingual Classrooms". *Latino Language and Communicative Behavior* ed. by Richard Durán, 109-131. Norwood, New Jersey: Ablex Press.

Zipper, J., ed. 1938. *Perets-shuln-bukh aroysgegebn tsum 25 yorikn yubiley*. Montreal: Peretz Schools.

Zondag, K. 1982. *Bilingual Education in Friesland*. Frjentsjer/Franeker: T. Weber.

Zondag, K. 1989. "Diversity and Uniformity in Six Bilingual Schools in Friesland". *Journal of Multilingual and Multicultural Development* 10.3-17.

Zubrzycki, J. 1988. "Australia as a Multicultural Society". *Siirtolaisuus/Migration* 4.9-16.

Contributors

Mohamed Hassan Abdulaziz is presently the Director of the Institute of Diplomacy and International Studies at the University of Nairobi. He holds undergraduate and graduate degrees from the University of London. At the University of Nairobi he has been Chair of the Department of Linguistics and African Language, and Dean of the Faculty of Arts. His publications are in the areas of Swahili language and literature, Swahili structure and sociolinguistics.

Hugo Baetens Beardsmore is Professor of English and bilingualism at the Dutch language Vrije Universiteit Brussel and teaches the sociology of language at the French language Université Libre de Bruxelles. He is a member of the Belgian Royal Academy, has published on many aspects of bilingualism and been a consultant in different parts of the world on issues relating to language planning and bilingual education.

Richard Benton is a New Zealander who has written and lectured extensively on language policy, bilingual education and the use of minority languages in education. After graduating from the University of Auckland, he taught in primary and secondary schools and did research into the English and Maori spoken by Maori school children. Benton obtained his M.A. and Ph.D. degrees from the University of Hawaii and since 1971 he has headed the Masters research program of the New Zealand Council for Educational Research.

Ursula Casanova was born in Puerto Rico and has been a school principal in Rochester, New York. She received her Ph.D. from Arizona State University and is presently an Assistant Professor there. Her research interests center on policy issues related to education and culture. She has co-authored a book, *Schoolchildren At Risk* (Richardson, Casanova, Placier and Guilfoyle 1989) and publishes a monthly column, "Putting Research to Work", with David Berliner for *Instructor Magazine*.

Michael Clyne is Professor of Linguistics at Monash University and Director of the Language and Society Center of the Languages Institute of Australia. His research areas are bilingualism/language contact, sociolinguistics, second language acquisition and cross-cultural discourse analysis. Among his books are *Transference and Triggering, Deutsch als Muttersprache in Australien, Multilingual Australia*, and *Language and Society in the German-speaking Countries*.

Jim Cummins is currently a Professor in the Modern Language Center of the Ontario Institute for Studies in Education. He has published several books related to bilingual education and minority student achievement including *Bilingualism and Special Education: Issues in Assessment and Pedagogy* (1984), *Bilingualism in Education: Aspects of Theory, Research and Policy* (1986, with Merrill Swain), *Minority Education: From Shame to Struggle* (1988, with Tove Skubnabb-Kangas) and *Empowering Minority Students* (1989).

Kenji Hakuta received his training under Roger Brown and Jill de Villiers at Harvard University, where he received his Ph.D. in Experimental Psychology in 1979. His main languages of interest are Japanese, Spanish and English, and he has drifted around various circumstances under which these languages are learned, used, and lost. He has held academic positions at Yale University, the University of California at Santa Cruz, and most currently at Stanford University, where he is Professor of Education and directs the doctoral training program in Bilingual Education following the path of Robert Politzer.

Nancy H. Hornberger is Assistant Professor of Education at the University of Pennsylvania. She holds degrees from Harvard University, New York University, and the University of Wisconsin, Madison. She specializes in sociolinguistics and bilingual education, with special attention to language minority populations in Peru and the United States. Her recent publications include a book, *Bilingual Education and Language Maintenance: A Southern Peruvian Quechua Case* (1988), and a special issue of the *International Journal of the Sociology of Language*, entitled "Bilingual Education and Language Planning in Indigenous Latin America" (1989).

Nathalie Lebrun is from the Belgian province of Luxembourg and studied languages and linguistics at the Université Libre de Bruxelles. She carried out the field work in the investigation into trilingual education in the Grand Duchy of Luxembourg under the direction of Prof. Hugo Baetens Beardsmore.

William Francis Mackey is currently CIRB Research Professor at the International Center for Language Management Research at Laval University, Quebec. He was the Founding Director of the International Center for Research on Bilingualism (CIRB). Mackey has also been Fellow of the Royal Society of Canada, Federal Commissioner of the Bilingual Districts Advisory Board, Head of Linguistic Research for the Royal Commission on Bilingualism and Biculturalism, Foreign Advisor of the Irish Language Attitudes Research Committee, and a Fellow of the Royal Academy of Belgium.

Christina Bratt Paulston is Professor of Linguistics and Director of the English Language Institute at the University of Pittsburgh. Paulston has published in the fields of language teaching, teacher training, language planning, bilingual education, and sociolinguistics. She holds degrees from Carleton College, the University of Minnesota, and Teachers College, Columbia University. From 1976 to 1981 she was trustee of the Center for Applied Linguistics.

David G. Roskies is Professor of Jewish Literature at the Jewish Theological Seminary of America. He is co-founder and editor of *Prooftexts: A Journal of Jewish Literary History* (1981-) and has published two books on Jewish responses to catastrophe.

Bonifacio P. Sibayan is Professor Emeritus of Linguistics and Education at Philippine Normal College. Sibayan has done research and written on bilingualism, bilingual education, language planning, methods of teaching language and other curricular subjects, language and identity and socio-economic development.

Tove Skutnabb-Kangas is Guest Researcher at Roskilde University, Denmark, and part-time sheep farmer. Her research topics include bilingualism, minority education, linguistic human rights, minority women and power, linguistic imperialism, modern forms of racism (ethnicism, linguicism). Skutnabb-Kangas has written and edited over twenty books and around two hundred articles.

Kamal K. Sridhar is currently Associate Professor of Linguistics and Director of English as a Second Language at SUNY-Stony Brook. She has taught courses on bilingualism, bilingual education, sociolinguistics, and English in international contexts at the University of Illinois, City University of New York (Queens College), and SUNY. She has published widely in the areas of language use and policy in multilingual societies, second language acquisition, non-native varieties of English and language maintenance/shift among Asian Indians in the United States.

Gerardo Torres is a graduate of the Escuela Normal of the Catholic University of Puerto Rico and did his graduate work in education at Teachers College, Columbia University. He has taught in the rural areas of Puerto Rico, the New York public schools, and is presently a teacher educator at The City College of New York.

Henry T. Trueba is presently Associate Dean of the College of Letters and Science and Director of the Division of Education at the University of California, Davis. He received his M.A. in Anthropology from Stanford University and his Ph.D. also in Anthropology from the University of Pittsburgh. His publications include *Success or Failure: Linguistic Minority Children at Home and in School* (1987), *Raising Silent Voices: Educating Linguistic Minorities for the 21st century* (1989), *School and Society: Learning Content Through Culture* (1988, with Delgado-Gaitan).

Albert Verdoodt is now with the Unité de Récherches Sociologiques of the Catholic University of Louvain at Louvain-la-Neuve, Belgium. A recipient of the Prix de l'Académie des Sciences Morales et Politiques of the Institut de France, he has published numerous works on the sociology of language. He has been a Visiting Professor at the University of Burundi (1966-1967) and at Laval University (1968-1970).

Koen Zondag is a senior officer for bilingualism and bilingual schooling at the Frisian Center for Bilingual Schooling, the Frisian Department of the Center for Educational Advice in Friesland. His main interest is the pedagogical and philosophical aspects of this type of schooling.

Index